GLOBAL LUXURY TRENDS

GLOBAL LUXURY TRENDS

Innovative Strategies for Emerging Markets

Edited by

Jonas Hoffmann

Associate Professor of Marketing, SKEMA Business School, France

and

Ivan Coste-Manière

Professor of Marketing, SKEMA Business School, France

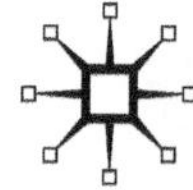

First published 2013 by
PALGRAVE MACMILLAN

Palgrave Macmillan in the UK is an imprint of Macmillan Publishers Limited, registered in England, company number 785998, of Houndmills, Basingstoke, Hampshire RG21 6XS.

Palgrave Macmillan in the US is a division of St Martin's Press LLC, 175 Fifth Avenue, New York, NY 10010.

Palgrave Macmillan is the global academic imprint of the above companies and has companies and representatives throughout the world.

Palgrave® and Macmillan® are registered trademarks in the United States, the United Kingdom, Europe and other countries.

ISBN 978–1–137–28738–0

This book is printed on paper suitable for recycling and made from fully managed and sustained forest sources. Logging, pulping and manufacturing processes are expected to conform to the environmental regulations of the country of origin.

A catalogue record for this book is available from the British Library.

A catalog record for this book is available from the Library of Congress.

10 9 8 7 6 5 4 3 2 1
22 21 20 19 18 17 16 15 14 13

Printed and bound in Great Britain by
CPI Antony Rowe, Chippenham and Eastbourne

CONTENTS

FIGURES AND TABLES

FIGURES

TABLES

CONTRIBUTORS

EDITORS

Dr. Jonas Hoffmann is Associate Professor of Marketing at SKEMA Business School in France. He has extensive experience in consulting and executive training, and has been a speaker at international luxury events. He has written several articles about marketing and innovation in the luxury industry. He is the co-editor of *Luxury Strategy in Action.*

Dr. Ivan Coste-Manière has extensive experience in the luxury industry; he has created eight companies in the fragrance, watches and marketing sector. He is Professor of Marketing and Director of the Master of Science in Luxury and Fashion Management at SKEMA Business School in France. He is the co-editor of *Luxury Strategy in Action.*

CO-AUTHORS

Joanna Chen holds a master's degree in Fashion Strategy Management. She is an expert in luxury retail-network improvement and luxury-malls creation in China. Based in Shanghai, China, she is now in charge of a new project of Hang Lung Properties.

Bernard Cova is Professor of Marketing at Euromed Management, Marseilles, France, and Visiting Professor at Università Bocconi, Milan, Italy. A pioneer in the consumer tribes field since the early 1990s, his internationally influential research has emphasized what he calls "the Mediterranean approach" of tribal marketing.

Anna Hoarau holds a double master's degree in Criminology from University College London, UK, and in Luxury and Fashion Management from SKEMA, France. She is currently acting in establishing art exhibitions in China in collaboration with Jean-Claude Novaro, the great French glass blower.

Betina Hoffmann holds an MSc in Marketing. She is currently Business Development Manager of a cosmetics company in Monaco. She also runs her own business where she designs and sells jewelry. She has previous experience in marketing and strategy in the luxury, fashion and cosmetics industries in Brazil and in France.

Francesco Giliberti Birindelli studied Law and Economics at the Catholic University of Milan, Italy. He is a founder of [Trust] Partners, a multinational advisory firm, and is responsible for managing worldwide taxes of the Gucci Group since 2006. He is also Vice-President of the Supervisory Board of Marbert since 2010.

Camille Jaganathen is a French student at SKEMA Business School, France. She studies International Business and Management at the Suzhou campus in China and is a former member of the island6 art collective in Shanghai, China.

Cedric Laforge holds an MSc in Luxury and Fashion Management of SKEMA, France, and is an Accredited Jewelry Professional (AJP) of the Gemological Institute of America (GIA). He is currently a junior international marketing and communication manager at Backes & Strauss London.

Laurent Lecamp graduated from Reims Management School, France, and GIA (Gemological Institute of America). He started his career with LVMH, before joining the world of watchmaking. He is the founder of an independent high-end watch brand, which has won many awards: CYRUS. He is also editor of luxury glossy magazines in Europe and Asia.

Yves R. Lucky holds a master's degree in Economics from Nice University, France. Currently Professor of Creative Marketing and Regulatory Issues at SKEMA Business School, France, he is running two companies that are among the leading ones in Europe in the fields of premiums, promotions and specialty advertising.

Daniela Milosheska is currently working in the field of event planning and management in the renowned agency P, with headquarters in Dubai, United Arab Emirates (UAE); Prague, the Czech Republic; and Skopje, Macedonia. She is collaborating with the world's leading PR gurus. She holds a master's degree in Fashion and Luxury Management from SKEMA, France.

Maureen (Mimi) Morrin, PhD (New York University), is Professor of Marketing at Rutgers University, School of Business, in Camden, New Jersey, USA. Her research, published in several top marketing journals, focuses on the sensory aspects of consumption behavior. Before becoming an academic, she worked in advertising and brand management.

Katrina Panchout holds a specialized master's degree in Strategic Communications Management. She is Professor of Marketing at SKEMA Business School, France, and Director for the International Master in Management Program. She has extensive professional experience, having worked for companies like Lacoste, Habitat and Weber Shandwick, in France and England.

Alessandro Quintavalle is a graduate in Management and Economics Engineering at Politecnico di Milano, Italy. He holds an MBA from EADA Business School, Spain. He has decennial experience in luxury goods, having worked for several companies in the horological industry. He is currently CEO of Thomas Mercer.

Mukta Ramchandani is a luxury and fashion consultant from India. She holds an MSc in Luxury and Fashion Management from SKEMA Business School in France. She currently works in Dubai, UAE.

Rasa Stankeviciute is a freelance marketing consultant, specializing in fashion and luxury goods. She holds an MSc degree in International Marketing and Business Development. She is a blogger on her blog *Fashion Population* (http://fashionpopulation.blogspot.com or www.fashionpopulation.com).

Sandeep Vij is the founder of Banyan Netfaqs! Private Limited (BNPL), an Indian online media group, and is the former CEO of DDB Mudra Group. He has one of the most fruitful careers in the Indian advertising industry.

Tae Youn Kim is Lecturer in Social Psychology of Fashion at Korea University, South Korea. She received a PhD in Sociology with a specialization in luxury consumption from the Department of Human and Social Sciences of the Sorbonne University, Paris 5 Descartes, France, in 2010.

INTRODUCTION

Jonas Hoffmann and Ivan Coste-Manière

The luxury industry is currently on a remarkable journey: quarter after quarter, Hermès, Louis Vuitton, Gucci and their counterparts announce record sales in a growing market with profits in double-digits.

Luxury companies, nevertheless, affirm unanimously that this journey is as challenging as it is exciting: the acceleration imposed by globalized markets, stock markets and digital technologies, to name but a few, demand velocity, agility and continuous adaptation.

Indeed, clients in "emerging" markets like China, Brazil or India are younger than the traditional luxury clientele, and are hungry for novelty. They are becoming more discerning, progressively raising their standards for quality and service, and looking more and more for luxury experiences.

How can this fascinating market be navigated? This book brings an international panel of luxury experts from 11 nationalities and four continents to provide a global perspective on the strategies, practices and companies that are changing the way we understand the luxury world.

Sailing yacht racing provides an appropriate metaphor to describe the current market situation. As in the America's Cup, there are competitors and capital flows from around the world in the market, technological breakthroughs emerge from time to time, regulations may be influenced by actors to a certain extent, and the weather conditions are akin to the ever-changing facet of the market in its economic, regulatory and demand components.

Some competitors are more powerful than others, but each team has a chance of winning a race if it makes the best use of its equipment and skills and if it has a little bit of luck on its side. People are what will ultimately define who achieves lasting success.

This book aims to be a valuable tool for luxury decision-makers. It provides some ready-to-use insights and best practices, but its main goal is to open horizons, inviting luxury sailors to question their operation modes and imagine new ways of bringing and capturing value.

Chapters cover mature luxury markets like Europe and the United States, but mainly the emerging markets of China, Brazil, India, Russia and South Korea. Trends like the impact of digital technology on luxury, luxury sustainability, luxury and arts, luxury and sports, luxury entrepreneurship, luxury consumption of ultra-high net worth individuals and luxury tribes are covered (Figure I.1).

The book is at the intersection of markets and trends, thus tacking Global Luxury Trends!

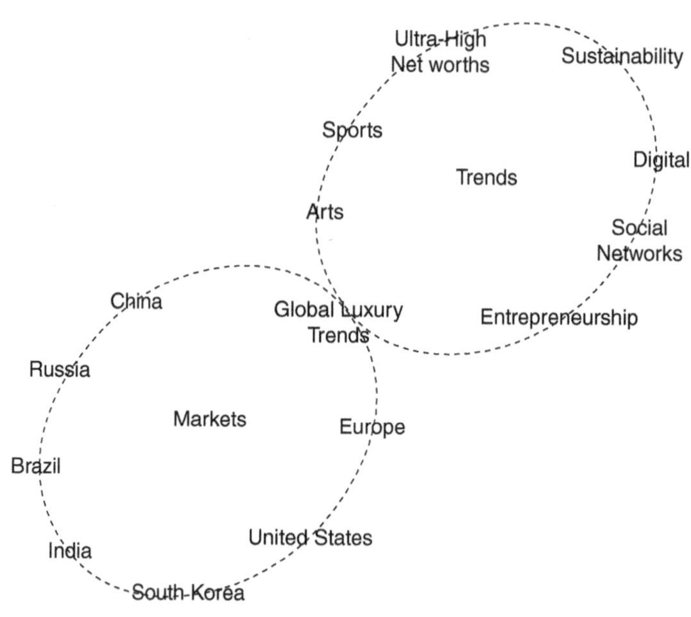

FIGURE I.1 **Global luxury trends**

These different lenses through which the luxury industry can be viewed make up a whole that can be symbolized by the infinity symbol or the number 8, reminding us that luxury is eternal as much as it is a symbol of wealth and fortune.

Like sailing in a beautiful archipelago, the reader can approach the book in different ways, reading the chapters in sequence or dipping into it as mood dictates. It contains the following chapters:

Chapter 1, "On Luxury Strategizing", explores business-model innovation, effectual luxury strategies and behavioral strategizing to understand the different ways actors, from luxury conglomerates to *maisons*, strategize.

Chapter 2, "Paths for the Emergence of Global Chinese Luxury Brands", analyzes the paths currently being followed by Chinese luxury brands to internationalize, showing that there is a way to accelerate this process, following "looking to the future" value propositions.

Chapter 3, "Luxo Brasil and Osklen's New Luxury", presents the fast-growing Brazilian luxury market and the case of Osklen, a company with a unique luxury-sustainable development policy.

Chapter 4, "Über Luxury: For Billionaires Only", takes a tour around the art and science of marketing luxury goods to individuals with a net worth superior to US$ 1 billion by unraveling the luxury consumption patterns of these Ultra-High Net Worth (UHNW) individuals.

Chapter 5, "Occupation Fashion Blogging: Relation between Blogs and Luxury Fashion Brands", presents the growing role of online networking sites and microblogs in the luxury fashion industry. It shows how companies act and react from the point of view of a professional fashion blogger.

Chapter 6, "Engaging with the Luxury Consumer in China", covers the growth of online in China: its definition and identification, its rapid growth, who is the Chinese netizen, the Chinese luxury consumer and how luxury and fashion goods can leverage this opportunity to create value-led and customer-driven touch points.

Chapter 7, "Luxury and Arts in China: The island6 case", presents the case of Shanghai-based island6 art gallery. An in-depth exploration of its unique concept provides hints on where the art and luxury market will head in China in the years to come.

Chapter 8, "Luxury Shopping Places in China", tackles a central issue of developing operations in China: where to go? It identifies the top five cities, the brands present in each and the key characteristics of luxury shopping places.

Chapter 9, "Perspectives on Luxury Operations in China", tackles two features of the luxury business in Asia: finance and licensing. The financial implications of luxury development are explored and the issue of licensing is thoroughly explained.

Chapter 10, "Luxury Consumer Tribes in Asia: Insights from South Korea", analyzes how in Asia the emergent luxury consumption appears to be a tribal one. These luxury tribes allow its members to know about luxury events such as private sales and fashion shows. This unique phenomenon provides new avenues to the marketing of luxury brands.

Chapter 11, "Luxury in Russia and in Countries of Eastern Europe", presents these markets, their potential and specificities. It provides advice on how to establish and expand a luxury business and how to deal with fortunate and bargaining clients.

Chapter 12, "Luxury in India: Seduction by Hypnotic Subtlety", presents the emerging Indian Luxury Industry, how to avoid stepping into the chasm between exclusive and ordinary and what brands need to do, to hasten the process of Darwinian evolution.

Chapter 13, "Polo as a Vehicle for Communicating on Luxury", analyzes how sports, and particularly polo, are a privileged vector exploited by luxury brands in order to communicate about their image, looking for notoriety, awareness and visibility.

Chapter 14, "Mimesis and the Nexus of Luxury Industry in India", shows how mimesis and desire, concepts that date back to the post-independence era, play a vital role in understanding the consumption of luxury brands in India.

Chapter 15, "Tesla Motors, The Reinvention of the Luxury Sports Car Industry", covers the story of how Tesla created its brand and how it has become, since 2005, the world's favorite electric luxury car.

Chapter 16, "Why Buy Luxury? Insights from Consumer Research", focuses on the desire to indulge, and the various psychological mechanisms and situational factors that can influence the consumer's decision to purchase a luxury good.

Finally, chapter 17, "ELIE SAAB: Strategic Presence in the Digital Luxury Space", takes an in-depth look at how luxury fashion house ELIE SAAB has developed its on-line strategy. Lessons and challenges for luxury brands going online are identified.

Challenging times reward entrepreneurial and tenacious talents. May this book be a source of inspiration for those shaping global luxury trends!

ACKNOWLEDGMENTS

The authors are grateful to the companies and brands that graciously granted us permission to reproduce their company images in this book: Andrew Winch Designs, Backes and Strauss, Cyrus, ELIE SAAB (agencies UZIK, Premices and Onrim), HAGI publishing, island6, Osklen, Tesla and Thomas Mercer. We warmly thank Sian Jones for her copyediting. Special thanks to Alessandro Quintavalle for his contribution and enthusiasm all along this project. We thank SKEMA Business School for their support. Finally, we thank Eleanor Davey Corrigan, Hannah Fox, Devasena Vedamurthi and Palgrave Macmillan.

1

ON LUXURY STRATEGIZING

Jonas Hoffmann

1.1 INTRODUCTION

Stand alone or merge? Be accessible or exclusive? Internationalize, but where? How fast?

Strategy is all about choice![1]

The first choice: what is your offering?
The second choice: who are your clients (and competitors)?
The third choice: how do you sustain a viable business?

In a landscape that is fiercer than ever,[2] these choices are critical and demand consistent implementation capabilities.

We explore some emerging paths on strategizing, that is, the way top-managers frame, practice and act to build a sustainable advantage for their companies. Along the lines of Richard Normann,[3] we approach strategizing through the lens of framing: framing the "map and the landscape", configuring the company and reconfiguring the mental space. Consequently, we do not offer best practices or ready-to-use formulas, but we will provide some food for thought, hoping that it might give you some insight into the minds of luxury decision-makers, be they top-managers or entrepreneurs. Maybe right away, maybe later, but, at one moment, to connect with some previous knowledge in your mind and... you reframe!

Which emerging paths are we interested in? The first path is that of business model innovation (BMI) in the luxury industry; we then explore effectual luxury strategies before finally moving to behavioral strategizing.[4] The first provides a map, the second is

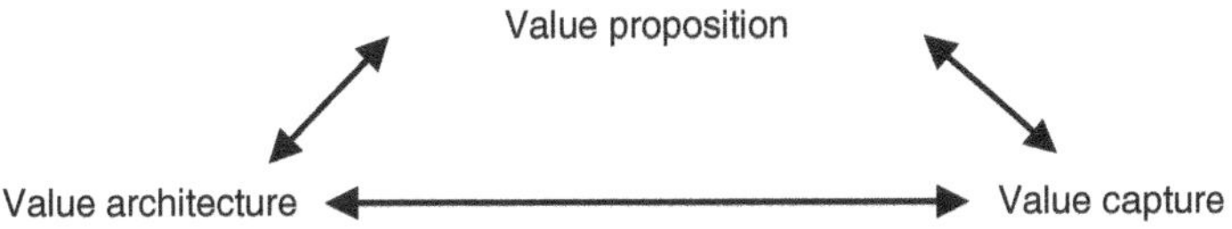

FIGURE 1.1 **Components of a business model**

about landscaping, the third promises a bridge between both. For each of these, we provide a brief definition of the concept, identify companies strategizing along these lines, and draw insights.

1.2 PATH I – BUSINESS MODEL INNOVATION[5]

A business model is "the logic of the firm, the way it operates and how it creates value for its stakeholders".[6] Three basic components can be identified in a business model: value creation, value architecture and revenue model.[7] Value creation integrates the definition of the value proposition, comprising "the targeted type of customer or the market segment addressed by the business activity, the product or service, and partners who create a link between the business and the customer".[8] It assumes that an offer has no value *per se*; the offer acquires value at the moment it is bought and used by a client in a certain context (Figure 1.1).[9]

Value architecture comprises the definition of the "value constellation required by the firm to create and distribute the offering, and determine the complementary assets needed to support the firm's position in this chain".[10] The revenue model specifies "the revenue generation mechanism(s) for the firm, and estimates the cost structure and profit potential of producing the offering, given the value proposition and value chain structure chosen".[11]

One interesting tool to articulate the presentation of a company's business model is the business model canvas proposed by Osterwalder and Pigneur.[12] It extends the three components of the business model into nine elements:

- Value creation:

  (1) Value proposition (What value does the company offer to customers?);
  (2) Customer segments (Who are the customers?)

- Value architecture:

    (3) Customer relationships (What sort of relationship does the company seek to establish with its customers?);
    (4) Distribution channels (How does the company distribute its products?);
    (5) Key activities (Which activities/processes are involved in the business?);
    (6) Key resources (Which resources does the company depend on?);
    (7) Key partners (Which external resources are involved in the company?)

- Revenue model:

    (8) Cost Structure (What is the cost structure like?);
    (9) Revenue Streams (What types of revenue streams are involved?)

When talking about value proposition it is important to bear in mind that we define it in the sense given by Kapferer and Bastien, and Chevalier and Mazzalovo,[13] that is, a luxury good must have a strong artistic content, be the result of craftsmanship and be unique; therefore, a luxury brand has an identity, not a positioning.

There is a dynamic interplay between business model components.[14] Some luxury companies (such as Burberry, Celine and Loewe) decided to outsource the production of some pieces (for example, jeans) to low-wage countries, like China. This involves a series of redefinitions in the company-value architecture: redefinition of the key activities performed in-house or in the home country and establishing new partnerships, for example. This will certainly impact (positively) the company's revenue model, but its consequences in the long term for the brand image are to be seen.

The decision to internationalize a company can be done in several ways (partnership, licensing or subsidiary), each one having consequences for the different elements of the business model. Brand licensing and extension decisions are at the heart of the value-creation process and will again impact the value architecture and the revenue model. Armani is probably stretching its umbrella too widely[15] and Pierre Cardin, despite his artistic genius, has long lost its luxury status through indiscriminate licensing.

Since luxury industry companies can (and do) compete for the same share of wallet, some common patterns can be observed in luxury business models depending on the company activity sectors and strategic group membership.

Boundaries and strategic groups in the luxury industry

The European Cultural Creative Industries Alliance (ECCIA) includes the following sectors in the luxury industry: watches & jewelry, fashion, perfumes & cosmetics, accessories, leather goods, gastronomy, furniture & furnishing, design household equipment, cars, yachts, wines & spirits, hotels and leisure experience, retail and auction houses, and publishing.[16] Chevalier and Mazzalovo[17] add to these the sector of private banking. Others identify a continuum from Product to Experience or Lifestyle, where watches and accessories would fall in the first category, and hospitality in the second category.[18]

Which companies compete with each other? The consulting company Precepta conducted a study in 2010 to cluster luxury companies in different strategic groups.[19] They identify five clusters:

1. "Breeders–consolidators": these are the likes of LVMH, PPR Gucci and Richemont. They have large financial means and their development is based either on acquisition of emerging or under-exploited brands, or the management of a portfolio of brands. They target strong growth and performance.
2. Independent Luxury *Maisons*: this group includes companies like Chanel or Hermès that are controlled by family capital or individuals, and have a patrimonial mode of governance. Their brands are managed according to strict principles, and heritage is a core claim.
3. "3ML (Mass-Luxury Fashion Houses)": the likes of Ralph Lauren, Armani or Hugo Boss are in this group that offers affordable luxury. Their strategy is based on market optimization by maximizing the umbrella brand image to enable brand extension and diversification.
4. Specialists: they include companies like Rolex or Mauboussin. These are brands with strong market legitimacy, although they are hardly as extensible as the previous group. Economic models are mainly based on strong margins and low volumes.
5. "FSMS (Specialized manufacturers multi-segments)": these groups primarily include cosmetics groups like L'Oréal, Estée Lauder or Coty.

(Continued)

They are present in several market segments from mass-market to luxury. Their model is mainly based on product innovation, marketing and managing a portfolio of brands, usually by licensing, to achieve economies of scale.

The strategic considerations of business-model components will weigh more or less heavily depending on the company's strategic group.

For instance, cost rationalization will weigh more for luxury conglomerates and other publicly traded companies (that is, "Specialized manufacturers multi-segments" and "Mass-Luxury Fashion Houses") but will be less important for specialists and *maisons*, where the strict respect of a certain brand philosophy will prevail. Richard Mille's conservative business model,[20] Chanel's strategy and Osklen's commitment to sustainable development are such examples. Luxury conglomerates are also under constant scrutiny from financial markets, and the temptation to stretch luxury brands is ever present in order to increase margins, treating them as "cash cows". Specialists, on the other hand, have the flexibility to react quickly to market changes. They are, however, under strong pressure in the face of the consequent means required for international expansion, and it is not rare to find brands like Sonia Rykiel welcoming partners in their capital as a consequence.

Among the key activities of luxury conglomerates are acquisitions integration. They show an interesting positive track in that respect, given that in other industrial sectors, mergers and acquisitions often end up with mixed results.[21] For instance, luxury conglomerates will use classic strategic tools of portfolio management as evidenced by LVMH's recent acquisition of Bulgari to strengthen its jewelry division.

Regarding the revenue model, a certain balance needs to be found between profitable and non-profitable brands within a portfolio of brands. As Blanckaert[22] observed, numerous are the luxury brands that make no profit at all.

Further on, BMI is a "reconfiguration of activities in the existing business model of a firm that is new to the product/service market in which the firm competes".[23] Apple is the ultimate example of BMI with the revolution it brought, for example, to the music, telecommunications and publishing industries. The iPod for instance, was a device with a revolutionary value proposition (e.g., seamless music experience) that, in association with the iTunes platform, completely changed the revenue model of the music industry. The same succeeded a few years later with the iPhone and the iPad. Several examples of value-creation innovation exist in the luxury industry. Richard Mille, Greubel Forsey and Cyrus are such companies in the watch industry.

Can we observe BMI in the luxury industry? It is not as disruptive or at the fast pace as in the information and communication technologies industry. The main BMI in this industry was the search for clout by the creation of luxury conglomerates in the last two decades; a consolidation movement that is far from over.

1.3 PATH II – EFFECTUAL ACTION[24]

Entrepreneurship, like luxury, is about people. It is about a person, in a certain context, with certain resources, who challenges the status quo. Two of this book's authors have recently launched new ventures in the luxury industry demonstrating, if necessary, the vitality of the sector. Nevertheless, literature on entrepreneurship in the luxury industry is scarce at best. This section explores the concept of effectuation and how it can help decision-makers not only in new ventures but also in companies going through severe change.

Effectuation is an expression coined by Saras Sarasvathy as a way of differentiating from causation or causal thinking. She wanted to understand the decision-making process of expert entrepreneurs in transforming an idea into a viable new venture. Results show that instead of following a traditional causal or strategic process, these entrepreneurs followed what she called an "effectual logic" or effectuation. The departing point in their reasoning was their actual means, represented by three questions:

(1) Who I am? (Traits, abilities and attributes);
(2) What do I know? (Education, experience and expertise); and
(3) Whom do I know? (Social and professional networks)

that lead to the identification of possible effects (courses of action) out of those means (What can I do?).

Early interaction with stakeholders is central in this approach. This interaction helps to get stakeholders "on board" (generating effectual stakeholder commitment) which consequently provides new means and redefines the goals of the venture. Goals are built "on the fly" and change as a consequence of interactions and contingencies. This process follows an iterative pattern where new means are the base for new interactions and so on. That does not mean an absence of strategy, but rather an openness to adapt given new opportunities and circumstances.

Expert entrepreneurs are shown to follow certain principles in their action:[25]

- affordable loss (finding ways to reach the market with minimum expenditure of resources such as time, effort and money),
- strategic partnership (building partnerships rather than doing a systematic competitive analysis),
- and leveraging contingencies (the ability to turn the unexpected into the profitable).

How does effectuation apply in the luxury industry? At least two strategic contexts can be suitable for the use of effectual logic: new venture creation and strategic turnarounds. It should be no surprise that effectuation could be a favored way to explain new luxury venture creation. The Richard Mille incorporation described in our previous book[26] could be explained through these lenses. Indeed, Richard Mille started out with its industry experience, its important network, and sought to create a unique time piece. By finding stakeholders who committed by funding its venture and the specialized craftsmanship to design and produce it, it then became possible to build the first RM 001. The early engagement of Formula 1 driver Felipe Massa opened new possibilities for RM and so on. Was it possible for Richard Mille back in the late 1990s to rationally anticipate such a path? Probably not. The driving force behind the brand expansion was Richard Mille's vision of the watch, its means and the effects he was able to generate along the process.

Effectuation also seems suitable to explain strategic actions in uncertain environments. For several independent luxury companies, that is exactly how the last 20 years can be described. From a family "niche" business in the triad countries (Europe, US and Japan), luxury has become a consolidated, globalized industry. Managerial requirements to operate in such a complex environment have become rather sophisticated and several family-owned businesses either disappeared or were sold.[27]

In such an environment, how should luxury companies under a severe crisis strategize? Analyzing PESTELs or 5-forces may not be of great help. This is where effectuation becomes an interesting alternative, as exemplified by Swiss mechanical music-box-maker Reuge,[28] and Germain porcelain-maker Meissen.

Reuge's renaissance

Reuge was founded in 1865 in Sainte-Croix, Switzerland. The company history followed the ascension and decline of the mechanical music box, finding itself at the end of the 20th century, surviving thanks to some loyal Swiss and Japanese clients. In the face of likely bankruptcy, a new management team came on board and developed an effectual approach.

Reuge's actual means in 2005: the attributes of a luxury product were still there – refined craftsmanship, unique *savoir-faire* and a strong heritage, but the brand had long been incapable of corresponding to anyone's dream; on the contrary, a Reuge music box was the kind of gift that most people would rather hide than exhibit. The diagnosis was clear: low perceived brand value, outdated management practices and so on, and as a consequence, a lack of financial means.

What to do: Based on this situation and the available means, the company studied several possible courses of action and ended up redefining the company's *raison d'être*. From the music box as a means of transporting music, the brand decided to shift towards lifestyle, a trendy product, a piece of interior design, while still maintaining the values of a traditional product, like being Swiss-made.

Effectual development: laborious execution followed this diagnosis, and the actions listed below were undertaken with the very limited financial means available to Reuge, following an affordable loss principle.

(Continued)

(1) Product redesign: This product was still developed for the traditional customer-base that was looking for a product strongly linked with Reuge's heritage. But a new line of clean and contemporary models was quickly developed to appeal to a larger clientele. Then came the question of the effect to be generated out of this new means (a redesigned music box)?

(2) Corporate business/VIP gifts: The idea of exploring the corporate business/VIP gifts was sparked by the company. Many top people in government as well as companies had a serious need to find a gift like Reuge, that is: (a) unique in its style; (b) possible to adapt to the corporate identity and (c) could be filled with emotion (and special music); in other words, a real luxury product. Examples of clients included The Peninsula Hotel in Tokyo, or personalities (like His Highness the Pope, the Princess of Japan or His Majesty the King of Spain), clients who became an important source of development and generated spontaneous word of mouth.

(3) Corporate partnerships: The customized Peninsula music box highlighted another possible effect to be attained: co-branding. That meant partnering with luxury brands sharing the same levels of Reuge for uniqueness, emotional intensity and top-level quality. Partners included telephone-maker Vertu, watchmaker Harry Winston, porcelain-maker Meissen and luxury-car-maker Maybach.

(4) From product to lifestyle: The question remained however, about the role of the music box as an item of furniture. Even though some clients continued to value a traditional music box, the goal was to rejuvenate the target, and make something that owners would be proud of exhibiting in a central place in their living rooms. This was the most recent development of the brand that was presented in March 2012 at the Basel World Fair: Reuge products for interior design as wall units and lamps.

Reuge could be presented as a success story: a company led by an extraordinary leader who had the vision and the stamina to change the destiny of a company. Although all these elements were present, not the least being the capacity of the work force to adapt and quickly react to the different opportunities that emerged, there is something more fundamental at play in the company's renaissance.

Even if at the onset, the new management team was able to envisage certain outcomes, the company's story was written on the fly.

It is the story of a transformation; it was the identification of the actual means, their possible effects, interaction with clients and the commitment of certain stakeholders to buy and promote the brand which made new means possible, resulting in new effects and so on.

Meissen is going through a similar process under the direction of CEO Christian Kurtzke. Once the favored porcelain of European Royalty, the company suffered a long decline until the management change introduced in 2010. The actual means of the company were not hard to identify: the company's molds covering 300 years of porcelain manufacture. New segments have since been effectually explored: jewels and accessories. That brought new clients to the company and enabled the development of new means like the opening of Villa Meissen in Milano. Finally, the company started to explore fine arts by, among others, partnering with contemporary artists to imagine what Meissen could look like in the years to come. Interestingly, we see in this example how effectuation and BMI interact, since it is the value proposition redefinition that is at the center of both Reuge and Meissen cases.

Effectuation does seem a suitable frame for luxury strategizing and marketing,[29] for both new venture creation and companies facing international, complex and uncertain environments. Isn't the decision to enter in the Chinese market made for most companies using such logic?

1.4 BEHAVIORAL STRATEGIZING

Whereas the concepts of BMI and effectuation have been around for a decade, the new psychology of strategy leadership, as Giovanni Gavetti puts it,[30] is in its inception.

Its departing point is the observation that firms typically cluster around a few strategic positions creating intense competition and diminishing returns. Other positions are however unoccupied, but they are far from the status quo and thus difficult to recognize. In the lines of effectuation and BMI, it takes the environment as a resource to be acted on. It is up to leaders to better use associative thinking, mixing rationality and intuition to reshape industries and competitive landscapes.

This approach provides the psychological rationale underlying the identification of blue ocean strategies.[31] It is about spotting "cognitively distant" opportunities, akin to BMI. It focuses on the leaders' mental processes that should be associated with market-forces analysis (e.g. Porter's five forces) in order to pursue distant opportunities.

In this respect, leaders need to combine three abilities:[32]

- Spot opportunities (Rationality)
- Act on opportunities (Plasticity)
- Legitimize opportunities and "shape" or "construct" the opportunity space (Shaping)

The first challenge lies in spotting opportunities. This calls into question established frames, values and ways of doing within a corporation. Richard Mille saw an opportunity to develop a 21st-century watch, Kurt Kupper and Christian Kurtzke saw the opportunity of going from a physical product to a lifestyle brand for Reuge and Meissen, Oskar Metsevaht conceived the opportunity for a new luxury with Osklen. However, many companies fail on this respect because entrenched practices and mental routines prevent managers from exploring the landscape.

Should a luxury company sell through Internet? E-commerce is developing: net-a-porter is probably the best example; Pomellato just announced that it would open its e-boutique. But how about luxury e-commerce in China? According to Aline Conus,[33] CEO of Chinese based e-luxury brands, e-commerce can be a good opportunity if companies accept one condition: the management analogy is less the "one stop shop" exemplified by a yearly contract with a provider like Fedex, but more like "pizza delivery", with drawbacks like no insurance and the need to deal with several logistic partners. But it does work and it can represent an interesting opportunity if the management is able to challenge its mental frame.

Secondly, plasticity tackles organization malleability, that is, the capacity to take action and get employees engaged. Sometimes, the opportunity fundamentally calls into question the company identity generating internal stakeholders' resistance. Moving from products to lifestyle means adding services to the offer and changing key performance indicators (KPI). Is the company able to commit to that? Expanding to new markets can be tempting, but is the company able to accept that local people manage the market that can potentially become its main one (e.g. Dunhill in China)? Along the same lines, several companies separate their brand and sales into geographical areas. However, how can they manage the fact that individual clients purchase luxury items outside their home country? Industry experts estimate[34] that about half the luxury purchases of the Chinese people are made outside of mainland China for tax reasons (as in Brazil). How can companies manage the fact that some country managers are building brand awareness and others collecting the fruits? How can fair KPI and Profit & Losses (P&L) be established at a managerial level?

As stated by Gavetti, "persuading a workforce that the company's historical identity needs to be reconceptualized is the most difficult of the many hurdles a leader may need to clear in bringing along internal stakeholders".[35] If this could be facilitated in contexts where failure is the likely outcome, it is less obvious in other contexts, especially during mergers and acquisitions.

Thirdly, the shaping ability means being able to legitimize opportunities with external stakeholders. As rightly pointed by Gavetti, financial stakeholders are among the most conservative and any strategic turnaround is first seen with skepticism. That can possibly deprive the company from the financial resources necessary to make the change.

Examples of legitimatization do exist. Louis Vuitton has so far successfully managed its product-line diversification. Osklen moved from sportswear to luxury fashion. Tesla is succeeding in creating a market for top-of-the-range electric cars. It took a while, but luxury car companies are now at the forefront of carbon footprint reduction.

How can these cognitive capacities be developed?

Associative thinking is the central psychological mechanism at play. Indeed, not the least of Bernard Arnault's competences was his capacity to frame and manage LVMH not as a *maison* but as a multinational quoted company where finance plays a central role. This enabled the company to seduce investors and pursue its aggressive acquisition strategy.

Which characteristics of leaders impact their capacity to develop analogies?[36]

The first one is the breadth of experience: the direct or vicarious experience in other industries may help to draw an analogy. Indeed, Henri Racamier and Bernard Arnault at Louis Vuitton, Christian Blanckaert at Hermès, among several other top-managers, had previous experience in construction, industry and manufacturing. This is also where consultants can be useful in supporting this process. The second characteristic is the depth of experience in the industry. An in-depth understanding of the industry can guide an accurate apprehension of the benefits associated with a strategic change. However, that can also prevent the leader from facing a new reality by focusing on a poor source of analogy, with potentially disastrous consequences. A third factor to take into account is the constraints set by policy and regulators.

Given the psychological preponderance of this approach, understanding representations and personal values of top managers may give interesting insights in the strategic directions likely to be taken. This is exemplified by the narrative of the rise and fall of family *maisons* in the 20th century.[37]

This approach also explains why effectuation is suitable in certain contexts. For instance, after a major shock (almost failure, industry completely changed), local search (and not far opportunities) may be the only effective mode of search that is available. Identifying actual means (core of the offer) and what could be done based on that (effectuation) is thus the most appropriate strategic option.

1.5 CONCLUSION

Which trends are going to shape strategizing in the years to come? Consolidation, digital and globalization are three obvious bets. Given that most clients in emerging countries are young, the importance of speed and change is likely to keep accelerating. A question remains about the role of financial capitals from emerging markets that may take a share in luxury companies corresponding to their market importance and role in the world economy, especially from Asia. How that is going to impact luxury companies' strategy remains to be seen.

A fundamental tension remains in the short-term demands of financial markets and the long-term construction of luxury brand equity. Since luxury brands and companies are built to last for generations, there should be a long-term view in how companies are managed. Failure is nevertheless a possibility, as demonstrated by Christian Lacroix or brands that opted for short-term licensing strategies and lost their luxury status, like Calvin Klein or Pierre Cardin.

Indeed, the luxury industry is a people business: creators, management, frontline employees in their interaction with clients will build the value brand. Economies of scale, lean management and "greater taylorism"[38] find limited application in this industry. Intangibles are central. We could even go further and suggest that the luxury industry could be a field of inquiry for strategy's next paradigm.[39]

As this chapter has tried to explain, there is no magical strategic tool that would fit every company; it is up to each company to understand its context and strategize accordingly.

Our aim was also to highlight the central role of conceptualizing for luxury leaders. BMI, effectual action and behavioral strategizing are three conceptualization efforts on strategizing and we looked at how they apply to the luxury industry.

As Richard Normann[40] insightfully proposed, there is a necessary balance between conceptualization capability and action orientation by top-level managers. Conceptualization without action means "paralysis", action without conceptualization means "hysterical hyperactivity".

Shall this chapter serve as an invitation for luxury strategists to explore new frames in their minds and markets.

NOTES

1. As emphasized by Michael Porter through all his books, see for example Porter, M. (1980), *Competitive Strategy,* New York: Free Press. A must read on strategy is Kiechel III, W. (2010), *The Lords of Strategy,* Boston: Harvard Business Press.
2. Blanckaert, C. (2011), *Luxe,* Paris: le cherche midi.

3. Normann, R. (2001), *Reframing Business*, Chichester: John Wiley & Sons.
4. This is certainly an arbitrary choice and other topics could equally deserve our attention. Gavetti, G (2010), Towards a Behavioral Theory of Strategy, *working paper*, provides a comprehensive review of the strategy field.
5. This business model literature has gained momentum in recent years and it is nowadays seen as an interesting alternative to the positioning (e.g., Porter five forces – Porter, M. E. (1985), *Competitive Advantage: Creating and Sustaining Superior Performance*, New York: Free Press), and resource based (e.g. core competences and capabilities – Barney, J. B. (1991), "Firm Resources and Sustained Competitive Advantage", *Journal of Management*, 17: 99–120) schools of strategy. Compared to these schools, the BM concept promotes an outside-in view instead of inside-out; it needs to be learned over time, which highlights the importance of experimentation in the discovery and the development of a new BM; and implicitly assumes that strategy itself is more often directed towards discovery than planning (McGrath, R. G. (2010) Business Models: A Discovery Driven Approach, *Long Range Planning*, 43 (2–3), 247–261).
6. Baden-Fuller, C., Demil, B., Lecocq, X. and Macmillan, I. (2010), "Editorial", *Long Range Planning*, 43(2–3): 143–145.
7. Yunus, M., Moingeon, B. and Lehmann-Ortega, L. (2010), "Building Social Busines Models: Lessons from the Grameen Experience", *Long Range Planning*, 43(2–3): 308–325.
8. Dussart, C. (2010), *Creative Cost-Benefits Reinvention: How to Reverse Commoditization Hell in the Age of Customer Capitalism*, London: Palgrave Macmillan.
9. A crucial question is what we understand by value? For the company, it is the reward for the entrepreneurial risk. For the client, it is what makes him better-off with the company offer. Following Richard Normann and Christian Dussart, we believe that long-term shareholder value is maximized by the creation of customer value; Normann, R. (2001) *Reframing Business*; Dussart, C. (2010), *Creative Cost-Benefits Reinvention*.
10. Chesbrough, H. and Rosenbloom, R. S. (2002) "The Role of the Business Model in Capturing Value from Innovation: Evidence from

Xerox Corporation's Technology Spinoff Companies", *Industrial and Corporate Change*, 11(3), 529–555.

11. Chesbrough and Rosenbloom, "The Role of the Business Model in Capturing Value from Innovation".
12. Osterwalder, A. and Pigneur, Y. (2009), *Business Model Generation*, Toronto.
13. Kapferer, J.-N. and Bastien, V. (2009), *The Luxury Strategy. Break The Rules of Marketing to Build Strong Brands*, London and Philadelphia: Kogan Page Ltd; Chevalier, M. and Mazzalovo, G. (2008), *Luxury Brand Management*, Singapore: John Wiley & Sons (Asia) Pte. Ltd.
14. Check also Storemark, K. and Hoffmann, J. (2012), "A Case Study on the Business Model of Chloé", *Journal of Global Fashion Marketing*, 3(1): 34–41.
15. Stankeviciute, R. and Hoffmann, J. (2011), "The Slippery Slope of Brand Expansion: Look to the Luxury Sector to Understand How Brand Extensions Affect Parent Brands", *Marketing Management*, Winter, pp. 26–31.
16. ECCIA (2012), The value of the cultural and creative industries to the European economy, June 2012 retrieved from http://www.eccia.eu/uploads/media/The_value.pdf on 10 June 2012.
17. Chevalier, M. and Mazzalovo, G. (2008), op. cit.
18. Presentation made by Denis Morisset at the Innoluxury Summit, Shanghai, on 12 January 2012; it was well the theme of the Financial Times Business of Luxury Summit in 2012.
19. Precepta (2010), Stratégies des groupes de luxe, 3 May 2010, available at http://www.xerfi.fr/XERFINEW_WEB/FR/Etudes_sectorielles_Precepta-Strategies_des_groupes_de_luxe_0DIS40.awp
20. Hoffmann, J. and Hoffmann, B. (2012), "The PIER Framework of Luxury Innovation", in Hoffmann, J. and Coste-Manière, I. (eds), *Luxury Strategy in Action*, London: Palgrave Macmillan.
21. See for instance in the IT sector, the mixed results of the merger between Alcatel and Lucent, or the partnership between Nokia and Microsoft.
22. Blanckaert, *Les 100 mots du Luxe*, Paris: Presses Universitaires de France.
23. Santos, J., Spector, B. and Van der Heyden, L. (2009), "Toward a Theory of Business Model Innovation within Incumbent Firms", *working paper*, Insead.

24. This section is based on Sarasvathy, S. (2001), "What makes entrepreneurs entrepreneurial?", *working paper;* Sarasvathy, S. (2008), *Effectuation: Elements of Entrepreneurial Expertise*, Chelteham: Edward Elgar; and several articles available at www.effectuation.org.
25. Sarasvathy, *Effectuation.*
26. Hoffmann and Hoffmann, The PIER Framework of Luxury Innovation.
27. Blanckaert, *Luxe.*
28. We present here an abbreviated version of the Reuge case explained at length at Hoffmann, J. and Kupper, K. (2012), Playing outside the Box: The Effectual Reuge-volution, *working paper.*
29. See also, Blanckaert, *Les 100 mots du Luxe*, pp. 85–8.
30. Gavetti, G. (2011), "The New Psychology of Strategic Leadership", *Harvard Business Review*, July 2011; Gavetti, Toward a Behavioral Theory of Strategy, *working paper.*
31. Kim, W. C and Mauborgne, R. (2005), *Blue Ocean Strategy*, Boston: Harvard Business Press.
32. Gavetti, "Toward a Behavioral Theory of Strategy".
33. Round-table at Walpole's British Luxury Summit, London, 9 July 2012.
34. Ibid.
35. Gavetti, "The New Psychology of Strategic Leadership".
36. Gavetti, G., Levinthal, D. and Rivkin, J. (2005), "Strategy Making in Novel and Complex Worlds: the Power of Analogy", *Strategic Management Journal*, 26: 691–712.
37. Blanckaert, *Luxe.*
38. Kiechel III, *The Lords of Strategy.*
39. Ibid.
40. Normann, *Reframing Business.*

3 Components of a business model

- Value proposition
- Value architecture
- value capture (revenue model)

2

PATHS FOR THE EMERGENCE OF GLOBAL CHINESE LUXURY BRANDS

Jonas Hoffmann and Betina Hoffmann

2.1 INTRODUCTION

China's luxury goods market will be worth an estimated US$ 27 billion by 2015, representing 20 percent of global luxury sales.[1] As observed in other sectors in China, the speed at which the market took off is impressive. Louis Vuitton entered the market 20 years ago, has currently more than 40 stores in China and is opening more at a fast pace.[2] No surprise that (Western) luxury groups are in great shape, reporting double-digit growth and profits.

This market big bang has been a bonanza for Western luxury conglomerates and companies and their commercial partners in Hong Kong and mainland China. Strong growth and high profit margins have of course attracted newcomers, but no local brand exists so far to challenge the likes of Louis Vuitton, Hermès, Gucci or Prada in China, and even less abroad. Given China's economic growth, rich craftsmanship tradition and growing availability of financial and managerial competences, there are grounds for such a development.

2.1.1 What are the potential paths for the emergence of global Chinese luxury brands?

An analysis of the three components of a business model[3] – namely value[4] proposition, value architecture and value capture – provides the basis for considering this question. This chapter shows that opportunities to create and make original value propositions in China do in fact exist but that the challenge lies in constructing, delivering and capturing this value.

2.2 LUXURY VALUE PROPOSITIONS

A luxury value proposition corresponds to someone's dream; it is a source of pleasure, a sign of status; it is unique and incorporates a certain heritage and refined craftsmanship. Identification with it does not stem from a customer need, but only when needs are satisfied do we enter the realm of desire. As we have said elsewhere,[5] a Chanel bag will serve to hold some small belongings, a Ferrari to move from Cannes to Monaco, a Richard Mille watch to check the time, but needs are not the main value drivers behind these products.

The value proposition expresses the potential of an offer to correspond to a client's dream. Value propositions are culturally framed: what people dream of in China is certainly different from what people dream of in Western countries. Indeed, while bamboo and jade have powerful meanings in Chinese culture, this is not the case elsewhere; it would therefore be relatively difficult to persuade or educate Western clients that bamboo, for example, is a "noble" material.

Alternatively, dreams can be framed by economic factors: a central tenet of marketing is its capacity to frame client expectations in favor of the company offer. Given the recency of the market economy in China and even more of the luxury market, there is room to frame client desires and luxury expectations in a sort of market "education" process. Hence the effort engaged in by Chanel, Louis Vuitton, Cartier, Hermès and others to present their long heritage of craftsmanship, *savoir faire*, innovation and exclusivity[6] in China.

Given this strong focus of luxury incumbents on heritage, a meaningful frame for newcomers from China or elsewhere is to differentiate three orientations of luxury value propositions: "looking to the past", "looking to the present" and "looking to the future" (Figure 2.1).

"Looking to the past" value propositions are those that draw inspiration from the rich Chinese history, revitalizing refined

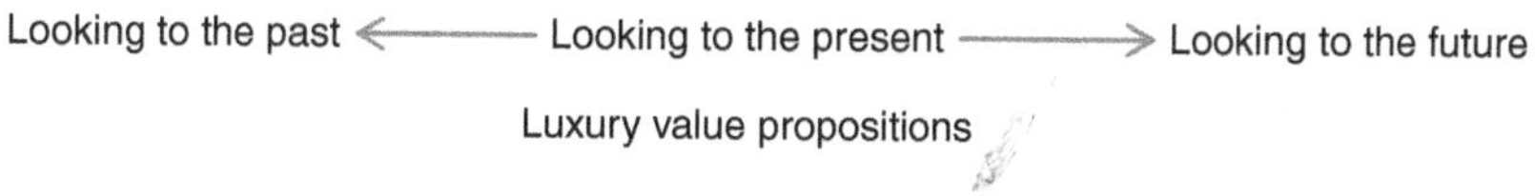

Looking to the past ⟵ Looking to the present ⟶ Looking to the future

Luxury value propositions

FIGURE 2.1 **Orientation of luxury value propositions**

craftsmanship and heritage. Indeed, the history of China shows that it excelled in those dimensions. Historically, merchants from Europe had long crossed Asia to trade Chinese silk, creating what came to be known as the Silk Road (or Silk Route). China has been an economic superpower for most of its history and this opulence has given birth to numerous refined crafts: silk, tea, porcelain, jade, bamboo, tailoring, tea and liquors, to name but a few.

Several Chinese brands exemplify this orientation. Moutai liquor has a history dating back many centuries and is characterized by the respect for ancient traditions; priced at more than US$ 200 a bottle, it is exported all over the world, mainly to the Chinese diaspora. Tea is another luxury product which draws on China's heritage, with some vintages costing hundreds of dollars per kilogram. Jewelry is another field of choice where brands like C-Jewelry create luxury pieces that are inspired by traditional Chinese crafts. The most representative example is probably that of Shang Xia.

Shang Xia[7]

ShangXia is a brand, created in 2008 by Chinese designer Ms. Jiang Qiong Er with the support of Hermès, which opened its first store in 2010. It presents as its vision: "SHANG XIA, Renaissance of Chinese Craftsmanship". Its first product line focuses on the home including decoration, accessories and "an extended experience of tea".

The brand naming attests to its value proposition: "Shang Xia" means "up" and "down", reflecting "the flow of energy from the past through to the future transmitting the essence of a culture and its aesthetics. Building on the inheritance of the culture and with the spirit of respect for the environment, it is in this continuum that Shang Xia strives to integrate the finest quality materials and consistent craftsmanship in the range of its product offerings. With flair and minute attention to detail and quality, Shang Xia integrates the warmth, balance and harmony of Chinese hospitality and grace".

(Continued)

Central to the brand project is the experience of its artistic director who comes from a family with strong links with the creative and artistic world and who studied in both China and France, thus giving her creative work a dual perspective. Finally, the choice of Chinese materials symbolizes this desire to accentuate heritage and craftsmanship: zitan wood, felt, bamboo, eggshell porcelain, cashmere, jade and agate.

"Looking to the present" value propositions are grounded in contemporary China, building bridges between East and West and focusing mainly on luxury lifestyles. Luxury hospitality is a sector where this approach has found fertile ground, as the overseas expansion of Mandarin Oriental luxury hotels bears witness. As Middle-Eastern countries have created an Emirati hospitality approach, symbolized for example, by the Burj al Arab seven-star hotel in Dubai, the Chinese architectural tradition expressed in places like the Summer Palace in Beijing or the Suzhou Gardens, could give birth to a new form of Chinese luxury hospitality. Other examples can be found in lifestyle brands such as Shanghai Tang, jewelry from Qeelin, shoes from Chengdu-based Sheme and fashion creators like Uma Wang or Shiatzy Chen.

Shanghai Tang[8]

Created in Hong Kong in 1994, Shanghai Tang belongs to the Swiss luxury conglomerate Richemont. The company value proposition states that the company pioneers a luxury, Chinese lifestyle. They aim to be a "global ambassador of contemporary Chinese chic", showcasing "the best of Chinese heritage and craftsmanship through a unique product universe and multi-sensory shopping experience".

One distinctive feature of the brand is its appeal to Shanghainese tailoring:

> Shanghai Tang's unique Imperial Tailoring collection offers made-to-measure service supported by a strong heritage of legendary Shanghainese tailoring – the only Chinese "Haute Couture" house

> with a unique fusion of east meets west silhouettes with exquisite vintage craftsmanship. Much of the Shanghainese tailoring skills and fashions were lost during the cultural revolution, with now only a fragment of houses employing the ancient techniques, Shanghai Tang being one of the last bastions.

The company therefore aims to interpret "Chinese culture and craftsmanship with a vibrant sophistication and dynamism of the 21st century, utilizing the best of Chinese materials from luxurious Chinese silk to the finest Mongolian cashmere and precious Chinese jade, to create a range of contemporary luxury lifestyle products that are proudly made by Chinese."

This is an example of how a company can delve into Chinese heritage to propose a brand aimed to please the Chinese today. We can notice that all the dimensions of a luxury brand are exemplified: heritage, craftsmanship, *savoir-faire*, innovation and exclusivity. Shanghai Tang has so far an international network of 40 boutiques in the world that became well-known for their multi-sensory approach.

Although "looking to the past" and "looking to the present" value propositions can eventually lead to global players, it will probably be a long process. Perception inertia and the cultural framing of "*made in* China" will take a certain time to evolve. (It is noticeable that both Shanghai Tang and Shang Xia are totally or partly owned by Western companies Richemont and Hermès.) "Looking to the past" value propositions in particular face issues of legitimacy vis-à-vis Western luxury incumbents: Europe has a long and strong luxury heritage, associated with refined craftsmanship; "*made in* France, Italy or Switzerland" are associated in consumers' perceptions with "true" luxury goods.

There is, however, an opportunity for Chinese luxury players to accelerate their international expansion (and at the same time overcome legitimacy issues) by developing "looking to the future" value propositions. This can be done by companies that propose a viable future view for a certain luxury category, reframing the meanings associated with a certain luxury product. While examples in China are lacking so far, they do exist in the Western luxury goods industry.

Richard Mille luxury watches offer one such example. This brand was created in 2001 with a value proposition of creating a 21st-century watch. According to Richard Mille, most luxury watches are geared toward the past, using today's materials to build watches inspired by the 19th century. By integrating new materials and composites – from the aeronautics and car industry for example – a certain artistic and architectural dimension and the best *haute horlogerie* enabled by Swiss fabrication, Richard Mille launched its first ultra-performing timepiece (RM001) in 2001. For the last decade, the company has kept pushing the boundaries of mechanical watch-making, creating numerous innovations along the way. As a consequence, it is recognized as one of the most innovative companies in the watch industry today. The reasons for this are numerous. Richard Mille's genius and charisma go without saying, but the brand's capacity to reframe the current industry's logic and develop a future-oriented value proposition is also central. Another example is provided by the brand Cyrus.

CYRUS – Value Proposition by Camille Coulibeuf[9]

The Cyrus watch was created after four years of development, by two double-cousins, Julien and Laurent Lecamp. They wanted to satisfy the need for a timepiece with a very eye-appealing design (strong identity), new ways of reading time (innovation) and a very unique story. They chose the name of CYRUS referring to CYRUS The Great, the first conqueror of the world, who represents the values of the brand driven by the spirit of conquest.

Each timepiece in gold is stamped – on the back – with a certified copy of one of the first coins in humanity (displaying a lion and a bull) developed under the reign of CYRUS The Great. The original coin (2500 years old!) belongs to the brand itself and required more than four months to be found. Luxury is into details . . . and luxury needs a true story.

Compared to most of the brands, CYRUS has famous ambassadors (sportsmen and businessmen) that spontaneously come to the brand as they are fans of it. This is the philosophy of the brand: not having customers but real fans. It makes all the difference.

Swiss watchmaker Jean François Mojon (awarded best developer-conceptor of the year 2011 at *Grand Prix de l'Horlogerie de Geneve 2011*) signed a ten years' agreement with the brand to develop all the complications of the timepieces. The different patents for the first two collections required three years of development: one of the main characteristics of the CYRUS KUROS collection is its patented eye-catching design that perfectly suits the wrist (with a patented double-angle sapphire too), whatever its size, while the CYRUS KLEPCYS represents a revolutionary mechanism patented – and a completely new way, in three dimensions, to read the time (on a linear basis), the date and the moon phases. The complications of the KLEPCYS only exist for the KLEPCYS itself which makes the brand all the more exclusive, explaining why it received the award "Best independent brand" at the *Nuit de l'Horlogerie de Monaco 2011*, a prize given by collectors from all over the world (Figure 2.2).

FIGURE 2.2 **Cyrus logo**

The Cyrus brand identity is reflected in its logo. The company strongly believed in the meaning/power of the logo for the success of a brand and paid particular attention to its development.

More than representing a component of a watch (the escape wheel), it has three branches, curved and rolling on the right side, meaning that the brand is future-oriented.

Each of the three branches lets the energy flow to the center of the logo (the heart of CYRUS) thanks to an opened extremity.

The CYRUS Geneve logo is clearly made of three elements: the logo, the name and the location. The "CY" and "US" form two halves of a circle and the "R" in the middle is the third element.

The number three is prominent in everything the company has developed. Why? Simply because it is connected to Cyrus The Great, who conquered three main territories before being considered as the King of the world, 2500 years ago. Once again, luxury is into details... and luxury needs a true story.

Last but not the least, the dial of the two collections is made of triangles (three angles and three sides) and they all have three functions

(Continued)

(time, chronograph and date for the Kuros; time, moon phases and date for the Klepcys); each timepiece has three different types of finish.

The philosophy of the double-cousins? "If you have to choose between 2 roads in your life, always take the less travelled by – even if it is the longest one – and it will make all the difference."

Defining the value proposition is a key step, but several challenges lie in building, delivering and capturing this value.

2.3 VALUE ARCHITECTURE

The value architecture comprises the definition of the resources and activities necessary to create and distribute an offering and to "determine the complementary assets needed to support the firm's position in this chain", including "the firm's suppliers and customers, and should extend from raw materials to the final customer". It also describes "the position of the firm within the value network linking suppliers and customers, including identification of potential complementors and competitors".[10]

What could be the specific challenges concerning the value architecture for Chinese luxury? The first relates to the existence of a refined and specific *savoir faire* to create and manufacture a luxury product. Assuming this resource exists, as the examples above suggest, another necessary resource is the availability of funding to support a project. This should not be a problem, given the funding available from public and private funding agencies to push "created in China" projects.

Related to the above-mentioned funding issue is the paramount importance of "Guanxi", that is, the network of interpersonal relations possessed by an individual both in the private and the public sector. This is the *sine qua non* condition for the development of a luxury business, given the high-profile target of such an offering.

Which activities should the company develop? Creation and design are at the heart of the offer and the booming art scene in China demonstrates that talent is emerging at a growing pace. The challenge will certainly lie in the managerial capabilities required to take an original luxury value proposition and turn it into a profitable marketable product. Birindelli[11] provides ample evidence of the management complexity of a luxury company, and given the lack of history in the development of such companies in China, this is one of the difficulties that should be addressed by the integration of skilled resources. This explains the partnership between Shang Xia and Hermès. These managerial skills are even more necessary in the case of brands intending to play abroad, where complex regulations, customs, tax and currency issues are at stake.

Logistics and distribution modes are also important. Given the power of landlords and the concentration of luxury outlets in specific areas, such as Nanjing Xi Road in Shanghai, choices concerning the ownership of stores, franchising or selective distribution have a considerable impact on cost structure, brand building, sales experience and ultimately, on the capacity to project a luxury image.[12]

Finally, the impact of counterfeits should not be underestimated. Even if they could be considered a sign of a brand's success, they still have a predatory effect on a brand's image. A company's capacity to interact effectively with the authority to prevent this burden is necessary.

Designing the adequate value architecture is not a simple exercise and the impressive expansion of luxury conglomerates in the last two decades is evidence of how a critical mass of resources and capabilities changes the power relations in an industry.

2.4 VALUE CAPTURE[13]

Capturing an adequate share of value calls into question the chosen revenue model. What are the costs? What is the pricing structure? All the choices in terms of the value proposition and value architecture will signal the viability of the business model.

Short-term success being the "offering of the moment" is more easily achievable than the construction of a long-term brand that will stand the test of time.

Defining adequate value capture mechanisms calls for sophisticated financial skills mastered by luxury conglomerates but they are in much shorter supply for small and medium players. Financial and tax issues should be carefully addressed, given the price differences between mainland China and Hong Kong, for example, and the fact that an important amount of luxury buying by Chinese residents is done outside of mainland China.

How about India?

India will represent a luxury market of €10 billion by 2015, according to A. T. Kearney. Like China, India has a long tradition of fine craftsmanship. The country is the biggest consumer of gold in the world and the jewelry industry has for long been a source of inspiration for Western players. Jaipur, for instance, is estimated to have between 200,000 and 300,000 workers involved directly or indirectly in the gemstone trade, and it is home to companies like the Gem Palace or Amrapali. Hospitality is another sector where the country excels, with chains like Taj and Oberoi.

A rationale similar to that in China applies. Global luxury companies could emerge in the long term if the country keeps up in its development path, but they are unlikely to appear in the near future. As in China, luxury giants are investing in local companies, like Moet Hennessy Louis Vuitton (LVMH)'s L Capital acquisition of a stake in Fabindia. Moreover, a continuous understanding of this market and its education about (Western-defined) luxury consumption is a top priority for established groups. For instance, Hermès has developed products for a local clientele (e.g., its sari line) and has partnered with the Khanna family, owners of the Oberoi chain of hotels since 2007. The same applies for Montblanc, with the Gandhi collection.

It could be risky for Western companies to neglect today's India and develop "looking to the past" value propositions. The 2011 Chanel Mumbai–Paris collection and the recent Louis Vuitton advertising campaign are evidence of this. Both look for the India of the Maharajahs, its palaces, its elephants and so on. Even if that is still the favourite tourist destination in the country, what today's young Indians are doing (see Bungalow 8 and Bombay Electric in Mumbai) could not be farther from this stereotyped foreign vision of the country.

2.5 DISCUSSION

The central point for the emergence of luxury created and made in China is the development of a distinctive luxury value proposition. Why can "looking to the future" value propositions inspire Chinese luxury players? The first reason is that, despite Western resistance, the future is somehow happening there: Shanghai and Hong Kong are on par with London, Paris or New York as magnets for young talented workers and creators. Luxury conglomerates are sending their most gifted resources to these markets, thus creating a critical mass favoring new ventures. The second reason lies in a kind of incumbents' dilemma: luxury conglomerates may be tempted to reproduce a model that has worked well so far and pursue their efforts to "educate" the market in Western-defined luxury codes. This may find its limits in emerging markets such as China, India and Brazil, where young adults make up the bulk of luxury consumers, presenting rapidly evolving luxury aspirations. As a consequence, brands that are not fine-tuned to these fast-evolving markets may find themselves challenged by newcomers.

How can one do it then? The examples from Richard Mille and Cyrus show one way: using technological developments (e.g., new materials). Another way is to draw inspiration from the arts scene. Louis Vuitton has mastered co-signing collections with artists, and German porcelain-maker Meissen is also on this track.

The value proposition is just a first step, and a consistent business model must rely on equally sound value architecture and value capture. Even if Guanxi is the starting point for that, there are several issues to be addressed and skilled resources are necessary to complete the creative team. These skills abound in luxury conglomerates and it is likely that the association of former employees from these groups with emerging talent will be a meaningful path, as evidenced by Qeelin.

2.6 CONCLUSION

The economic epicenter has shifted to the Pacific, and this is where the next pages of the luxury industry will be written.

Besides producing hungry luxury consumers, China will play an ever-increasing role in this industry.

When will we see global Chinese luxury players? The answer certainly depends on which time frame we choose. In the short term, probably not, but in the long term, the answer is certainly yes.

For the foreseeable future, luxury conglomerates like LVMH, Richemont and PPR will continue scanning the luxury environment to spot emerging "stars", making the likelihood of the emergence of a pure Chinese player quite random. On the other hand, it is also likely that luxury conglomerates' shareholders will increasingly come from China, given its clout. Mergers and acquisitions present one way of realizing that presence, as exemplified by the acquisition of Italian yachtmaker Ferrety by China's SHIG-Weichai and of a stake of French fashion house Sonia Rykiel by Hong Kong's Fung Brands. The recent introduction of Prada in the Hong Kong stock exchange is a clear sign of this trend. All in all, the diffused capital structure of most luxury conglomerates may make the question of who the luxury company owner is less relevant.

This cannot be said of the "created and made in" label. Given the strategic assets it represents and the premium price it allows companies to command, this will continue to be a major issue for years to come. What entities like the European Cultural and Creative Industries Alliance (ECCIA)[14] do will influence our perception of where "true" luxury comes from. The frame presented above presents a path for Chinese luxury companies to grow and profit with *"created and made in* China" luxury products.

Conversely, it also presents some paths for the maintenance of luxury incumbents' competitive advantage. This can be achieved by insisting heavily on heritage, the *"made in"* label, refined craftsmanship ("looking to the past") and continually renewing the brand by integrating new materials and interacting with artists, as a brand like Louis Vuitton has successfully done in recent years.

ACKNOWLEDGMENTS

The authors thank Malcolm Parker and Sian Jones, for their help in improving the chapter, and Laurent Lecamp, for his review of the Cyrus case.

NOTES

1. McKinsey & Company (2011), *Understanding China's Growing Love for Luxury*.
2. www.louisvuitton.com.
3. Moingeon, B. and Lehmann-Ortega, L. (2010), "Creation and Implementation of a New Business Model: A Disarming Case Study", M@n@gement, 13(4): 266–297; Osterwalder, A. and Pigneur, Y. (2009), *Business Model Generation*, Toronto.
4. What is value? For the company, it is the reward for entrepreneurial risk. For the client, it is what makes him better off with the company offer. Following Richard Normann and Christian Dussart, we believe that long-term shareholder value is maximized by the creation of customer value. Sources: Normann, R. (2001), *Reframing Business*, Chichester: John Wiley & Sons; Woodruff, R. (1997), "Customer Value: The Next Source for Competitive Advantage", *Journal of the Academy of Marketing Science*, 25(2): 139–153; Dussart, C. (2010), *Creative Cost-Benefits Reinvention: How to Reverse Commoditization Hell in the Age of Customer Capitalism*, London: Palgrave Macmillan.
5. Hoffmann, J. and Hoffmann, B. (2012), "The PIER Framework of Luxury Innovation", in Hoffmann, J. and Coste-Manière, I. (eds), *Luxury Strategy in Action*, London: Palgrave Macmillan.
6. Hoffmann, J. and Hoffmann, B. (2012), op. cit.; Comité Colbert (2011), *Press Report*, downloaded on 24 October 2011 at http://www.comitecolbert.com/internet/images/stories/Presse/Dossier%20institutionnel/Presse_FR_2011_HD.pdf.
7. All the information and citations in this section are from the institutional website of Shang Xia: www.shangxia.com, accessed on 24 October 2011.
8. All the information and citations in this section are from the institutional website of Shanghai Tang: www.shanghaitang.com, accessed on 24 October 2011.
9. Camille Collibeuf is a 2011 graduate from SKEMA's Luxury and Fashion Management Master of Science program. He wrote about the Cyrus business model in his dissertation under the supervision of Prof. Jonas Hoffmann.
10. Chesbrough, H. and Rosenbloom, R. S. (2002), "The Role of the Business Model in Capturing Value from Innovation: Evidence from

Xerox Corporation's Technology Spinoff Companies", *Industrial and Corporate Change*, 11(3): 529–555.

11. Birindelli, F. G. (2012), "Luxury Business: Multinational Organizations and Global Specializations", in Hoffmann, J. and Coste-Manière, I. (eds), *Luxury Strategy in Action*, London: Palgrave Macmillan.
12. Quintavalle, A. (2012), "Retailing in the Luxury Industry", Hoffmann, J. and Coste-Manière, I. (eds), *Luxury Strategy in Action*, London: Palgrave Macmillan, pp. 74–107.
13. Given that in our previous book Pizzini has developed this point at length, we will just provide a brief exposition: Pizzini, G. (2012), "Financial Survival Guide: Value Creation and Piña Coladas", Hoffmann, J. and Coste-Manière, I. (eds), *Luxury Strategy in Action*, London: Palgrave Macmillan.
14. Including Comité Colbert (France), Fondazione Altagamma (Italy), Walpole British Luxury (UK), Meisterkreiss (Germany) and Circulo Fortuny (Spain).

3

LUXO BRASIL AND OSKLEN'S NEW LUXURY

Jonas Hoffmann

3.1 INTRODUCTION

This chapter aims to take a tour around Brazil's flourishing luxury market. It starts by presenting an overview of the market before delving into the emblematic case of Osklen's new luxury.

3.2 BRAZIL LUXURY MARKET: FACTS AND FIGURES

The Brazilian luxury market is progressing at double-digit rates and was evaluated to be worth US$ 7.59 billion in 2010.[1] McKinsey[2] has estimated that 3 million Brazilians can afford luxury goods, while Forbes has identified 30 billionaires in Brazil, half of them self-made and the other half inherited.[3] The market has really taken off in the last five years, with demand for luxury goods remaining vigorous despite the global financial crisis of 2008. Most luxury groups have recently entered the market or are in the process of doing so, and the biggest brands are now in the process of entering Brazil's "2nd tier" cities such as Belo Horizonte, Brasilia or Curitiba, after establishing themselves in São Paulo and Rio de Janeiro.

3.2.1 Main venues

São Paulo is where it is all happening. It concentrates more than half of Brazilian GDP and is home to most Brazilian high net-worth individuals. Main venues for luxury consumption are Oscar Freire's street, close to the financial district of Avenida Paulista, and the close neighborhood of Jardins that is home of most luxury cars dealerships and Cidade Jardim Mall. Other shopping places in São Paulo include NK Store, JK Iguatemi and Iguatemi São Paulo. Cidade Jardim Mall is probably the world's first luxury mall to host a public library.[4] Besides São Paulo, the above-mentioned Rio de Janeiro, Brasilia, Curitiba and Belo Horizonte are other cities with a thriving luxury market.

Entering the Brazilian market is however complicated due to the so-called cost Brazil:[5] red tape, different taxes, high real-estate cost, expensive labor, high logistic cost and strong protectionism. Being able to count on a good network including local lawyers, import/export trading companies and, potentially, a local partner is important for foreign companies.

3.2.2 Consumer behavior

McKinsey[6] identifies three main categories of luxury consumers in Brazil: High Net Worths, AAAs and Aspirationals. In the high net worth group are the 13,700 households (0.1%) with an income of at least R$ 46,500 per month ($ 25,200), mainly new and self-made money. The AAA group includes the 182,500 households with an earning between R$ 20,925 and 46,500 per month ($11,346–$25,200), characterized by a high level of education and sophistication. Thirdly, the Aspirational group comprises 662,600 households with earnings of more than R$ 11,630 ($6,303).

A common trait: Brazilians like to spend and show off. As stated by McKinsey, "being seen to be rich is an important part of *being* rich". The reasons for this are numerous. As in other emerging countries like India and China, the group plays a central role in Brazilian's life: the family and friends. Brazilians are as individualistic as they are other oriented. And they have long waited for the promise of being the "country of the future". So now that they see themselves as the country of the present and the future, they want it all and they want it now.

Also, for long, the fortunate classes had to fly to the United States and to Europe to get access to luxury goods, creating a mimetic desire of the middle classes to have access to those same goods. Now they have them in Brazil.

Contributing to this mimetic desire, akin to India's Bollywood, there is a strong celebrity culture related to Brazil's entertainment industry, the so-called telenovelas (soap operas). And those celebrities are central to the image construction of luxury brands, supported by a dedicated "celebs" media industry, including Brazil's "People" magazine, *Caras* ("Faces"), *Vogue*, *Elle* and the more generalist press, including titles like *Veja* or *IstoÉ*.

The cult of the body, the importance of appearance and ostentation all contribute to this culture. Part of this is due to the weather and beach culture, all strongly reinforced by the media and the star system. Isn't Brazil's cosmetic surgeon, Dr Ivo Pitanguy, known as the Michelangelo of the scalpel, a national treasure?

Among other characteristic traits of Brazilian luxury consumers are the following:

- Brazilians love credit, and even those who can afford to pay up front prefer to pay through instalment plans.
- Clients are ready to pay the price: given taxes and import cost, the price of several consumer goods is often double that found in the US and Europe. That makes for nice profit margins for retailers. It also motivates Brazilians to travel overseas (New York, Miami or Paris) to acquire those goods.[7] In Miami, Brazilians are kindly referred to as "Walking Stimulus Packages".
- Service is fundamental. Throughout their history, Brazilian elites have been able to afford full-time maids and servants. This has created high expectations regarding service at luxury shops and the need to feel truly distinctive as luxury shoppers.

3.2.3 Purchases

Given this show-off culture, highly visible items like cars and accessories are largely praised. Despite Brazil's security deficit, to put it mildly, luxury car sales are booming. Porsches, Ferraris and the like have found one of their fast-developing markets in Brazil. What is hard to believe for those living in Europe or the United States is that most of those cars are armored.

Given São Paulo's constant traffic jams, helicopters are a must have for high net worth Brazilians. Indeed, according to industry experts, the city has one of the world's largest private helicopter fleet in the world. Lifestyle luxury is well represented by several top-level hotels including the Fasano in São Paulo, and several world-class resorts in the Brazilian coast and the Amazon region. Top-level gastronomy is a recent development in Brazil and the 4th position of D. O. M. at the 'world's best restaurant' ranking is particularly appreciated.[8]

This show-off logo orientation could suggest a mimicking orientation towards US- and Europe-defined luxury codes. That would make for an easy stereotype. Brazil is much more than that. It has a mosaic, vibrant, contrasted, young and dynamic culture. Brazilians are, generally, smiling, warm-hearted, welcoming and informal people. And history has taught them that they can only count on themselves and their network, resulting in a strong entrepreneurship culture.

At a broader level, the country is blessed by Mother Nature, able to nourish part of humanity, with a fabulous biodiversity and clement weather. The country prides itself as a champion of sustainability. At the same time it is violent, continuously fighting corruption, has insufficient infrastructure and struggles to be able to nourish all its citizens.

It is in this context that Osklen emerged. It is not the first Brazilian luxury brand to gain world notoriety – jewelry-maker H. Stern has been there for much longer; but it uniquely symbolizes the potential for a different luxury, what Osklen calls a "new luxury". We shall explore this unique brand in the following section.

3.3 OSKLEN

Founded by Oskar Metsavaht, Osklen is a Brazilian fashion company that has been gaining momentum in the last years because of its distinguished proposition of a "new luxury". We present below the company, a profile of Oskar Metsevaht, and a view of a new luxury item.

3.3.1 Company profile[9]

The company was founded in 1989 and its style "is expressed in the crossover of the different elements that are part of the daily life of its Creative Director, Oskar Metsavah. Fashion, art, culture, design and the environment are all a part of Osklen's inspiration, and make it not only a brand, but a vehicle of communication for a lifestyle."

The legend is now well-known but is worth presenting: Oskar was originally a sports-medicine physician and passionate about outdoor sports like alpinism, surfing, snowboarding and skating. When he was a member of the first Brazilian team to climb the Aconcagua in the Andes in mid-1980, he used his medical knowledge to design a high-tech anorak. This anorak was ergonomically adapted for climbing in very low temperatures and was aesthetically appealing. After the expedition, it became an object of desire. The response was so good that a few years later he quit his profession to create high-end sportswear inspired by his love for snowboarding and surfing.

For the first ten years, sportswear was the main identity of the brand. From 2000 onwards, it began to focus more on fashion design and luxury, with the issues of environmental conservation and socio-environmental education present throughout the history.

Oskar remains at the helm of the creative (art and style) direction, not because he considers that he is the most creative, but because Osklen and the Instituto e projects are the concrete manifestation of his vision: "it is my way of writing what I think, imagine and believe".

Osklen "finds itself between the dynamism of the metropolis and the exuberance of Brazilian nature, giving life to a style based on the harmonization of contrasts. The brand represents the lifestyle of contemporary women and men in a world where urban and nature, global and local, organic and technological live together."

It aims to integrate nature, culture, society and refined aesthetics offering a casual-chic style that aims to be "an authentic and genuine Brazilian lifestyle both contemporary and cosmopolitan at the same time". It looks to make "clothes with a meaning made for people who identify with the lifestyle" it offers.

Since 2003, Osklen has presented its collections at Sao Paulo Fashion Week, the biggest fashion event in Latin America. Its latest collections are:

- Fall/Winter 2010: Tropic of Capricorn
- Spring/Summer 2010: Samba
- Fall/Winter 2011: Fenix
- Spring/Summer 2011: Oceans
- Spring/Summer 2012: Royal Black

Every collection has its own importance and history, but the Fenix and Royal Black had a special meaning. The first was inspired by the tragic fire which burnt down Osklen's headquarters in February 2010. It voiced the rebirth of the brand after its history had been reduced to ashes. The Royal Black is a tribute to Afro-Brazilians and came out of a long work of immersion in Brazil's black culture.

A central point in Osklen's identity is its sustainability engagement in all the steps of its business process (see more below). The brand gained momentum in 2008 when it was identified by the WWF–UK as a "Future Maker" in a report where most established luxury groups were criticized by their lack of transparency regarding their sourcing processes. Recognition has been mounting since Osklen was considered one of the ten most influential and inspiring brands in the world by WGSN, the fourth most creative company in Brazil, and the Emergent Luxury Company of Year (2011) by the Luxury Briefing Awards.

Osklen has nowadays 62 stores in Brazil, two stores in Milan, two in Tokyo, one in Rome, one in New York, one in Miami, one in Buenos Aires and a season store in Punta del Este. Besides its showrooms in Italy, Greece, Australia and the United States, the brand is present in France, England, Germany, Korea and the Middle East.

Osklen is the first ever fashion retail chain in Brazil to have offset its retail and headquarters' carbon emissions by the purchase of social carbon credits at CantorCO2e (affiliate to Cantor Fitzgerald, world leader in carbon credits trade).

Forbes[10] has recently estimated Oskar's fortune, a close proxy to Osklen value, to be US$ 400 million.

3.3.2 Oskar Metsavaht[11]

Oskar Metsavaht is a multidisciplinary creator who dwells in areas such as fashion, audiovisual, furniture design, socio-environmental actions and expeditions.

"My creative process starts with a scene, a story, a style, a concept. I create from something I wished or lived. From this point on, I create the mood, the atmosphere, the looks, and the attitude. Most of the time, I conceive the campaign even before the collection. Maybe that's why I love making the art direction of the photo shoot. I create the atmosphere, of the story and make my own movies, through which I can share the scene I imagined in the beginning of the process. The pieces are designed to be the costumes for my movie, and it's possible to 'watch' it in each detail of the collection. I'm only satisfied when the elements proposed for each piece, the colors, the textures, and silhouettes are worn by the characters of the movie I created", says Oskar Metsavaht.

His lifestyle connected to the urban, to nature, to the arts and to the board sports, united with his constant need for experimentation, brought him to also create projects such as the snowboarding expedition trilogy – Surfing the Mountains. As his ideas and projects are always intertwined and mutually influence each other, the trilogy served as inspiration for collections and documentaries directed by Oskar Metsavaht.

Through Om.art, his Creation and Design office, new developments of his ideas came from invitations to create projects for Brazilian and international clients, such as the Andy Warhol Foundation of Art, the special edition of the Jeep Cherokee for Chrysler Brazil, the series of watches for H.Stern entitled Arpoador, commercialized in Brazil and abroad, besides the creation of the sandals Ipanema RJ, a worldwide launch of the line inspired in the most authentic contemporary carioca lifestyle.

Oskar Metsavaht has been recognized as one of the forerunners of the movement for sustainability, bringing into the market the idea of "new luxury". He is frequently invited to participate as a keynote speaker on the theme in world conferences such as the Milano Fashion Summit and the Ethical Fashion Paris. Oskar was invited by Anna Wintour from American Vogue to participate in the Runway to Green event, a charity runway show to promote sustainability in luxury fashion brands.

Founder of the Instituto e, a non-profit organization located in Rio de Janeiro, dedicated to the promotion of human sustainable development, he developed the *e-fabrics* project that, in partnership with businesses, institutions and research centers, identifies fabrics and materials developed according to socio-environmental criteria. Oskar Metsavaht was also named in 2011 as a UNESCO Goodwill Ambassador.

3.3.3 Instituto e

The Instituto e is a Civil Society Organization of Public Interest for human sustainable development based in Rio de Janeiro. It aims to facilitate projects in six areas, the so-called 6 e of the Instituto e:

- earth: it relates to ethics, responsibility and mission. It includes indicators based on the Earth Charter Initiative.
- environment: it relates to environmental impact, natural-resources management and conservation programs. It includes indicators based on the Convention of Biological Diversity.
- energy: it relates to climate change, energy efficiency and renewable energy. It includes indicators from the Kyoto Protocol.
- education: it relates to knowledge diffusion, education and communication. It includes indicators from the UN's Millennium Development Goals.
- empowerment: it relates to local development, revenue generation and quality-of-life improvements. It includes indicators from the Rio's 92 Agenda 21.
- economics: it relates to sustainable development and corporate social responsibility. In includes indicators related to the triple bottom line.

A central project is *e fabrics* aimed at the individuation of eco-friendly and sustainable raw materials, especially in the area of textile and fashion industry. Its goal is to spread the use of sustainable raw materials in order to protect biodiversity. Analysis of raw materials, impacts of production processes, biodiversity conservation and social aspects are among the main selection criteria for classifying the e *fabrics* products. The mapping of e *fabrics* was developed in partnership with Brazilian companies, institutions, research centers and supported by the ABIT – Brazilian Association of the Textile Industry.

e *fabrics* include materials such as vegetal leather, fleece from recycled PET, organic cotton, natural latex from Amazonia, pirarucu fish leather, jute canvas, organic silk and others.

Another central project of the Instituto e is TRACES – the social and environmental footprint-assessment of six Osklen *e-fabric* product life cycles. It is co-developed with the Italian Ministry for the Environment, Land and Sea (IMELS), in partnership with Forum das Americas and with the collaboration of Senai-Cetiqt. The project was launched in the framework of the 2004 environmental cooperation agreement between Italy and Brazil aiming to identify, through a specific case study, the social and environmental impacts in textile production, a sector which currently employs 30 million people in developing countries and significantly contributes to land, water and energy consumption, and has one of the largest carbon and social footprints in the manufacturing industry.

It started auditing an organic cotton t-shirt and then tracked 6 Osklen's products life cycle in Brazil (by geographical region):

(1) In the Amazon, where:

- Pirarucu fish skin is collected and treated for bags, shoes and other accessories;
- Jute is cultivated and treated as a raw material for many Osklen products.

(2) In the south of Brazil, where:

- Organic cotton and silk are cultivated;
- In several industries located all around Brazil where cotton and textile are collected and recycled;
- In Osklen distribution centers and shops.

The project measured the impacts of the Osklen products with two main objectives:

- identify the measures that the company will have to implement to reduce the impacts of its products;
- inform the consumers and support the growth of sustainable consumption models, through quality brands and communication campaigns in all Osklen stores in Brazil and in the other countries where Osklen is present, including Italy.

So far, the results are the following:

TABLE 3.1 **TRACES assessment of Osklen e products life cycle done by the Italian Ministry for the Environment, Land and Sea (IMELS), Instituto e, Forum das Americas and with the collaboration of Senai-Cetiqt**

Material	Carbon footprint per product	Carbon footprint total product production
Pirarucu bag	38.674 grCO2eq	3.519kgCO2eq
Silk tennis shoes	10.704 grCO2eq	7.878 kgCO2eq
Eco canvas dock side	4.874 grCO2eq	1.569 kgCO2eq
e-bag jute bag	18.943grCO2eq	3.787kgCO2eq
Recycled pet and cotton Backpack hood	15.100grCO2eq	1.510kgCO2eq
Organic cotton T-shirt	4.081grCO2eq	6.823kgCO2eq
Total	92.376 grCO_2eq	25.086 kgCO_2eq

All the results related to carbon footprint have been certified by Rina (an independent auditor).

This deep commitment to sustainability makes Osklen a role model on how luxury fashion companies can orient their activities in a time of resource scarcity, a "Future Maker" in the words of the WWF–UK. That is paving the way for something with broader implications.

3.3.4 The new luxury philosophy

Oskar Metsavaht and Osklen firmly believe that luxury brands are regarded as such because they are associated with noble values. For traditional European luxury brands those noble values have been a commitment to quality, employment, innovation, contemporary, forward thinking and the holders of a societal meaning. But in the brand's eyes, during the last decade, several of these luxury brands have lost their noble values by outsourcing from their home country, by just selling to the huge demand on emerging markets (the primacy of the logo), by searching short-term financial profits and compromising on the brand identity – in short, forgetting their initial ethos and brand meaning.

This goes along with a societal awakening that the company calls "a 'new' new order", represented by values associated with Agenda 21 and social and environmental sustainability. For the luxury industry this implies the need to marry these new values (contemporary attitudes such as "simple is better", well-being; sustainable products; fresh creativity from emergent cultures) to the European luxury design and manufacture know-how. All that leads to a definition of a New Luxury.

As stated by Oskar Metsavaht[12]:

> There is a need to transform the luxury management to combine environmental respect for raw materials (sourcing) to aesthetic appeal and craftsmanship in order to transform luxury consumption, for clients to develop a perception of what values luxury really stand for: a New Luxury!
>
> I am considered a pioneer (actually, others call me a pioneer, but I see myself as more of a leader among others) and I see the future of luxury consumption, not in a certain snob European luxury, or the iconography of the American Dream/Way of Life, or the consumption of cheap products made in China without any creativity. That is going to change and in China, for example, a new generation of designers is going to draw in their millennial culture and long-term view, to develop its own original content and approach.
>
> And there lies a great opportunity and challenge for Brazil. If Brazilian companies and brands are able to materialize our way of life, our *joie de vivre*, our sensuality, informality and health, that I call, since the 1990s, the Brazilian soul, in association with raw materials from a sustainable socio-environmental origin

coming from highly symbolic regions like the Amazon, and helping low revenue communities (like the favelas or Amerindians or Black communities) to improve their quality of life conditions, that can be a breakthrough and can project a differentiated Brazilian approach globally.

The world is looking forward to experimenting with this Brazilian soul. Our sympathy, "de bem com a vida", is well integrated with nature, with the knowledge of several cultures through our ethnic foundations: European, African, Oriental and Amerindian. We have this unique facility to blend, to mix: dance, food, music, race and even religion! We are a "fresh civilization" with a new, different creativity for other societies and cultures. We represent, and are the health, the life of the planet. If we can materialize that as the Americans have done with the American Dream ...

It is through this Brazilian soul in association with a sustainable approach of our unique resources that we can achieve a unique place in the world. We do not have industry and labor to compete on cost with China, the luxury know-how of Europeans, or the American strength in marketing and communication. And our way is certainly not through selling our commodities with no intellectual or creative aggregated value.

My vision, our opportunity, is through our creativity and sustainability to empower craftsmanship and manufacturing. Conceptually: Ipanema + Amazonia + São Paulo

And elevate the *made in Brazil* luxury standard to create the dream and desire for our contemporary society to experiment our way of life through the "Brazilian Soul" and sustainable products that preserve this rich planet region to remain strong to nourish the future. Feeling Brazilian in this way is certainly a luxury...

3.4 CONCLUSION

The previous chapter about luxury in China presents in detail a frame to distinguish among three luxury value propositions:

"looking to the past", "looking to the present" and "looking to the future", given the strong focus of luxury incumbents on heritage. Osklen is a company that greatly symbolizes a "looking to the future" value proposition in its attempt to reframe the meaning associated with luxury itself. It is an inspiring brand that has been gaining momentum and is profiting from Brazil's take-off to reach new heights. It somehow shows a path for the development of the Brazilian luxury market as clients will gradually move from buying just a logo to becoming interested in the quality and soul of a luxury brand.

Challenges are numerous: internationalization and capital requirements to enter foreign markets like China are just the first of many. Will it remain independent or join a larger group? If it becomes part of a publicly traded company, this will bring tension regarding quarterly profit reports and long-term brand construction to the company's management.

As Brazil becomes in the near future the fifth-biggest world economy, its economy is going to overtake that of France or the United Kingdom, for example. An interesting question is who will be the source of inspiration for Brazilian elites who have been historically attached to US and European models? It is a whole new challenge that is opening in Brazil's history that consists in no longer being better than someone at a standard defined by someone else, but being able to build its own standards and values. To take a sports metaphor, not being the fastest to climb a mountain, but imagining a new way to climb a mountain, or even more radical, to create a new outdoor mountain sport. Oskar Metsavaht and Osklen are showing the way for a creative generation of young Brazilians craving to write their history, contributing to creating a better tomorrow, and to become present and future makers themselves.

ACKNOWLEDGMENTS

I dedicate this chapter to Betina Hoffmann. I warmly thank Oskar Metsavaht, Nina Braga, Nelson Camargo, Renata Koga and Fabiana Dias from Osklen and Instituto e, and Cristina Afonso from UbiFrance.

NOTES

1. MCF Consultoria e Conhecimento & GfK Brasil (2009), The Luxury Market in Brazil 2009/2010.
2. McKinsey & Company (2012), "What Companies Need to Know about Brazil's Luxury Consumers", *Consumer and Shopper Insights*, January, Retrieved on 3 March 2012 from http://csi.mckinsey.com/knowledge_by_region/americas/brazil_luxury_consumer_retail_trends
3. Forbes Insights (2012), Global Wealth and Family Ties: A worldwide study of how fortunes are founded, managed and passed on.
4. In the words of Christian Blanckaert, former vice-president of Hermès, "this is a shopping mall that understood that luxury is about nourishing the soul". We thank Christian for bringing this example to our attention.
5. Interview with Cristina Afonso, manager of the department Fashion, Housing and Health at Ubifrance São Paulo.
6. McKinsey & Company (2012), op. cit.
7. American Express released statistics at the 2012 Financial Times Business of Luxury Summit showing that up to 70 percent of Brazilian luxury purchases are made abroad; retrieved 28 June 2012 from http://luxurysociety.com/articles/2012/06/luxury-is-now-for-the-masses-and-the-classes.
8. http://www.theworlds50best.com/.
9. Sections in quotation marks come from Osklen website, corporate documents or press releases.
10. Forbes Inc. (2012), The World's Billionaires: Ones to Watch, 26 March 2012, p. 76.
11. This section comes from a company press release and its presentation as such is validated by Oskar Metsavaht.
12. Statements collected on 6 April 2012 by the chapter author.

4

ÜBER LUXURY: FOR BILLIONAIRES ONLY

Alessandro Quintavalle

4.1 INTRODUCTION

In the last quarter century the luxury industry has enjoyed incredible growth, increasing in size a good ten times during this very limited timeframe. On the one hand, an increasing population of wealthy people was a favorable condition for this expansion. On the other, the savvy introduction of new business models and brand-management techniques made it possible to broaden significantly the client base and appeal to it by offering a wide spectrum of new products and modes of consumption.

In the first decade of the new millennium, diversification and extension were the main drivers of growth for luxury brands, and this expansion was not limited to the lowest rungs of the client pyramid but spread evenly throughout. Furthermore, one of the effects of globalization was the rise of a category drawn from the new international social class of the hyper-rich, which has quickly swelled the ranks of the exclusive "Billionaires' Club", a group that has also increased tenfold during the last 25 years.

The Swiss Horological magazine *EuropaStar* renamed this category the "über-rich"[1] to reflect how this group has really propelled the ultra-high luxury industry and created incredible opportunities for special "toys" such as mega yachts, supercars and pluricomplicated watches; even though these objects numerically represent only a "small slice of the pie", the same cannot be said for the revenues and profits they generate.

The goal of this chapter is to present this often-mentioned – but still relatively unexplored from a consumer perspective – world of the ultra-rich, and to offer insights into their relationship with the world of luxury which, by affinity, intrinsically belongs to the same universe.

The chapter begins with a quantitative analysis of the demographic of billionaires which will explain how they have created and managed their fortunes, and why this group plays an important role in the luxury industry.

This will be followed by a more detailed insight into the client (with an analysis on the way this special group approaches luxury) and the factors that are relevant for successfully offering a product or service. The misconception about the ultra-affluent buying everything simply because of their spending power will be further challenged and the reverse will be demonstrated, particularly how great attention is dedicated to the investment value of the purchase – across all passion categories.

Finally, a broad overview on where and how billionaires choose to invest their money of passion will conclude the chapter.

4.2 BILLIONAIRES, WEALTH AND LUXURY

The correlation between luxury and economic trends is quite an intuitive and straightforward one: yet, in order to better understand how the two are linked, it is interesting to analyze how the luxury market has been influenced not only by the wealth creation of billionaires, but also by their actual number. In the figure below (Figure 4.1), the growth of the luxury industry (personal goods) during the decade 2000–2010 is compared with that of the number of High Net Worth Individuals (HNWIs) (defined as those individuals having investable assets of US$1 million or more), and with the growth of the overall wealth in their possession.[2,3] Yearly figures of each variable are normalized on the corresponding base value of 2000.

As well as the aforementioned correlation between the luxury market and the other variables, two further observations can be made:

(a) The luxury goods market's trends indeed follow a pattern similar to that of their counterparts, but with an average delay of one year;
(b) Of the two counterparts, the number of HNWIs shows a pattern closer to that of the luxury goods market and can therefore be considered as a qualitative predictive factor in the trends of the latter.

The World Wealth Report by Capgemini-Merrill Lynch shows how the category of Ultra-High Net Worth Individuals (UHNWIs) (those having investable assets of US$30 million or more), although comprising a mere 0.94 percent of the total population of 10.9 million of HNWIs worldwide, accounts for a good 36.1 percent of the total net-worth of the population.

By narrowing the analysis down to the select cluster of billionaires[4] – the target of this study – it can be noted that in the same year 0.01 percent of the population accounted for 8.4 percent

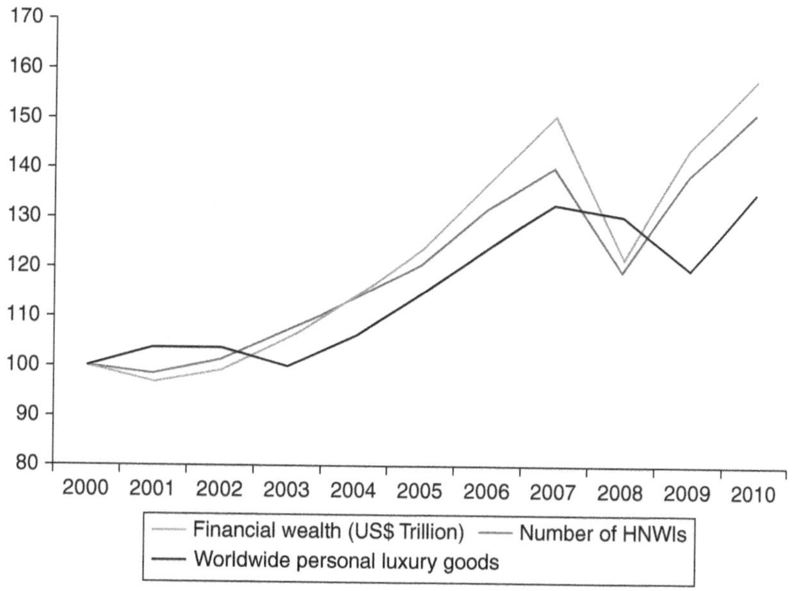

FIGURE 4.1 **Luxury market versus financial wealth and HNWIs growth (base 100 in 2000)**

Source: Bain, Cap Gemini, Merrill Lynch.

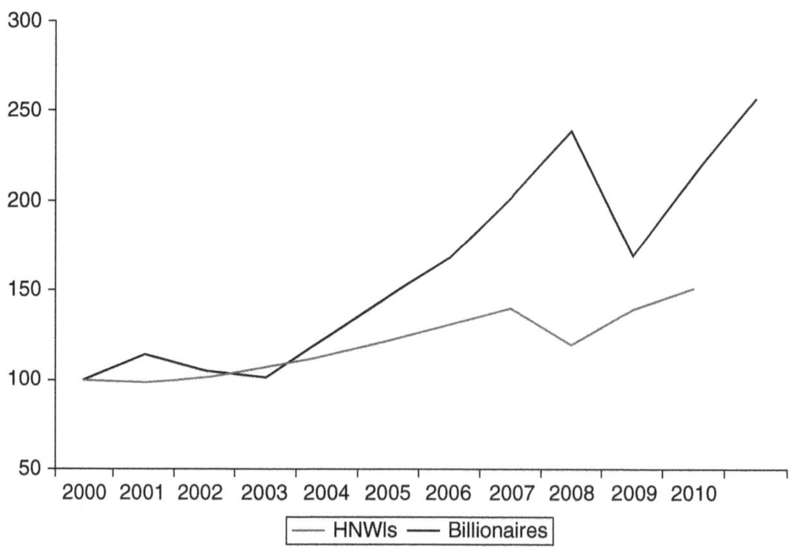

FIGURE 4.2 **HNWIs versus billionaires' growth (base 100 in 2000)**
Source: Forbes, Gemini, Merrill Lynch.

of the total worth, with this percentage increasing year by year. The same result is not only confirmed, but accentuated when comparing the growth of HNWIs versus that of the billionaires: since 2000 the latter group has grown more than twice as fast (115% versus 57%) as the former. This result, coupled with the correlation between the number of ultra-affluent prospects and luxury consumption, explains on the one hand the rise of the Über-luxury market and its brands, and on the other hand how billionaires are definitely a trend worthy of close scrutiny in years to come (Figure 4.2).

In purely numerical terms, the billionaires' club grew by a factor of almost 8 and topped 1,226 members in 2012, with the United States leading the rankings (35%) and Russia and China following with an 8 percent share each. As regards age, the United States stays just above the average of 62.5 years whereas Russia and China, with respectively 50 and 52 years, are among the youngest in the rankings (Figure 4.3).

On a more qualitative basis, a research made by Forbes[5] on the world's biggest fortunes provides several insights into how billionaires establish, manage and pass on their fortunes:

- 58 percent of the biggest fortunes are run by individuals, with families – whose involvement varies by region and industry – constituting the remaining 42 percent;
- Mature markets have more fortunes that are run with family involvement and more inherited fortunes than emerging markets;
- Family-managed fortunes are clustered in certain regions of the world (Hong Kong, India, France and Middle East), and hardly exist in others (Russia, China and the UK);
- Technology sector fortunes are owned by billionaires who are self-made and younger than average, whereas the real estate sector is very much a family affair;
- Individually run fortunes tend to grow faster;
- Management of wealth varies significantly across the world, with hedge funds popular in the United States, real estate in Russia and a more conservative approach in Asia.

4.3 ÜBER-LUXURY CLIENT: INSIGHTS

Billionaires are by definition out-of-the-ordinary people and their uniqueness is equally reflected in their personality – each of them is one of a kind – and in the very limited number which forms this special club; while it would be paradoxical to label them, it is nevertheless possible to outline some shared characteristics.

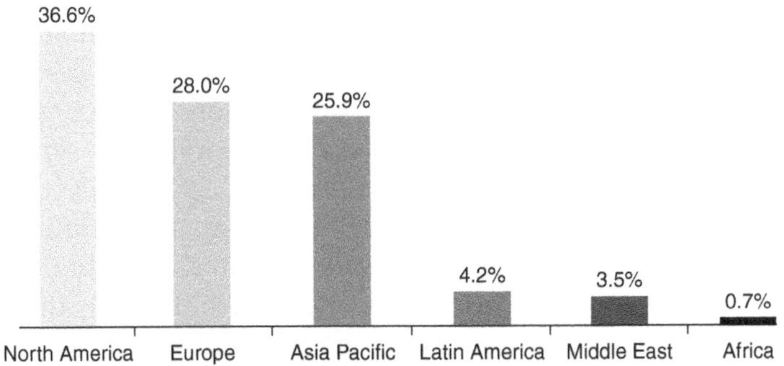

FIGURE 4.3 **Billionaires' distribution by region (2012)**
Source: www.forbes.com/Billionaires.

In terms of traits, three points are common to all billionaires:

- They are financially highly educated, this being a mandatory condition for creating and managing these fortunes; the saying "Billionaires don't know the value of money because they are extremely rich" is actually true in reverse: "Billionaires are extremely rich because they know the value of money" – and therefore they are very savvy and demanding customers. Nevertheless, they are not always alumni of top universities and business schools – many are examples of "famous college drop-outs" or people that reached the top without a formal education.
- They are not afraid to fail:[6] risk is necessary to reach the real heights of wealth, and the higher the risk, the higher the reward – but one should bear in mind the concept of "educated risk", that is "gathering solid information and facts in order to take the best possible decision within a given time constraint".[7] This even applies to investments of passion, for which they still frequently carry out back-up research.
- They tend to look creatively at opportunities[8] and therefore continually explore other avenues of their wealth,[9] as both investors and consumers.

Having an extremely high disposable income does not mean any price will be paid for a given product or service. The first prerequisite is individuality: billionaires want to purchase something utterly unique, that not only they themselves have not seen before but also that their best friends do not possess. If, in the case of collectibles (vintage cars, works of art) and brand new products, uniqueness is definable by a combination of price, scarcity and market value, in the case of bespoke products or services – very popular among these groups – that are specifically tailored for the clients, the mix of features becomes more difficult to match. Their profound financial awareness will always, in the end, lead billionaires to appreciate a product's worth, but this does not mean the object in question has to be triple-gilded: *cost* is a consideration but the primary concern is *value* – a concept different to *price* – combined with the highest standard of design and functionality. Billionaires are really not used to thinking in terms of *either/or*, but rather of *both*[10] (or, if more than two attributes are in question, in terms of *all*).

Once the value is recognized in the product or service, spending big sums is not a concern as long as one last condition is met: the quality delivered must be impeccable, since any failure whatsoever would be unacceptable and mean losing the client's trust. To better understand this point, it is necessary to explore further the concept of value, which has to be interpreted through the relationship billionaires have with time. Über-luxury prospects have very busy lives and time is a very limited resource: with such a proven ability to generate high incomes, every second must be leveraged because it can make the difference over the long term; hence the frequent use of a dedicated team of people organizing and optimizing the prospect's schedule. In consequence, any time spent dealing with unnecessary matters – even just delegating them – not only negatively affects the customer experience but also represents an opportunity cost that is, in the case of billionaires, by definition, very high: a classic example of the proverb "time is money".

In the next section, the way in which these special people invest their money in passion will be broadly discussed.

4.4 INVESTMENTS OF PASSION AND ÜBER-LUXURY

In their renowned "World Wealth Report", Capgemini and Merrill Lynch every year dedicate a section to the so-called Investments of Passion, an overview on how HNWIs allocate their "passion money" across the following categories:

- Luxury Collectibles: automobiles, boats, jets and so on;
- Art;
- Jewelry, gems and watches;
- Other Collectibles: coins, wine, antiques and so on;
- Sports Investments: sports teams, sailing, race horses and so on;
- Miscellaneous: club memberships, travel, guns, musical instruments and so on;

According to the research, emotive variables such as aesthetic value and lifestyle/status appeal generally drive these preferences, yet HNWIs also view many investments of passion as alternative ways of diversifying their portfolio and protecting – if not even increasing – their capital over time.[11]

The pattern for UHNWIs is generally slightly different: they tend to allocate respectively less money to jewelry, gems and watches and more to Art and Sports Investments than their counterparts,[12, 13] but what is generally common to both groups are the trends (the amount of money flowing into these categories vary according to the overall level of wealth) and the inclination toward investments with a low correlation with financial markets, to reduce the risks involved.[14]

The object of this section is to present, for each category of investment of passion, an insight into at least one of the markets belonging to that category and, for each market selected, to analyze the top of its pyramid, that is, to define its "über-luxury" segment both qualitatively and quantitatively.[15]

4.4.1 Luxury collectibles

4.4.1.1 Superyachts

The worldwide pleasure-boat market in 2010 had an estimated worth of €14 billion,[16] with Europe alone accounting for more than 90,000 units.[17] During the last years Europe saw the highest relative growth as European-based boat-makers gained market share in large-sized boats,[18] indeed superyachts – universally defined as leisure sail- or power-boats larger than 30 m/100 ft[19, 20] – representing one of the most emblematic category of "luxury toys", experienced an incredible growth, increasing their population from 2.490[21] to 3.228[22] units between 2007 and 2010.

This small segment, that in 2010 delivered 195 units with prices ranging from €5 million up to more than €300 million,[23] generated revenues of €4.5 billion[24] in consequence of an astounding €23 million as average unit value, and even when restricting the analysis to the segment of crafts over 70 meters, the principle is still valid. Mr Paolo Vitelli – president of Azimut/Benetti Group[25] – as early as 2005 was defining this "superniche" as a decidedly attractive, appealing market: "At the moment around ten boats a year are being produced, and if we consider that each one of these costs a good deal more than €100 million, let's say even 150/180 million, overall business in this sector well exceeds a billion Euros, despite the small numbers involved."[26] As it is established practice not to invest more than 10 percent of one's own liquid assets in a yacht – the famous 10 percent rule[27] – it goes without saying that these wonderful boats, demand for which has remained steady despite the economic crisis, are accessible only to the select club of billionaires. Consequently, superyachts continue to increase in size: the average length of the 100 largest crafts actually rose from 78.52 m to 94.63 m during the decade 2000–2010,[28] and the minimum size required to enter this special ranking moved, during the same period, from 50.5 to 73,5 m.[29] In testament to this dynamic race toward the bigger, new words such as Megayacht and Gigayacht appeared in the maritime vocabulary and, while there is an energetic ongoing debate as to how this superniche should be sub-segmented, one thing is clear: soon the expression *Terayacht* will be necessary to grace the arrival of the first unit above 200 m.[30]

4.4.1.2 Business jets

In contradistinction from the other luxury collectible categories, where aesthetic value takes precedence over the functional, private jets feature several attributes which make them valuable for both leisure *and* business reasons: they offer fast, flexible, safe, secure and cost-effective on-demand access to destinations around the world, together with the ability to conduct in-flight business meetings in private. In other words they cannot simply be considered as "big toys for the big boys" and these crucial differences explain their success.

In 2010, the worldwide fleet of business jets consisted of approximately 18,000[31] units, divided into three principal segments:[32,33]

- Small Cabins (42%): purchase price up to $18 million and range up to 3,100 nautical miles;
- Medium Cabins (33%): purchase price between $18 million and $42 million and range from 3,100 nm to 5,000 nm;

- Big Cabins (25%): purchase price higher than $42 million and range over 5,000 nm

In 2010, 763 jets were delivered – for a total $18 billion[34] – and the large cabin segment accounted for 40 percent in units and 76 percent in value.[35] Fully-owned units represented approximately 60 percent while the remainder divided into fractional ownership (10–15%) and branded charter operators (25–30%).[36]

The very top end is represented by the Large Corporate planes, often referred as to Bizliner (contraction of "business airliners") which are based on or converted from airliner types, but with completely revamped interiors. The average price of these jets ranges from $70 million to over $400 million for a totally refurbished VIP wide-body such as the Airbus A380 and the Boeing 747–8 VIP,[37] which can carry 25–50 passengers in VIP comfort and can be configured with offices, boardrooms and bedrooms. With 26 Bizliners delivered in 2010,[38, 39] the two enterprises alone exceeded $2.5 billion,[40, 41] testament to the importance of these models.

According to the General Aviation Manufacturers Association, the largest jets category has been the most resilient during the economic downturn with a recorded sales increase of 23 percent in units from 2007 to 2011, as opposed to the smallest and medium which have fallen 58 percent and 43 percent respectively.[42] The importance of the large segment should stay strong in the future where, in the next ten years it is expected to account for more than 60 percent in revenues and benefit against a five percent CAGR growth of the whole sector.[43]

4.4.1.3 Ultra-luxury cars

According to the Altagamma 2011 Worldwide Markets Monitor, the world luxury car market in 2010 was equal to €245 billion[44] and spread into the following segments:

- Absolute (1.5%)
- Aspirational (12.5%)
- Accessible (86%)

In quantitative terms, in 2010 this market accounted for approximately 3 million cars[45] (out of a global light vehicle market of 72 million units sold[46]) with a growth rate that not only recorded above average values,[47] but also with the Absolute segment – the most volatile – outpacing the other two.[48] With prices ranging from €100,000 to €2 million,[49] the ten prestigious brands[50] that in 2011 entered the "Top 100" ranking of the World Luxury Association[51] alone totaled 30,000 cars and over 5€ billion[52] in value. In response not only to increasing demand[53, 54] – which presents the dilemma of preserving exclusivity – but also to the client's quest for ever more individuality, ultra-luxury car manufacturers are currently striving to broaden the offer of customization services, with the goal of placing almost no limits on the personalization and design of the vehicle. When uniqueness is paramount, the names of these programs have to follow suit, therefore "Bespoke",[55] "Tailor Made",[56] "Ad Personam",[57] "Special Operations"[58] "Q"[59] are just a few examples of how every little detail counts when dealing with über-luxury.

4.4.2 Art

In economic terms, art can be considered a luxury good since it features high-income elasticity of demand, that is to say, it increases proportionally to people's income.[60]

Growing over 7 percent from 2010, the global market for fine and decorative art in 2011 reached a volume of 36.8 million transactions and generated a turnover of €46.1 billion, split equally between auctions and commercial gallery sales.

Notwithstanding a severe dip following the global recession which led to a downturn of 35 percent between 2007 and 2009, the market still managed to more than double its value in the past ten years.[61, 62] China is for the first time leading with a 30 percent share, followed by United States (29%) and the United Kingdom (22%). The Modern[63] and Contemporary[64] sectors combined accounted for nearly 70 percent of the fine-art market, whereas the Old Masters[65] – regarded as potentially less volatile to invest in – witnessed an impressive growth. If on one hand its finite supply limits expansion, the degree of scarcity has on the other a positive impact on prices, causing an overall increase.

Research and consulting firm Art Economics in 2009 conducted a survey with a group of the world's top art collectors and found that while their main motivations for collecting art were centered "on aesthetic, decorative, intellectual or historical reasons, many described it as a passion and most concurred that art was an excellent long-term investment."[66] Furthermore, the global recession did lead a shift in the HNWI's luxury purchasing habits with a trend toward long-term tangible value assets such as art.[67]

"Art prices are not correlated to sudden swings in stock markets but their prices tend to match changes in wealth creation and destruction. I'm not surprised by this growth, as we are not seeing the wealth damage of 2008–2009", says Michael Moses, creator of an eponymous index that tracks the prices at which individual works of art sell over time, using repeat sales data. The Mei Moses® All Art index, indeed, has beaten the S&P 500 in six of the last ten years, with an average annual return of 7.8 percent compared with 2.7 percent for the benchmark US index,[68] proving that art can be considered an asset as well as an alternative form of investment.

By limiting the analysis to the global art auction market only, statistics for which are more complete owing to data being publicly accessible, it can be noted that the market is highly concentrated in the very top of the pyramid: according to the "Art Market Trends 2011" by ArtPrice, the most expensive "one percent" of all lots sold generated 58.5 percent of the world's total auction revenue in 2011[69] with 1,675 artworks selling well above the $1 million threshold and no fewer than 59 above the $10 million threshold.[70]

While the most-valued works of art can be considered as trophies providing an incredible "recognizability factor" as well as "visceral rewards, emotional satisfaction" second to none,[71] passion alone would not entirely explain collections whose value for the top collectors can be in excess of 1$ billion[72] and in some case tying up almost the totality of these top collectors' net worths.[73, 74]

4.4.3 Jewelry, gems and watches

According to the Federation of the Swiss Watch Industry, the five main producer countries exported finished watches for over

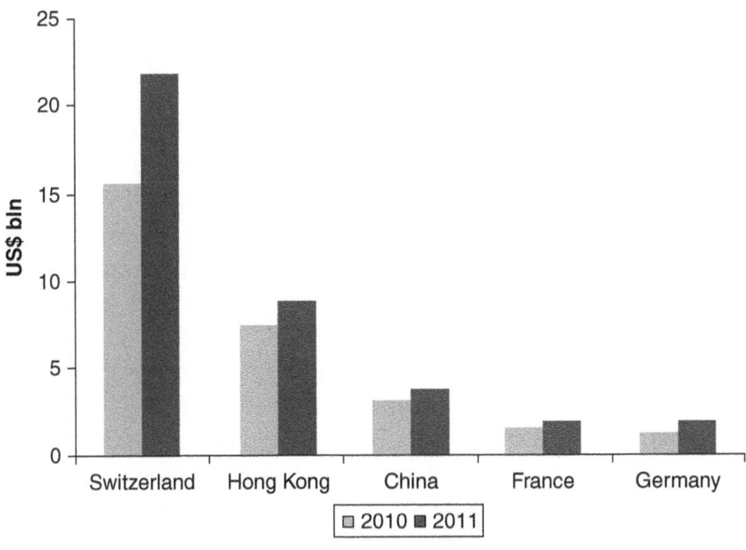

FIGURE 4.4 **Main watch-exporting countries**
Source: The Federation of the Swiss Watch Industry FH.

$38.2 billion[75] in 2011 and recorded a growth of 32.7 percent[76] over the previous year (Figure 4.4).

Focusing the analysis on Switzerland only – the most important market and by definition the "country of origin label" – 2011 saw 29.6 million units delivered and a turnover of 18.1 billion francs.[77] The sector, which accounts for ten percent of the Swiss industrial export,[78] enjoyed an incredible rebound from the crisis and, in just two years (2009–2010) rose 47 percent in value and 37 percent in quantity respectively;[79] in addition, the outlook seems very positive as confirmed by the many important players planning a capacity expansion through the construction of new premises and production facilities.[80]

The Federation of the Swiss Watch Industry (FH) divides the high-end market into three segments:

- Luxury watches: retail price between CHF 4,500 and 9,000;
- Prestige watches: retail price between CHF 9,000 and 18,000;
- Fine watches: retail price over CHF 18,000.

The three sub-segments together, with less than 10 percent in units, account for approximately three quarters of the total volume[81] of Swiss exports; even more impressively, fine watches alone, with a share of less than one percent in units[82] and an estimated average retail price of over 60,000 Swiss Francs, constitute almost 40 percent of total exports. This result is not surprising considering the contribution of the acclaimed über-watches – the special class that provided the name of this chapter – which can count on more than 100 models with prices in excess of €250,000[83] and with a maximum tag of €4 million.[84]

The purest expression of the newly-born über-watch niche, and probably the most innovative, is Greubel Forsey, the Swiss horological brand established by master watchmakers Robert Greubel and Stephen Forsey in 2004. Their timepieces are an unparalleled example of pure rarity, craftsmanship and exclusivity: just over 100 units are produced every year, superbly finished and built around one core idea; the Tourbillion mechanism, arguably the most significant horological invention in history, made by the most-famous watchmaker of all time – Abraham-Louis Breguet.

Until Greubel Forsey arrived on the scene, ultra-luxury watches had mainly been the domain of either small artisan workshops or important manufacturers, using such out-of-the-range products as exercises in technical supremacy to reinforce the brand aura and add value to their more mainstream product lines, according to the renowned principle of alternating accessibility with exclusivity.

Thanks to their stunning technical innovations, Greubel Forsey succeeded not only in introducing an interesting business model focused on the real top of the pyramid (their timepieces range from €300,000 to €600,000),[85] but also in becoming – extremely difficult when such limited numbers are involved – a brand of worldwide renown.

Their success did not go unnoticed and in 2006 Compagnie Financière Richemont of Switzerland, the top luxury goods holding company, acquired a 20 percent stake, proving how this niche of the market is paramount in terms of prestige and endorsing a new trend that will shape the industry in years to come.

4.4.4 Other collectibles

During the years 2008–2010 the category of Other Collectibles (coins, wines, antiques, etc.) stood out from all the other *passion of dollar* investments because rather than a dip, it actually recorded the highest growth of the period.[86] The reason is quite simple: while equity portfolios can lose much of their value overnight,[87] investments of passion – as well as prime property – can still be enjoyed when prices are deflated thanks to their tangible nature. Clearly, in times of economic uncertainty, physical assets with limited availability such as rare stamps, antique coins, fine wines and classic cars tend to increase their prices and demand thanks to their uniqueness which is a warranty of value.[88, 89] Interestingly, Art, another par excellence alternative investment, did not match the impressive result of Other Collectibles in the previous paragraph.

According to the Historic Automobile Group International (HAGI), the long-term return investment on classic cars looks very impressive: the HAGI index, which measures the performance of the 50 key-collectable classic cars, has increased by a factor of 30 during the last 30 years, which is equivalent to a compound annual growth rate of 12 percent; gold, by contrast, only managed 2.17 percent per annum (Figure 4.5).[90]

By looking at a shorter window frame, during the turbulent five-year period 2006–2011 the S&P 500 was down 18 percent whereas the average price of the vehicles sold by Auctioneers Gooding & Co – which in 2011 sold 27 cars at values greater than $1 million – increased 22 percent (Figure 4.6).[91]

The HAGI Index – which rose some 29.5 percent since its introduction in early 2009 – tracks only the top 100 historic cars of the market, a segment that generated in 2008 an annual turnover of £1.07 billion.[92] The select club that is the HAGI Top Index, composed – among other criteria – of cars each with a "limited edition" of no more than 1,000 and worth at least £100,000 individually,[93] covers a spectrum of over 47,000 cars totaling a market capitalization of £10.1–12.3 billion, which corresponds to an average value per vehicle of more than £250,000.[94] The average collector is estimated to have between five and ten cars, corresponding to between five thousand and ten thousand collectors.

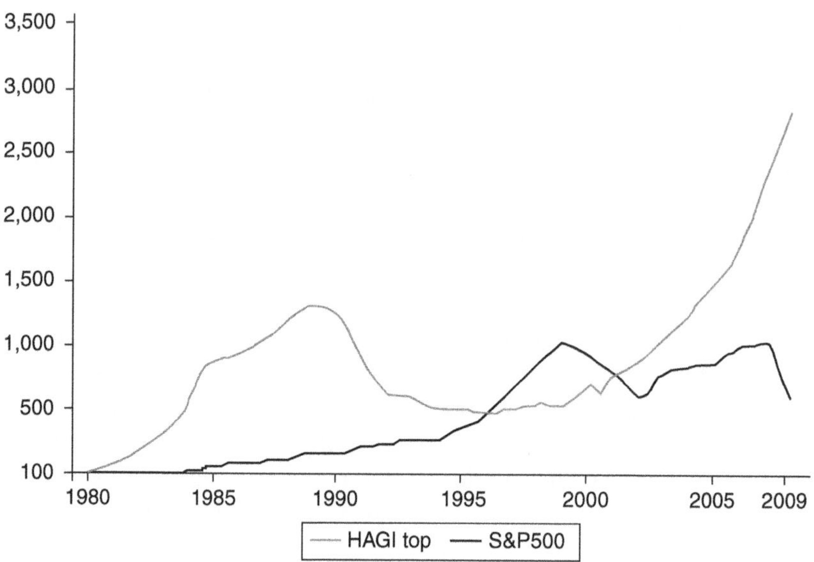

FIGURE 4.5 **HAGI Top Index versus S&P 500 growth (base 100 in 1980)**
Source: Reproduction, with permission of HistoricAutoGroup.com (HAGI Publishing).

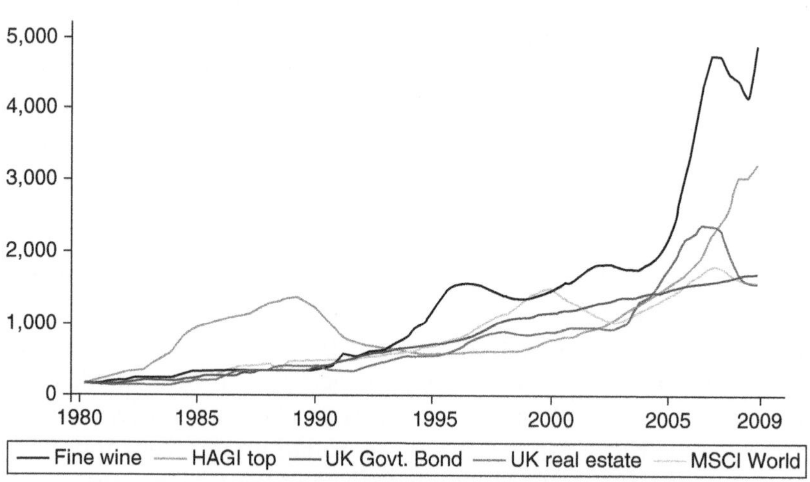

FIGURE 4.6 **HAGI Top and other asset classes (base 100 in 1980)**
Source: Reproduction, from "Better than Gold: Investing in Historic Cars" Dietrich Hatlapa, 2011 (HAGI Publishing).

Fine wines – whose tradable portion in 2010 was by comparison £3 billion – also recorded excellent growth during the decade 2001–2011, as shown in the comparison between the S&P 500 and the Liv-Ex (London International Vintners Exchange) Fine Wine 100 Index, the fine wine industry's leading benchmark which tracks the movement of 100 of the most sought-after fine wines.

Even though vehicles are still a niche market and not immune to declining in price (maintenance costs and deterioration can also decrease the returns on such an investment), this type of collectible can not only represent an excellent complement to an investor's portfolio – especially in addition to art and private equity – but also possesses two big advantages: cars can be enjoyed and touched and one needn't understand the mechanics of complex financial algorithms in order to collect them.[95]

4.4.5 Sports investments

Owning a favorite sports team is unmistakably one of the most satisfactory investments in terms of ego and prestige and, additionally, the number of UHNWIs combining the love of the game with financial returns has gradually increased in recent times. Indeed, if a precise plan is followed, it is possible to make money out of these activities.[96] It is no surprise that among the owners of the 50 most-valuable sporting franchises in 2011[97] – a special ranking compiled by Forbes – a good 24 were billionaires.[98] In numerical terms, a top team can exceed $2 billion worth and reach $700 million of yearly revenues[99] and, with regards to income, the NFL alone, for instance, generates yearly revenues of $9 billion. Sports teams, sailing and motorsports – these all represent interesting types of passion investments, yet the most emblematic one is horseracing, an activity with legendary roots. Horse-breeding is truly an ancient art and racing is the natural outcome of human attempts to produce the fastest horses to win battles. Horseracing occurred at least as early as the empires of Babylon, Syria and Egypt, and the event was included in the Olympic games of 664 B.C.

The tradition continued with the Romans and Arabs until arriving in England where, in the 17th century, racing of thoroughbreds was called the "Sport of Kings" to underline how ownership of horses was the exclusive domain of kings and nobility. And of course today, like any high-risk, high-stakes activity, it still keeps attracting the privileged super-rich who attend bloodstock auctions to select the best breeds and try to gain the fame and prestige of one day being crowned the winner of the top races. In 2010, according to the International Federation of Horseracing Authorities[100] 237,416 racing events[101] worldwide offered total wagers of €3.9 billion and generated €88 billion revenues in the betting industry alone. In terms of the top pyramid, horseracing is no exception, with the 0.1 percent of the competitions totaling 6 percent of the total purse thanks to 154 races with a prize over $1 million and with the highest rank of the podium occupied by the Dubai World Cup, worth $10 million.

4.4.6 Miscellaneous

According to the Altagamma 2011 Worldwide Markets Monitor, the world luxury Hôtellerie sector was estimated at around € 93 billion in 2010 and it was forecasting interesting growth prospects (+19%) owing to concurrent rebound from the downturn and the development of the Asian market. At the top of the pyramid, the absolute segment accounted for 20 percent[102, 103] in value.

With hotels representing one of the most advanced models in the "rental" market, an analysis that could be offered by analogy is that of the luxury yacht charter market. Superyachts can not only in effect be considered as five-star floating hotels (they too provide room, food, service and a crew to look after the guests) but also similar indicators can be applied to measure profitability: occupancy level (OCC), average daily rate (ADR) and RevPAW (Revenue per Available Week).[104] Due to the very high maintenance and operational costs – on a yearly basis usually between seven percent and ten percent of its replacement value – many owners charter their yachts to offset such costs; the rental rate generally reflects this figure and is set with the target of breaking even at 10–12 rental weeks.[105] Above that threshold, boats start generating revenue.

By applying the same segmentation as to superyacht building, 24 percent of the existing fleet of 3,228 yachts of +30 m was available for charter[106, 107] in 2010, a share which generated 2,035 weeks which in turn sold for $320 million. It is a very tiny market, although it may be compared to the very top hôtellerie both qualitatively and quantitatively: the average price per week of the 50+m segment (27% in quantity and 54% in value) was of $330,000,[108] an amount that, spread over an average of six cabins, corresponds to almost $8,000 per night per room. Even when focusing on the ultimate expressions of über-luxury, the comparison still obtains: €58,000 for the most luxurious suite in the world, of 1,680 m,[109] is in line with €840,000[110] per week for a superb 82 m, six-cabin yacht featuring 1,250 m of living space, to which, of course, one must add outdoor beach club and swimming pool. All with one big difference: you can take the boat wherever you like and the 300,000 liter fuel tank affords a range of over 5,000 nautical miles.

4.5 CONCLUSION

The previous paragraphs have analyzed the prospects' profile, the way in which they spend their passion dollars. Knowing for instance that the average Russian billionaire owns a $40 million private jet, a $30 million town house in Belgravia, a $40 million yacht moored in Antibes and a $50 million villa in Cote d'Azur[111,112] (where all the super-sports cars are parked) is of course helpful information but not decisive for selling an über-luxury product to him/her.

As already stated, über-luxury clients are extra-ordinary people and being unique means that the concept of value, which we have discussed throughout, differs completely from one individual to another, and indeed value is what drives purchase. And even if one could identify the magic formula for striking a chord with them with a given product or service, the other side of the "extraordinariness" coin would enter into the reckoning: über-luxury prospects are very hard to access, with many competitors striving to do the same.

It is often said that "The luxury business is a people business" and the point is doubly valid: subjectively, *it's all about the client,* and objectively, a solid network of people is paramount. All this requires skill, dedication, perseverance, sensibility and of course time, which is precious also to the non-billionaire.

NOTES

1. Maillard, P. (2008) "The Über-watches", retrieved February 29 from http://www.europastar.com/magazine/features/1003717967-the-x00dc-ber-watches.html.
2. Bain & Company (2011) Altagamma 2011 Worldwide Markets Monitor, retrieved from http://affaritaliani.libero.it/static/upload/bain/bain.pdf.
3. Cap Gemini, Merrill Lynch (2006–2011) World Wealth Report (editions 2006–2011).
4. www.forbes.com/billionaires.
5. Forbes (2012) Global Wealth and Family Ties: A Worldwide Study on How Fortunes Are Founded, Managed, and Passed On.
6. Rein, S. (2010) How to be a Billionaire, retrieved February 17 from http://www.forbes.com/2010/02/17/billionaire-wealth-how-leadership-careers-rein.html.
7. Harv Eker, T. (2005) Secrets of the Millionaire Mind: Mastering the Inner Game of Wealth, (pp. 86, 87) Harper Business, New York.
8. Rein, S. (2010) How to be a Billionaire, retrieved February 17 from http://www.forbes.com/2010/02/17/billionaire-wealth-how-leadership-careers-rein.html.
9. The Superyacht Group (2012) The New Wave of Superyacht Owners: Younger, Richer, retrieved April 4 from http://luxurysociety.com/articles/2012/04/the-new-wave-of-superyacht-owners-younger-richer.
10. Harv Eker, T. (2005) Secrets of the Millionaire Mind: Mastering the Inner Game of Wealth (p. 137) Harper Business, New York.
11. Cap Gemini, Merrill Lynch (2011) World Wealth Report 2011, p. 20.
12. Cap Gemini, Merrill Lynch (2007) World Wealth Report 2007, p. 13.
13. Cap Gemini, Merrill Lynch (2010) World Wealth Report 2010, p. 22.
14. Cap Gemini, Merrill Lynch (2011) World Wealth Report 2011, p. 21.
15. As general approximation, the same considerations on trends valid for HNWIs and UHNWIs will be extended to Billionaires.
16. Lucintel. Lucintel (2011) "Global Recreational Boating Industry Analysis and Forecast 2010–2015", www.lucintel.com.

17. Interconnection Consulting (2011) European Pleasure Boat Market has the wind in its sails again, retrieved September 13 from http://www.interconnectionconsulting.com/index.php?lang=en&presse=3.
18. Lucintel. Lucintel (2011) "Global Recreational Boating Industry Analysis and Forecast 2010–2015", www.lucintel.com.
19. Camper & Nicholsons (2008) (The Super) Yachting Index Superyacht Index First Edition, p. 10.
20. Mallet, V. (2012, January 6). Super-rich buying ever larger yachts, *Financial Times*.
21. Camper & Nicholsons (2008) (The Super) Yachting Index Superyacht Index First Edition, p. 15.
22. Camper & Nicholsons (2011) (The Super) Yachting Index Superyacht Index Fourth Edition, p. 18.
23. Daily Mail (2009) Admiral Abramovich launches his £300million mega-yachtski: The world's biggest (and it even has its own submarine), retrieved June 15 from http://www.dailymail.co.uk/news/article-1192640/Admiral-Abramovich-launches-300million-mega-yachtski-The-worlds-biggest-submarine.html.
24. Camper & Nicholsons (2011) (The Super) Yachting Index Superyacht Index Fourth Edition, p. 33.
25. Azimut-Benetti is the world producer of superyachts, with 187 boats deliver from 2002 to 2011. (Source: http://www.superyachttimes.com).
26. Petrone, F. (2005) Azimut/Benetti FincatieriPartnership – Not Only Megayachts, retrieved Janaury from www.nautica.it/superyacht/513/cantieri/azimut.htm.
27. Camper & Nicholsons (2008) (The Super) Yachting Index Superyacht Index First Edition, p. 27.
28. http://www.superyachts.com.
29. http://www.superyachts.com.
30. Royal Institution of the Naval Architects (2010, April), Superyacht, Megayacht, or Gigayacht? Rina Affairs, pp. 9–11.
31. JetNet iQ (2011) Business Aviation Marketing Intelligence (NBAA 2011 Update), www.rollandvincent.com.
32. JetNet iQ (2011) Business Aviation Marketing Intelligence (NBAA 2011 Update), www.rollandvincent.com.
33. Bombardier (2011) Business Aircraft | Market Forecast 2011–2030, www.bombardier.com.

34. JetNet iQ (2011) Business Aviation Marketing Intelligence (NBAA 2011 Update), www.rollandvincent.com.
35. Rolland Vincent LLC (2011) Business Jet Trends, Demand Drivers, and Outlook www.rollandvincent.com.
36. Bombardier (2011) Business Aircraft | Market Forecast 2011–2030, www.bombardier.com.
37. Higdon, D. (2010, February) Top Guns: Bizliners remain popular choice with huge flexibility. *World Aircraft Sales*, pp. 68–74.
38. Speed News (2011) Aviation News: Boeing Deliveries 2010. www.speednews.com.
39. Airbus (2011) Airbus delivers record number of corporate jets, retrieved January 27 from http://www.airbus.com/newsevents/news-events-single/detail/airbus-delivers-record-number-of-corporate-jets/.
40. Air Travel Genius (2012) Boeing Business Jet/Airbus Corporate Jet Airliners, retrieved from www.airtravelgenius.com/ar/boeing-airbus-business-jet-airliners.htm.
41. Air Travel Genius (2012) Boeing & Airbus VIP Widebody Airliners, retrieved from http://www.airtravelgenius.com/ar/boeing-airbus-vip-widebody-airliners.htm.
42. New York Times (2012) A Private Jet with Space for Both the Rolls-Royces. Retrieved April 4 from http://dealbook.nytimes.com/2012/04/04/a-private-jet-with-space-for-both-the-rolls-royces/.
43. Honeywell (2011) 2011Business Aviation Outlook, www.honeywell.com.
44. Bain & Company (2011) Altagamma 2011 Worldwide Markets Monitor, retrieved from http://affaritaliani.libero.it/static/upload/bain/bain.pdf.
45. Author's Estimate.
46. Industry Week (2011) Global Light-Vehicle Sales Reach Record Level in 2010 February 16 from http://www.industryweek.com/articles/global_light-vehicle_sales_reach_record_level_in_2010_23915.aspx?cid= NLQMN.
47. PricewaterhouseCoopers LLP (2011) Autofacts® 2011 Automotive Review, retrieved December 7 from http://www.pwc.com/us/en/press-releases/2011/2011-autofacts-forecasts.jhtml.
48. Bain & Company (2011) Altagamma 2011 Worldwide Markets Monitor, retrieved from http://affaritaliani.libero.it/static/upload/bain/bain.pdf.

49. Forbes (2011) The Most Expensive Cars of 2012, May 5 retrieved http://www.forbes.com/sites/hannahelliott/2011/12/05/the-most-expensive-cars-of-2012/.
50. Rolls-Royce, Bentley, Ferrari, Lamborghini, Maserati, Aston Martin, Bugatti, Spyker, Pagani and Koenigsegg.
51. http://www.top100luxury.com/wla/100/.
52. Author's Estimate from official press releases, market reports, news from specialized websites and portals.
53. Rolls Royce (2012) More Rolls-Royce Ghost Clients turn to Bespoke Personalisation, retrieved January 24 from https://www.press.rolls-roycemotorcars.com/pressclub/p/rr/pressDetail.html?outputChannelId= 4&id= T0124549EN&left_menu_item= node__6048.
54. Rolls Royce (2011) Rolls-Royce Expands Bespoke Operation due to Growing Demand, August 10 retrieved from https://www.press.rolls-roycemotorcars.com/pressclub/p/rr/pressDetail.html?output ChannelId=4&id=T0118993EN&left_menu_item=node__6048.
55. https://www.press.rolls-roycemotorcars.com/.
56. http://tailormade.ferrari.com/.
57. http://www.lambocars.com/.
58. http://www.mclarenautomotive.com/.
59. http://www.astonmartin.com/q-by-aston-martin.
60. Mac Andrew, C. (2010) The Global Ast Market in 2010, p. 121, Tefaf, Helvoirt.
61. Mac Andrew, C. (2012) "The International Art Market in 2011, Observations on the Art Trade over 25 Years" Tefaf, Helvoirt.
62. Mac Andrew, C. (2010) The Global Ast Market in 2010, p. 21, Tefaf, Helvoirt.
63. Modern art is herewith referred as all works of fine art created by artists born between 1875 and 1945.
64. Contemporary art is herewith referred as all works of fine art created by artists born after 1945.
65. Old Masters is herewith referred as all works of fine art created by artists born between 1275 and 1875.
66. Mac Andrew, C. (2010) The Global Ast Market in 2010, p. 128, Tefaf, Helvoirt.
67. Mac Andrew, C. (2010) The Global Ast Market in 2010, p. 123, Tefaf, Helvoirt.

68. Mathurin, P. (2012) Gold feels weight of Paulson Curse, *Financial Times*. January 8 retrieved from http://www.ft.com/intl/cms/s/2/265ff0e4-37d0-11e1-a5e0-00144feabdc0.html#axzz1s2Dys68c.
69. ArtPrice (2012) Art Market Trends 2011, p. 22, January 18 retrieved from http://imgpublic.artprice.com/pdf/trends2011_en.pdf.
70. ArtPrice (2012) Art Market Trends 2011, p. 6, January 18 retrieved from http://imgpublic.artprice.com/pdf/trends2011_en.pdf.
71. Esterow, M. (2011) The Global Appetite Is Increasing, 15 August retrieved from http://www.artnews.com/2011/08/15/the-global-appetite-is-increasing/.
72. http://www.forbes.com/2009/07/24/top-billionaire-art-collector-picasso-lifestyle_slide_2.html?thisspeed=25000.
73. http://www.forbes.com/profile/philip-niarchos/.
74. Blankfeld, K. (2011) Connecting With Art: An Inside Look into A Billionaire's Art Collection, 21 September retrieved from http://www.forbes.com/sites/kerenblankfeld/2011/09/21/connecting-with-art-an-inside-look-into-a-billionaire-art-collection/.
75. http://www.fhs.ch/statistics/watchmaking_2011.pdf.
76. Figures for the each country are converted from local currency to US dollars and the rate change applied is that of the year of reference.
77. http://www.fhs.ch/statistics/watchmaking_2011.pdf.
78. http://online.wsj.com/article/BT-CO-20120202-704262.html.
79. http://www.fhs.ch/statistics/watchmaking_2010.pdf.
80. Europa Star (2012) 2012 – AAA, March 7 retrieved from http://www.europastar.com/magazine/editorials/1004084674-2012-aaa.html.
81. http://journal.hautehorlogerie.org/en/echoes/economy/swiss-watch-exports-for-the-first-quarter-2011-2700/.
82. Author's estimate.
83. Tourbillon (2012) Orologi Meccanici Più Prestigiosi al Mondo.
84. Hublot (2012) The "$5 Million", March retrieved from http://www.hublot.com/wwwdata/news/pdf/2012/mars/2012_03_05_5million/2012_03_05_5million_ENG.pdf.
85. Tourbillon (2012) Orologi Meccanici Più Prestigiosi al Mondo.
86. Cap Gemini Merril Lynch (2011) World Wealth Report (p. 21).

87. Shirley, A. (2012) The Wealth Report 2012: A Global Perspective on Prime Property and Wealth (pp. 52–54), Knight Frank London.
88. Simon, E (2012) Classic cars – a viable alternative investment?, February 4 retrieved from http://www.telegraph.co.uk/finance/personalfinance/investing/9058922/Classic-cars-a-viable-alternative-investment.html.
89. Contemporary Art, for instance, has a non-finite supply.
90. Simon, E (2012) Classic cars – a viable alternative investment?, February 4 retrieved from http://www.telegraph.co.uk/finance/personalfinance/investing/9058922/Classic-cars-a-viable-alternative-investment.html.
91. Bozzo, A. (2011) Wide World of Investing, retrieved November 1 from http://www.cnbc.com/id/44979182/.
92. Hatlapa, D (2011) Better than Gold: Investing in Historic Cars, p. 32, Hagi Publishing, London.
93. Williams, D. (2011) Class Cars a Better Investment than Gold date retrieved November 7 from http://www.telegraph.co.uk/motoring/classiccars/8841453/Classic-cars-a-better-investment-than-gold.html.
94. Hatlapa, D. (2011) Better than Gold: Investing in Historic Cars, p. 32, Hagi Publishing, London.
95. Bozzo, A. (2011) Wide World of Investing, retrieved November 1 from http://www.cnbc.com/id/44979182/.
96. Shirley, A. (2012) The Wealth Report 2012: A Global Perspective on Prime Property and Wealth (p. 54), Knight Frank, London.
97. Badenhausen, K. (2011). The World's 50 Most Valuable Sports Teams, retrieved July 7 from http://www.forbes.com/sites/kurtbadenhausen/2011/07/12/the-worlds-50-most-valuable-sports-teams.
98. http://www.forbes.com/billionaires/.
99. Ozanian, M. (2012) The World's Most Valuable Soccer Teams, retrieved April 18 from http://www.forbes.com/sites/mikeozanian/2012/04/18/manchester-united-again-the-worlds-most-valuable-soccer-team/.
100. http://www.horseracingintfed.com.
101. Jump, trot and flatting.
102. Bain & Company (2011) Altagamma 2011 Worldwide Markets Monitor, retrieved from http://affaritaliani.libero.it/static/upload/bain/bain.pdf.

103. Luxury segment comprises rooms with average room-rate per night above of $ 125 whereas the absolute luxury segment those above $300.
104. Camper & Nicholsons (2011) (The Super) Yachting Index Superyacht Index Fourth Edition, p. 48.
105. Camper & Nicholsons (2008) (The Super) Yachting Index Superyacht Index First Edition, p. 24.
106. 2011 Camper & Nicholsons (2011) (The Super) Yachting Index Superyacht Index Fourth Edition, p.18,46.
107. 2010 Camper & Nicholsons (2010) (The Super) Yachting Index Superyacht Index Third Edition, p. 35.
108. 2011 Camper & Nicholsons (2011) (The Super) Yachting Index Superyacht Index Fourth Edition, pp. 49–50.
109. http://www.bang-olufsen.com/president-wilson.
110. http://www.edmistoncompany.com/yacht-charter/alfa-nero-1/.
111. Klebnikov, P. (2004) Live Like A Russian Billionaire, retrieved April 22 from http://www.forbes.com/2004/07/21/cz_pkl_0721 russianlifestyle.html.
112. Figures have been adapted to reflect inflation.

5

OCCUPATION FASHION BLOGGING: RELATION BETWEEN BLOGS AND LUXURY FASHION BRANDS

Rasa Stankeviciute

5.1 INTRODUCTION

Social media are changing so quickly that when one is asked to write about them, there is always at least a slight risk that by the time the paper is published, the statistics provided and the stories told will already be out of date. With this in mind, this chapter will present a brief introduction to the rise of the fashion blog, compare fashion blogs to fashion magazines, explore the relation between fashion blogs and luxury/fashion brands, and will look to the career opportunities for bloggers involved in different fields of fashion.

Describing blogging as someone's occupation and a blog as a business and a full-time job might initially sound strange for someone unfamiliar with the blogosphere. Nevertheless, fashion blogging has become an appropriate way to start a career in the fashion industry for some, a full-time job for others, and a great marketing opportunity for the brands.

Fashion bloggers involved in different fields, such as fashion journalism, fashion styling and fashion photography, have become trendsetters, influencing not only ordinary fashion consumers but also fashion designers as well as renowned luxury and fashion brands. And if being a taste-maker or opinion leader is not quite enough for fashion bloggers, they have now gone even further. "The bloggers have moved from commentators to creators; gone from front row next to Anna Wintour [American *Vogue*'s Editor in

Chief] to backstage next to Alber Elbaz [creative director of Lanvin] in but one calendar year."[1]

The relation between the three main types of fashion blogs (fashion news and reviews blogs, personal-style blogs and street-style blogs) and luxury/fashion brands will be studied in this chapter.

5.2 THE RISE OF THE FASHION BLOGS

"In the past few years, the fashion industry has been seriously shaken up by a new generation of influencers: the bloggers."[2] Although the first fashion blog was thought to have been launched in 2003, the rise of the fashion blog arguably started in 2006 when 40 selected fashion bloggers were given press passes to New York Fashion Week. Later, the designers Domenico Dolce and Stefano Gabbana took the pioneering decision to put the fashion bloggers in the front rows. The bloggers were placed next to Anna Wintour, Suzy Menkes and Hamish Bowles at the fashion house's Spring Summer 2010 Ready-to-Wear shows in Milan. What is more, they were provided with laptops, so that they could blog or tweet live from the shows. True, this might have only been a well-judged marketing strategy rather than a real interest in the bloggers, as the novelty of this decision in the industry attracted huge attention to the Dolce and Gabbana brand and its shows from the press. However, today it is no longer surprising to see the bloggers in the front rows of shows or to be treated by the press relation officers as if they were editors-in-chief of the most influential fashion magazines. "Fashion bloggers, like the cool kids in school, have become a kind of elite band."[3]

The luxury brands' interest in the bloggers has resulted from a huge number of followers that the blogs attract. Each month over 342 million people view more than 2.5 billion pages on Wordpress.com,[4] over 30 million blogs on Tumblr drives more than 13 billion page views every month[5] not counting the other blogging platforms.

Fashion consumers were becoming bored with being persuaded by advertisements and understood that the celebrities or professional stylists might be biased when endorsing one brand or another. The fashion consumers were more enticed by the user-generated recommendations and personal opinions provided by fashion bloggers. Consequently, the bloggers are poised to take a large piece of the major marketing and advertising budgets from the industry's leading brands, and each year more dollars are shifted into social media and celebrity endorsements are replaced by user-generated recommendations.[6]

However, almost a decade since the first blog was founded, the user-generated recommendations have become questionable. The bloggers do not pretend to be unbiased; more often than not, they are unabashedly self-promoting.[7] "As I've always declared, most of the new items you see on the blog are gifts that are given to me from brands in part to show support toward my blog and in part to reach more visibility online",[8] admits one well-known Italian personal-style blogger. And this example perfectly illustrates the situation of many famous fashion bloggers worldwide. The question is whether the bloggers' advice still remains as impartial as in the beginning of the blogging boom? It is a tricky subject, as when one sees an advertisement, at least one knows that it is a sponsored story.

This said, fashion bloggers are seen as influencers and opinion leaders. Therefore, after recognizing the need to become more reachable, the luxury and fashion brands saw fashion blogs as the perfect way to approach a wider audience. And according to Head Fashion Editor of *The Herald Tribune*, Suzy Menkes,[9] it is smart for the companies to look to bloggers, who are of a younger generation.

5.3 FASHION BLOGS VERSUS FASHION MAGAZINES

Fashion blogging has prompted a certain amount of discussion about the new versus the traditional media, in other words, about the "subjective" opinions of non-professional bloggers versus the "objective" perspectives of established editors.[10] Both blogs and magazines have their pros and cons. While magazines are able to provide their readers with a more professional content, they may be short of impartial opinion on the topics, as magazines usually depend on the companies they advertise. On the other hand, blogs are able to provide their readers with personal opinion, insights and user-generated recommendations – valuable experience for the modern-day consumers, but at the same time, they may lack the creative side of magazines.

However, fashion blogs claim big followings, and the brands are looking for wider audiences than magazines have ever been able to offer. Therefore, with luxury brands developing online stores, brands have begun to see the blogs as a new marketing opportunity.

When considering blogs versus magazines, four elements should be taken into account: investments, accessibility, frequency of blog posts and magazine issues and the personal touch.

From a business point of view, fashion blogs can be created for free, while it takes investments to publish a fashion magazine. From a consumer point of view, although one can now subscribe to many of the fashion magazines regardless of where one lives, the accessibility of printed magazines is still quite limited and expensive in comparison to the fashion blogs. Printed fashion magazines are usually published monthly, quarterly or semi-annually; fashion blogs, on the other hand, can be updated daily. And all that is needed to access any blog is an Internet connection, so with today's smart phones and tablets, blogs are easy to access from anywhere, even on the go.

True, fashion magazines have found a few solutions to overcoming limited accessibility. Though magazine applications on an iPad do not provide free-of-charge content, the online websites of the fashion magazines do. The webpage of Italian *Vogue*, which, according to *Industrie* magazine, is "the most maverick of the Big Four Vogues" is available in Italian and English languages and attracts 1.6 million page hits per month.[11]

Fashion bloggers usually work independently and, unlike magazine writers, they are not tied by the constraints of copyrighters or editors of the magazines. Readers of the blog are able to comment under the articles, like and share the posts, while the author is able to comment back and establish a close connection with the readers. Such a personal touch usually has a huge positive impact on the readers' engagement. The once-amateurish fashion blogs have all the opportunities to become professional information sources. And as the best books become movies, the best fashion news and reviews blogs may become influential online media-outlets.

The US-based Fashionista.com and the UK-based Businessof fashion.com are two of many worth checking out. *The Business of*

Fashion, founded in 2007, began as a project of passion, aiming to fill the void for an informed, analytical and opinionated point of view on the fashion business,[12] and five years later, the blog has been praised as an industry authority.[13]

Nevertheless, it is unlikely that the printed magazines will disappear from the market, as there will always be sentiments felt for turning the paper pages, seeing the printed photographs of the photo-shoots and collecting the magazines by the fashion enthusiasts.

5.4 CAREER OPPORTUNITIES: THE RELATION BETWEEN THE BLOGS AND THE BRANDS

5.4.1 Emerging brands

Bloggers are considered not only to have democratized the fashion industry, but also to have helped many emerging fashion designers to become known by spreading the word or reviewing their collections on the blogs. I talked to Eglė Čekanavičiūtė (eglecekanaviciute.com), an assistant women's-wear designer at Maison Martin Margiela, about the impact bloggers have on the recognition of young designers. The St Martin's graduate, who has already shown two collections of her own, assured me that having her personal work travel through blogs worldwide really helps her and other young designers, as it is a 24-hour access coverage that does not cost anything. "The culture of blogging is expanding mega fast, as it's available to everyone, and is becoming a popular source of research even for famous designers; this makes your work visible to people and companies that might want to work with you one day", says the fashion designer. According to Čekanavičiūtė, the ability to express one's opinion about one piece of work or another in public makes it honest advertising that sometimes works better than *Vogue* magazine's pages.

The recognition of Chiara Ferragni's blog *The Blonde Salad* (theblondesalad.com) has given the personal-style blogger an opportunity to establish her own business. The Italian blogger launched her shoe line *Chiara Ferragni* in 2010.

5.4.2 Renowned brands

"Blogs posting things about us, going viral, spreading throughout the Internet . . . it has an extraordinary impact on the business", says Jack McCollough of the renowned Proenza Schouler duo.[14] True, the important benefit that the brands get from the fashion blogs is the most effective form of marketing – word of mouth. Take Florence-based luxury retailer Luisa Via Roma, which also has an online store. Twice a year, for three consecutive years, it has organized an event Firenze4Ever, which, according to Camilla Gennari, a web-marketing manager at the luxury retailer, is a platform for interaction between bloggers, major brands and emerging talents. The bloggers get an opportunity to meet the designers, while the designers, in turn, have an opportunity to be well-communicated on the fashion blogs. The event offers both the bloggers and the luxury brands the potential to meet face to face and raise their profile online, according to Gennari. "Overall, the rise of the fashion blogs is a natural evolution that is beneficial for all involved", confirms Gennari. She also admits that the bloggers have helped increase popularity of the Luisa Via Roma brand.

Digging deeper, if you are getting into blogging to make money, you are in it for the wrong reasons.[15] But once a hobby, blogging may become one's part-time or full-time job and source of revenue. Once the blog starts attracting a significant number of visitors, there are several options to consider when thinking about monetizing it.

5.4.2.1 Advertising

Selling advertising on the blog is usually the bloggers' main source of income. Although the advertising can also appear in a form of text links or RSS, most fashion bloggers choose banner ads. The blogger can get involved in affiliate marketing or can sell an advertising place on the blog for a negotiated fee. Getting paid the negotiated fee for the advertising spot on the blog generates the guaranteed revenue.

Renowned street-style blogger Scott Schuman of *The Sartorialist* (thesartorialist.com) sells advertising place on his blog for a negotiated fee. To date, 75 percent of Schuman's revenue comes from advertising.[16] According to *The Business of Fashion*, "if current traffic levels are sustained and if a significant portion of the advertising inventory on *The Sartorialist* is sold, it could theoretically make Scott Schuman fashion's first million dollar a year blogger".[17] Luxury fashion brands and retailers such as *Net-a-porter.com, Bottega Veneta, Tiffany & Co* advertize on Schuman's blog.

Affiliate marketing is a performance-based online type of marketing. Its supply chain consists usually, but not always, of an advertiser (the brand), an affiliate network, the affiliate (the blogger) and the consumer. The affiliate gets paid a commission fee; the amount paid is based on the amount of either sales, or traffic, driven to the advertiser's website from the blog. At length, the blogger gets paid either per click on the banner (consumer's visit to the advertiser's webpage generated from the blog) or per sale on the advertiser's webpage generated from the blog.

5.4.2.2 Creating external products

Imagine the blogger launching a product, or think of a collaboration between the fashion blogger and a luxury brand to launch a product. If people care enough to follow the blog everyday and follow the life of the blogger, they are naturally a target group of consumers for that product, and a big part of all supporters will definitely become the buyers of the particular product.

In 2011 Scott Schuman collaborated with the American skin care brand *Kiehl's* to create a kit of *Kiehl's* products. As the outcome of the collaboration was meant to be launched for Father's Day, the street-style blogger took photographs of fathers and their children in New York's Central park for the advertising campaign of the collaboration.

Creating and selling external products is frequent among fashion bloggers, whose blogs generate huge traffic of visitors. By external products I mean both tangible and intangible ones. According to Robinovitz, co-founder and CCO of Digital Brand Architects,[18] when the brand works with a blogger in a way that it would work with any influencer such as a photographer, a stylist, or a public endorser of the brand, the brand has to compensate as it would compensate anyone for such work.

Regarding the intangible products, if you are a personal-style blogger, you might end up designing fashion pieces, as Ferragni did, or working as a stylist on various projects, what would mean the sale of your skills. Leandra Medine of *The Man Repeller* blog (themanrepeller.com) obtained paid partnerships include styling *Christian Louboutin* shoes in the window of *Saks Fifth Avenue.* Kelly Framel of *The Glamourai* blog obtained paid partnerships include styling the BCBG MaxAzria Brand's Ready-to-Wear Resort 2013 presentation.[19]

The turning point of a street-style blogger's career includes, but is not limited to, becoming a fashion photographer. In 2009, Schuman of thesartorialist.com was approached by the British luxury fashion brand Burberry, who tasked him to shoot a social media-advertising campaign "Art of the Trench". The blogger took photographs of 100 people all wearing the legendary Burberry trench coats. "We cast some of the people; we got people from the blog. Some people had their own Burberry coats, some people we gave them",[20] says the street-style photographer. According to the brand's CEO Angela Ahrendts,[21] the idea of the campaign was to show on the website different people wearing the Burberry brand's signature coats. Actually, on the specially designed networking website, users were also welcome to submit their own photos wearing the Burberry trench coat and people are able to like, share and comment under all the photos. "Together we are creating a body of images reflecting personal style from across the globe",[22] states the introductory part of the website.

In 2009, Yvan Rodic of *Face Hunter* (facehunter.com) was approached by the French apparel company Lacoste with a task to photograph around 100 people on the streets around the world wearing Lacoste clothes.

In 2011 the *Armani Group* hired Rodic to make a video about real people on the streets wearing *ARMANI* eyewear for the project called "Frames of your Life". Rodic was not the only blogger hired by *GIORGIO ARMANI,* as Tommy Ton of the *Jak and Jil* street-style blog (jakandjil.com) was previously hired by the luxury brand to photograph an advertisement campaign for the same project.

My street-style blog *Fashion Population* (fashionpopulation.com) has given me prospects to sell my photographs for various printed fashion magazines, to work for the online fashion-media outlets and to be involved in many different projects. It has also given me the opportunity to write this chapter.

Trends in Luxury and Digital by Christophe Pradere[23]

Digital can be seen as the conciliating factor between the underlying paradoxes of luxury:

1. Tradition/Innovation

While most luxury brands are over a hundred years old and base their promise on their heritage, they also have a duty of innovation. Thanks to new technologies, they are able to bind together their legacy to a projective modernity.

Prospective route:

The idea is to deliver information about brands' patrimonial attributes thanks to additional contents provided via augmented reality. For example, Louis Vuitton sets up an exhibition: additional content can be visualized through augmented reality by scanning the QR code of the piece cartel. Standing in front of an iconic Louis Vuitton trunk, you could launch a video on your smart phone and watch, in 3D, a trunk-maker assembling the trunk, a tanner dyeing leather, and visualize the different materials in detail, almost being able to feel their textures.

2. Openness/Closeness

Luxury brands rely on a principle of openness meaning that notoriety and desirability are necessary to fuel consumers' imagination. They are also tightly linked to closeness, meaning that selectivity and exclusivity are key drivers of their category. They are highly receptive to trends while remaining true to their essence.

In this sense, digital provides brands with both accessibility and rarity, mass diffusion and ultra-customization enabling them to operate like permeable and self-centered systems.

Prospective route:

The idea is to uncover luxury places, places that are hard to access by essence.

(Continued)

The brand would search for talents and ideas among digital users by implementing a crowd-sourcing platform of reflection about consumers' customs. This platform would be considered as a real R&D tool manageable by the brand. For example, Aston Martin Consumer Lab.com.

3. Expertise/Lifestyle

If specific know-how (processes, materials etc.) is constitutive of luxury today, brands belonging to the category also aspire to a promise that goes beyond expertise and wish to develop a lifestyle offer.

To manage that value transfer, new technologies are essential as they are at the root of any thought about new uses.

Prospective route:

The idea is to develop the theme of curating.

The brand gleans different objects from all over the world and sets up ephemeral galleries. The content of these galleries can be purchased on the web.

The brand develops its expertise in curating and moves its activity onto the field of art to become a lifestyle symbol.For example, Hermès Curating

4. Local/Global

Luxury brands more than any others have to deal with both localization (their cultural and geographical anchorage from which they draw their inspiration and strength to build knowledge) and globalization (the exportation of this knowledge to an Elsewhere where they would be considered as an iconic and universal reference belonging to a worldwide elite).

Digital is based on "deterritorialization", it gets rids of borders to focus on one specific consumer, highly self-centered and nomadic.

Prospective route:

The idea is to develop partnerships with local artists.

The artists create pieces that are only available on the brand's web-store of their native country. Those web-stores are designed by the artists themselves and inspired by the countries they are from.

For example, CartierDesignmyLondon.com proposes a ring designed by Damien Hirst. On the website, he explains how the city of London was an inspiration for his creation.

NOTES

1. Friedman, V. (10 January 2011). *Fashion Blogger Snags next H&M Collaboration.* Material World. http://blogs.ft.com/material-world/2011/01/10/fashion-blogger-snags-next-hm-collaboration/#axzz1kxpfAfcQ Retrieved 10 January 2012.
2. Ziv, Y. (2011). *Fashion 2.0: Blogging Your Way to The Front Row- The Insider's Guide to Turning Your Fashion Blog into a Profitable Business and Launching a New Career,* CreateSpace. https://www.createspace.com/Products/Book.
3. Copping, N. (13 November 2009). Style bloggers take centre stage. FT.COM http://www.ft.com/intl/cms/s/0/89f8c07c-cfe0-11de-a36d-00144feabdc0.html#axzz1kxDRyFio Retrieved 5 January 2012.
4. http://en.wordpress.com/stats/.
5. Ton, T. (2012). *The Fashion Media A-List: An Interview with Rich Tong.* Industrie Magazine, Issue 4.
6. Ziv, Y. (2011). *Fashion 2.0: Blogging Your Way to The Front Row- The Insider's Guide to Turning Your Fashion Blog into a Profitable Business and Launching a New Career.* Yuli Ziv.
7. Strugatz, R. (5 June 2012). *To Pay or Not to Pay: A Closer Look at the Business of Blogging.* http://www.wwd.com/media-news/digital/a-closer-look-at-the-business-of-blogging-5942163?page=3.
8. http://www.theblondesalad.com/2011/11/when-you-find-items-like-these.html.
9. Amed, I. (22 January 2010). *Fashion 2.0 | Suzy Menkes on the Growing Influence of Fashion Blogs.* http://www.businessoffashion.com/2010/01/fashion-2-0-suzy-menkes-on-the-growing-influence-of-fashion-blogs.html.
10. Hanssen, K. and Nitzsche, F. (2010). *Fashion Blogs: From Musings On personal Taste To Style Reports around the Globe.* Zwolle, The Netherlands: D'jonge Hond.

11. *The Fashion Media A-List: Vogue.it.* Industrie Magazine, Issue 4 (2012).
12. *The Business of Fashion. About.* http://www.businessoffashion.com/about, retrieved 14 January 2012.
13. Vogue Italia, *The Business of Fashion. About.* http://www.businessoffashion.com/about Retrieved 14 January 2012.
14. http://the-coveted.com/blog/2011/02/22/proenza-schouler-sees-extraordianary-impact-of-fashion-bloggers/
15. Mischief, A. (5 October 2010). *The Money Myth of Fashion Blogging (And How To Monetize Your Blog).* Independent Fashion Bloggers. http://heartifb.com/2010/10/05/the-money-myth-of-fashion-blogging-and-how-to-monetize-your-blog/
16. Strugatz, R. (5 June 2012). *To Pay or Not to Pay: A Closer Look at the Business of Blogging.* http://www.wwd.com/media-news/digital/a-closer-look-at-the-business-of-blogging-594163?page= 3
17. Amed, I. (3 October 2011). *The Business of Blogging | The Sartorialist. The Business of Fashion.* http://www.businessoffashion.com/2011/10/the-business-of-blogging-the-sartorialist.html#more-25486 Retrieved 9 October 2011.
18. Strugatz, R. (5 June 2012). *To Pay or Not to Pay: A Closer Look at the Business of Blogging.* http://www.wwd.com/media-news/digital/a-closer-look-at-the-business-of-blogging-594163?page= 3
19. Strugatz, R. (5 June 2012). *To Pay or Not to Pay: A Closer Look at the Business of Blogging.* http://www.wwd.com/media-news/digital/a-closer-look-at-the-business-of-blogging-594163?page= 3
20. Amed, I. (3 October 2011). *The Business of Blogging|The Sartorialist. The Business of Fashion.* http://www.businessoffashion.com/2011/10/the-business-of-blogging-the-sartorialist.html#more-25486 Retrieved 7 October 2011.
21. Zucker, S. (11 November 2009). *Burberry Extends Its Brand By Networking, Socially. Brand Channel.* http://www.brandchannel.com/home/post/2009/11/11/Burberry-Extends-Its-Brand-By-Networking-Socially.aspx#continue, Retrieved 1 September 2011.
22. Art of the trench. http://artofthetrench.com/, retrieved 2 November 2011.
23. CEO BETC Design.

6

ENGAGING WITH THE LUXURY CONSUMER IN CHINA

Katrina Panchout

6.1 INTRODUCTION

The transformation of luxury goods from the privilege of the elite to an attainable 21st-century dream has seen dramatic changes in targeting strategies used by luxury goods to reach consumers and geographical markets.

An ever-expanding economic and geographic market plus changing attitudes across the consumer landscape are resulting in a disintegration of boundaries, both geographical and socio-demographic. Product-range stretching and extension are adding to a general democratization of consumer attitudes to, and uses of luxury goods. The luxury sector has gradually moved from being perceived as a fairly restricted, elitist dream based on design creativity, to a massive economic sector with sharp retailing skills.

6.2 A TIMELESS CONCEPT

Derived from the Latin *Lexus*, meaning the indulgence of the senses, the symbolic aura surrounding luxury brands remains intact regardless of cost. The development of self, via self-construal through brand identification and consumption, is not new. However, the construction of self-concept as well as the concept of luxury itself is better understood when viewed through a socio-psychological framework. Shining through this cultural prism are the core values of luxury; product excellence, craftsmanship, exclusivity, authenticity, heritage and innovation; definitive codes in social differentiation and emulation. However, the strategies used to communicate and manage the luxury brand concept have radically changed.

6.3 A CHANGING INTERNATIONAL LANDSCAPE

Driving an international marketing strategy that produces global sales while protecting the notion of exclusivity and establishing culturally resonant customer engagement remains one of the strategic challenges of this decade for luxury brands. Where once luxury goods brands were relatively small in number, with a clear value proposition of heritage and tradition and a targeting strategy aimed at the happy few within a mainly Western population, the latter part of the 20th century has seen an explosion in the luxury goods sector with a clear trading down for certain brands. New markets have emerged, particularly in Asia. Cultural, geographic and demographic forces now shape this new luxury brand universe, driving product development and marketing practice.

As the line between limited accessibility both geographically and socio-demographically, and the idea of exclusivity and expensive becomes blurred, the concept of pure luxury has given way to a more segmented and democratized approach. The dream still exists but it is marketed and carefully managed across different product categories and customer segments. New luxury brands have entered the market and many brands are extended into new categories or stretched in order to capture a rising economic and population growth with a thirst for luxury goods. Luxury goods are now descending the social ladder, leading to a democratized trading up and down of the market. Masstige is now an integral part of many luxury goods product management.

A younger, international and dynamic audience has also changed the perception and attitudes of consumers towards luxury goods. The new luxury consumer is much younger, more discerning without being particularly loyal, and with a high disposable income. Gone are the days of an elitist, hierarchical relationship between the brand and consumer. Nowadays, the luxury consumer sees himself at the heart of the marketing process, seeking an authentic experiential connection with the brand.

6.4 IDENTIFYING NEW TOUCHPOINTS

What is new is the use of online technology to leverage this self-expression through brand differentiation, brand ambassador recruitment, customer loyalty and the deepening of brand relationships with its consumers through online brand communities.

As luxury brands become more democratized, they need to shift from product-focused to customer-focused marketing strategies and look for more original ways in which to connect and resonate with these brand-savvy consumers. Brand management practices therefore need to evolve, taking into consideration the changing marketing and digital environment. Luxury brand managers need to seek out touchpoints[1] during the decision-making process whereby brands may engage with the customer to create added value and clear differentiation points. Building strong brands demands a high level of consumer awareness with strong favorable and unique brand associations. Building these associations is key to establishing the brand long term in the consumer's mind, and so gain competitive advantage. Enhancing this brand equity over time requires innovation and key differentiators.

Luxury brands today must constantly evolve their brand management and communications strategies in order to meet the challenges thrown up by this new dynamic marketing environment. One of the most important recent structural changes in luxury marketing strategies has been the use of online media and digital technology to tap the potential of luxury brand strategy in the 21st century.[2] Brands are realizing the value that this medium offers in order to reach brand-led reference groups and develop deeper brand understanding via more precise targeting strategies. They have also identified its potential as a tool to reinforce customer-relationship management through customer engagement. Likewise, digitally native consumers, empowered by this technology, are using it in a way that puts them at the heart of the marketing process. They are no longer passive consumers and their expectations have been dramatically raised.

6.5 CHINA: A NEW LUXURY CONSUMER

Despite a general global economic downturn, China enjoys substantial growth with a burgeoning middle-class segment. By 2012, China is expected to become the fourth-largest market in terms of wealth, reaching 4.4 million wealthy households with an annual growth rate of 16 percent.[3] By 2020, the number of luxury consumers on the Chinese market is estimated to be 180 million people and many of them will be under 50 years of age. While most of this wealth may be found in the largest and most-developed cities, this wealth is expanding out from Tier I cities to Tier II, III and beyond.

China remains a country that places great importance on its cultural heritage and traditions. The traditional flat structure of Chinese society allows luxury brands to be used as amulets, instantly recognizable and acknowledged as a sign of personal success and social status. Consumer behavior is underpinned by this symbolism and these values. There is therefore a striking resonance for the Chinese consumer between himself and the symbolic values of brands and in particular luxury brands.

The role of symbolism as a leverage for brand associations can be seen in the ownership of luxury brands. Their symbolic values of quality, exclusivity, craftsmanship, heritage, authenticity and product excellence are just as important as the functional benefits of the brand itself. Ownership of these brands and the appropriation of brand meaning by association allow the Chinese consumer to differentiate himself, build self-concept and create individual self-expression. The link between brand user and self-image associations defines the notion of self-concept and serves as a uniform, denoting membership of certain reference groups and by definition, selected brand communities.[4]

6.6 LITTLE EMPERORS

Over 89 percent of Chinese luxury consumers today are under 45 years of age, many not more than 35 years.[5] Digitally native, they have developed an understanding and awareness of brand heritage and codes. Often only children, these solitary "Little Emperor" consumers have been educated to a high standard and raised to expect the best that money can buy. As a result, they are brand literate and brand recognition is high. Their attachment to brands is moving from this cultural display of self-expression: "Yi jin huan xiang" (return home in golden robes), into a mainstream cultural phenomenon encompassing complex emotional and psychosocial considerations. Social media tools form an integral part of their lives. As only children, they use social media to enter into an extended family that they can trust and to source, locate, communicate, congregate and validate. From a brand's perspective, this consumer education through online research and communications, peer-to-peer validation and engagement in brand communities has given way to a more relaxed but discerning attitude towards luxury consumption and wealth display.

6.7 THE CHINESE LUXURY NETIZEN

The online behavior of this young, luxury consumer shows an informed but protracted and drawn out approach to the purchase decision process. Information research and evaluation may take as long as 2–3 months before the purchase is actually made. They want the best that their money can buy and which reflects their own personality and individuality. This is hardly surprising given the average luxury goods expenditure balanced against monthly income. Online is the principal source of this search and is perceived as an important and credible source of information via the company website or through peer-to-peer feedback and referencing via social networks. Moreover, there has been a real shift from consumer analysis of basic product functions to more emotional considerations and in particular the role of the brand in self-expression of the individual and membership of a chosen reference group or brand community. Brand experience and lifestyle enhancement motivations play a particularly important role in this process. The core values of luxury brands; superior craftsmanship, exclusivity, quality, heritage, innovation and international standing are perfectly coherent within this changing frame of reference. High prices are seen as a guarantee of quality and peer-group evaluation via e-communities is crucial.

Given the tendency of eastern cultures to focus on interdependent self-construal, the line between collective self and brand communities is easily blurred.[6] Sharing and maintaining brand relationships via peer-to-peer diffusion and networks uphold the goals of the individual and these communities.[7] Members of this population have wholeheartedly embraced the Internet as a multidimensional medium that allows them to do just this; communicate, congregate and connect around brands and their peers, thus reaffirming their place within the peer group.

6.8 IDENTIFYING BRAND COMMUNITIES

Brand communities are non-geographically bound communities, based on a structured set of social relationships among brand users.[8] This structure includes shared rituals, traditions and a collective moral conscience that provides cohesion to this group and the choices it makes; creating brand ambassadors and brand vigilantes too. Shared meaning and experiences strengthen the fabric of these communities underscoring brand/consumer mutual appreciation. Customer-centered experience sharing and interaction between members of brand communities help lock in customer loyalty, providing a clear exit barrier. Contextual customer-centered relationships thus allow the consumer to develop a deeper understanding of brand heritage values and develop a clear sense of self-concept and expression. This has significant leverage value in a collective society, such as China.

Brand communities are often found online and the development of online media and, in particular, social media in China has helped further enhance this consumer behavior. It has also brought a closer and more relaxed relationship between luxury brand and the consumer. However, what makes this online growth of particular interest is its convergence between this army of Chinese netizens and the growing numbers of increasingly younger and Internet-savvy luxury consumers.

6.9 THE CHINESE DIGITAL ENVIRONMENT

In June 2010, China had already over 420 million Internet users, many accessing the Internet via mobile technology[9] ; this is five times as many as in India, and nearly double that of the United States according to management consultants, McKinsey. By 2015, this figure is expected to reach nearly 750 million, turning China into a powerhouse of online activity.[10] The growth in social media and digital technology represents a golden opportunity to provide valuable levers to identify and enhance value creation across retail strategy, brand management and customer-relationship marketing.

There are many reasons that explain this digital growth. As more people leave rural areas to work in Tier I/II/III cities, the geographical size of China and the long-distance travel required to sustain family relationships and friendships make maintaining those contacts quite difficult. Online communication facilitates the quality and perennity of these community links. Similarly, while China might register thousands of television stations, there are very few national networks.[11] Broadcast media are fragmented, driven by regionalization and linguistics. Renowned for the restricted availability of information and widely viewed to be under strict government vigilance, traditional media have ceded their place to social media as a credible source of information. In turn, social media has evolved from an under-positioned medium used more often for music, videos and gaming, to establishing itself as a credible source of information and two-way communications. Its role as brand advocator and reference source has grown particularly due to the gap between urbanization and retail development. Rich populations are arising outside the traditional Tier I cities, driven by urbanization.[12] Yet many foreign brands are still unavailable outside key Tier cities. Official brand information is often scarce and not available in Chinese. In the absence of luxury stores outside the main Tier I and II cities, "clicks 'n mortar" replaces the more physical "bricks 'n mortar". The virtual shop window and online experiential marketing allow the brand to develop its retail strategy and communicate superior customer service.[13] Forming an open forum, social media allow Chinese consumers to discover brands, their heritage and social benefits plus share shopping experiences.

This is particularly important for brands with a relatively small retail footprint in the Chinese market.

6.10 EMBRACING DIGITAL OPPORTUNITIES AND CHALLENGES

Digital opportunities do not come without some considerable strategic challenges. Luxury and prestige brands need to be aware that the social media and online landscape in China is radically different from that of more mature markets such as mainland Europe and the United States. Many recognized that names such as Google and Facebook have no real presence in this market. There is no dominant global leader but rather a fragmented ecosystem comprising search engine Baidu, social networking sites such as RenRen and Kaixin, microblogging sites Sina Weibo and Tencent Weibo, videosites Youku and Tudou as well as the online marketplace TaoBao. Sina Weibo is much more advanced than the microblogging site Twitter, with well-developed video and photo-sharing functions. Both are under the constraint of 140 characters; however, Chinese characters will allow a brand to say a lot more than with the same number of alphabetical ones. Many netizens access the Internet via their mobile phones and there are a growing number of iPhone and Android applications. Improved broadband connectivity enables the development of richer, more tailored content management but what is key to this market is developing "local" Chinese sites. The search engine market is particularly important as most will use Baidu as a search engine starting point. A brand that has not paid for search on Baidu in one of its brand zones is practically invisible for the Chinese consumer.[14]

While there are a growing number of international star players on the Chinese market, notably Burberry, BMW, and certain cosmetic brands, many prestige and luxury brands have failed so far to seize the importance of this medium as a strategic tool to leverage brand development or provide value creation at particular touchpoints.[15] Moreover, many have failed to appreciate the key drivers and challenges for digital success within the Chinese market.

6.10.1 A multi-dimensional approach

Burberry,[16] already renowned in Europe for its innovative approach to digital marketing, quickly recognized the potential of this media. It conjugates clicks 'n mortar with bricks 'n mortar via its own e-commerce enabled, Chinese-language site offering live streaming of runway shows, subtitled versions of the Burberry Acoustic Video Series, a Chinese-language mobile site and in-store touch screens and iPads. This digital competence is enhanced by an integrated social media strategy that includes live streaming of fashion shows on Youku, a presence on microblogging site Sina Weibo thus allowing over 182,000 followers to pick up on news, celebrity sightings, product videos and so on. Douban members can listen to its music channel or follow the acoustic video series, while Kaixin creates e-community traffic.

This multi-dimensional approach allows the brand to build and deepen brand knowledge and understanding through experiential marketing and community management. It was one of the first fashion brands to launch e-commerce on its Chinese site.

6.10.2 Digital engagement

Both BMW and Audi are also developing highly interactive and integrated digital marketing campaigns for the Chinese market. In addition to its own online presence, BMW enhances its brand experience through customer rewards and gratification. Fourzone equivalent, Jiapeng, rewards site visitors with a badge and the opportunity to participate in contests for attractive prizes. What many Chinese customers want is to engage with the brand, undertake a brand experience and to be able to share this experience with their peers. Reward-structured competitions or video customization plus the provision of user-generated tools such as online drawing material, cartoon paint cell, scripting features and online personalized-editing allow the customer to take the brand experience and make it their own via social network platforms. Land Rover has been particularly good at this approach with its 360 digital campaign, "The Evoque Effect": A half-digital, half-animated video mini-action series which can be customized before sharing across social-network platforms and mobile applications. Series related questions provide the opportunity to win a MacBook Air or design a poster while the Sina Weibo page drives traffic to the Evoque microsite.

Sharing the experience promotes viral and buzz marketing activities. Lamborghini, which has no official online window other than its "market" page on Taobao, provide background details on the brand's heritage, with detailed photographs and car specifications, all in Chinese. A $1 million car is up for sale and while Lamborghini has yet to see an actual sale, over 8,000 requests for further information about the brand underscores the use of this site in creating interest and buzz via peer-to-peer diffusion.

6.10.3 A new form of experiential marketing

The individual experience, if positive, will be shared, and this brand–consumer interaction leverages brand knowledge and understanding. Games, competitions, badges and invitations to move offline to collect bracelets in-store, all create excitement and a buzz around the brand.[17] Badges in particular, awarded on the basis of the number or type of visit, are quickly replacing carrier bags as status symbols of brand belonging and peer-group recognition. These badges may be backed up by activities such as geolocalization and seasonal activity-based tips or used simply as a passport to a competition and a more-complex reward structure. Estee Lauder complements badging with a competition theme running through its RenRen page. Users may collect coins and gain additional points by sharing with friends. Top scorers win prizes and all activity is linked to its e-commerce-enabled site.

Badges and on-page testimonials quickly transform brand novices into knowledgeable brand ambassadors.[18] Estee Lauder's El-Lady encourages a sense of community around the brand via editorial content, interactive games, community-led product recommendations, videos and online shopping. To encourage diffusion, content may be shared and peer-to-peer comments and validation is actively encouraged via skin surveys and online quizzes. The integrated, content managed approach of these brands underlines the importance of using a carefully considered, differentiated digital strategy rather than drowning online platforms with multiple but unrelated messages.

6.11 CONCLUSION

The use of online and social media as a strategic tool in luxury brands marketing cannot be ignored. A convergence between the development of online and an increasingly youthful luxury consumer provides valuable strategic opportunities for luxury brands to leverage and enhance brand value via these new touch points. Digital investment now will help deepen the brand experience and in the long term to build brand equity. In order to do this, however, brand management practices need to consider the local cultural and economic dynamics that shape the Chinese market. A deeper brand understanding and attachment will only come through glocal activity – Chinese-language-based and cultural adaptation within the overall architecture of the brand. In the long term, this investment will also help build brand strength thus protecting against the albeit distant arrival of home-grown Chinese luxury brands onto the local market.

Should brands adapt to the local characteristics of the Chinese digital landscape, they will reach out to the luxury consumer, pulling this digitally native netizen into the brand universe and turning out a brand advocate.

NOTES

1. Court, D., Elzinga, D., Mulder, S. and Vetvik, O. J. (2009) "The Consumer Decision Journey", *McKinsey Quarterly*, June 2009.
2. Atsom, Y., Dixit, V. and Wu, C. (2011) "Tapping China's Luxury Goods Market", *McKinsey Quaterly*, April 2011.
3. Farrell, D., Gersch, U. A. and Stephenson, E. (2006) "The Value of China's Emerging Middle Class", *McKinsey Quarterly*, June 2006.
4. Markus, Hazel and Shinobu Kitayama (1991) "Culture and the Self: Implications for Cognition, Emotion and Motivation", *Psychological Review* 98(April): 224–253.

5. Atsom, Y. and Dixit, V. (2009) "Understanding China's Wealthy", *McKinsey Quarterly*, July 2009.
6. Aaker, J. and Schmidt, B. (2001) "Culture Dependent Assimilation and Differentiation of the Self", *Journal of Cross Cultural Pyschology*, 32(5): 561–576.
7. Kampmeier, Claudia and Simon, Bernd (2001) "The Role of Independence and Differentiation", *Journal of Personality and Social Pyschology*, 81(3): 448–462.
8. Muniz Albert, M. Jr and Thomas C. O'Guinn (2001) "Brand Community", *Journal of Consumer Research*, 27(March): 412–432.
9. Sethi, A. (2010), "Chinese Consumers in 2010", *TNS Global Research China*, Tnsglobal.com.
10. Bain Study (2010) China Luxury Market Study 2010, Greater, *China Retail Practice, Bain & Co*, November.
11. Galloway, S and Guthrie, D. (2010) L2 Digital IQ Index: China, *L2thinktank.com*, 16 June 2010.
12. Scherer, M. (2010) China market entry strategies – bypassing 1st Tier cities, *Labbrand.com*, 26 June 2010.
13. Fenn, A. (2011) Social Media in China: why and how, *thomascrampton.com*, 28 February 2011.
14. Strangeloop, (2011) Why Luxury websites are disappointing Chinese consumers, *Strangeloop Networks Inc*, 2011.
15. Okonkwo, U. (2009) Sustaining the luxury brand on the Internet, *Journal of Brand Management*, 16: 302–310.
16. Burkitt, L. (2011) Burberry Stores in China get digital makeover, *Wall Street Journal*, 14 April 2011.
17. Penhirin, J. and Philippe, L. (2004) Understanding the Chinese consumer, *McKinsey Quarterly*, July 2004.
18. Sethi, A. (2010) Social Media in China – Great expectations, *TNS China*, Tnsglobal.com, 18 June 2010.

7

LUXURY AND ARTS IN CHINA: THE ISLAND6 CASE

Camille Jaganathen

7.1 INTRODUCTION

Since Deng Xiaoping started opening China's markets to international trade in 1978, the economy has undergone rapid growth. Thirty-four years later, China has become the second-largest economy in the world after the United States.[1]

The number of citizens in China with assets over a million dollars has risen in tandem, reaching approximately 1,110,000 million in 2011.[2] Shanghai, one of China's economic hubs, boasts 132,000 millionaire inhabitants (one Shanghainese out of 175 is a millionaire[3]) and as the saying goes, money attracts money.

One of the consequences of the booming economy in China has been the development of the luxury market. Luxury goods are currently enjoying tremendous popularity among Chinese people. The overseas Chinese spending during the 2012 Spring Festival reached a record $7.2 billion; according to the World Luxury Association as reported in *China Daily*,[4] Chinese purchases account for up to 62 percent of the European luxury market. *The Economist* reports that "overall consumption in China . . . will rise by 11 percent annually over the next five years".[5] The art sector is, however, not experiencing the rapid growth seen in the other sectors of the luxury market. In the most established areas of Shanghai, it is easy to find European designer stores, as China becomes Louis Vuitton's largest market.[6] The art sector has had markedly less success than the luxury market when targeting the *nouveaux riches*.

Such a discrepancy of growth is worth the interest of economists and luxury specialists.

China is a new market for luxury goods. Most Chinese have only recently been able to shop on the basis of desire, rather than necessity. For the art market to succeed, therefore, the Shanghainese must regard art as a way to diversify their luxury acquisitions and emulate Western peers. However, there are signs of change: Chinese auction houses are now selling works at a pace formerly associated with those in London and New York and the sale of Picasso's "Femme Lisant" for $21.3m to a Chinese bidder is testimony to how much a few are willing to pay to compete in the international market. With an Education Department that emphasizes practical studies over cultural learning, and syllabi that are often characterized as rigid and unimaginative, unawareness of the art world dampens the market.

In this chapter, I will briefly explore the interaction of the art market with the rest of the luxury sector, and the situation of those markets in contemporary China. I will then offer a guided tour of island6, a growing innovative Shanghai-based arts collective. The visit will conclude with an interview with Thomas Charvériat, founder and owner of island6 arts collective.

7.2 ART AND LUXURY

Art and other areas of the luxury market often overlap. For example, artists have often provided inspiration to fashion designers. Yves Saint Laurent's iconic wool jersey dress in bright color blocks of white, red, blue and yellow, designed in the autumn of 1965 was inspired by the Dutch painter Mondrian. *Dali*, a unique collector's bag was designed by Lancel in the early 1970s with the collaboration of Salvador Dali in honor of his love and muse, Gala.[7] In 2011, the now world-renowned brand re-released the *Crazy for Daligrammes* collection, featuring the monograms created by Dali. The aim of this collection was to take inspiration from the universe of the Surrealist and very productive artist.

But the relationship between art and other luxury markets extends beyond providing inspiration – it is mutual. As well as drawing inspiration from art, the Luxury sector often collaborates with it. When Louis Vuitton decided to renew its fashion house logo in 2002, Marc Jacobs, Vuitton's Art Director, turned to famous Japanese artist Takashi Murakami. The result was the rainbow Superflat Monogram, used for the hugely successful limited edition series of Eye Love Monogram bags. Louis Vuitton has also privately patronized the art world; for example, in his Espace Louis Vuitton in Hong Kong, he has hosted work from Damien Hirst, Jeff Koons, and Jean-Michel Basquiat.

Similarly, museums have devoted exhibitions to great designers such as Alexander McQueen's retrospective "Alexander McQueen: Savage Beauty" opened on May 2011 at the Metropolitan Museum of Art that had a final attendance count of "661,509...making it the eighth biggest show on record at the Metropolitan Museum of Art".[8] In 2006, the Parisian gallery Almine Rech exhibited "Stage", a series of photographs taken by Hedi Slimane, the former artistic director of Dior and new Yves Saint Laurent house's creative director, who was seen as an artist in his own right, independently from his work at the Haute Couture fashion house. By exhibiting famous creative and art directors from fashion, art acknowledges them as members of contemporary artistic movement.

We have seen therefore that through the process of research and creation art and fashion closely interact. As the Chinese people grow accustomed to luxury products, therefore, they become familiar with the art world.

7.3 ISLAND6 ARTS CENTER

In Shanghai, the art district of No. 50 Moganshan Road, commonly known as M50, located along Suzhou Creek, started out as a retreat for starving artists who could not afford studio space elsewhere. The former factories and warehouses are now a thriving and trendy setting for the Shanghai art scene, bringing together contemporary artists, galleries, art schools and design studios, along with cafés and restaurants. In this unexpected district blossom all kinds of creations. Tourists, art collectors or business professionals can all find what they are looking for, from small artist studios in which one can take part in the invention, conception and production of the artwork, to large workshops where art galleries and design companies have decided to settle in order to benefit the fertile artistic atmosphere.

Calling island6 Arts Center a gallery does not begin to describe the truth; it is, in fact, also a workshop, shooting and digital-effects studio, and, occasionally, a dining room or strip joint. But it is, above all, the home of the Liu Dao Art Collective.

The island6 Arts Center and the Liu Dao Art Collective were founded simultaneously in 2006 as a not-for-profit gallery exhibiting its own homemade artworks. The name was taken from the art center's original location in the Fou Foong Flour Mill, the lone building number 6, standing amidst a sea of debris and run-down shacks. Encircled by Suzhou Creek, it loomed dramatically in the middle of an empty field of rubble like an island raising from the depths of the sea – hence its name. The main goal of island6 was to support the production of "Made in China" artworks in a context of growing egocentrism and commercialization in China. More than simple *chinoiseries*, the Liu Dao Art Collective is an international, multidisciplinary group of individuals specialized in their own field, presenting unique technological multimedia artworks, often featuring beautiful scenes of glittering animated LED.

The collective, named Liu Dao (a Pinyin phrase meaning "island number 6" in Chinese六岛) was founded in 2006 by the island6 Arts Center under the direction of French curator Thomas Charvériat "who decided to revive the communist idea of danwei, or the work unit".[9] Each member of the collective is involved in the creation of artworks, and composes it. Only a brand new contemporary-art market such as China could have allowed such experimentation. The Liu Dao Art Collective gives the possibility for anybody skilled enough to participate and to make art just for the beauty of it. Their work focuses on interactive art installations exploring the effects that "technologies have on our perception and modes of communication".[10] The astounding observation concerning this collective is its shining diversity. The members of the collective come from all around the world (China, France, Singapore, Austria, Hong Kong, the United States, and more than 21 different countries since the beginning), and from such diverse fields as Modern History,

English, Art, International Business or Film. It is the collaboration and interaction of such different people that has permitted the cutting-edge results of such stature.

The management style of this collective does not rely on the strict rules typical of most professional organizations. Rather than a small group of decision-makers, island6 has a strong entrepreneurial culture and pushes every individual of the collective to take decisions, allowing the gallery to move forward. Rules and authority are informal, as, with the exception of the owner, everyone is on the same level, and members, working on a volunteer basis, are as casual about their schedule as about their dress code. The island6 Arts Center being the home of the Liu Dao Collective has been organized to enable volunteers to spend as much time as they wish in the gallery, with no obvious separation between work and free time. As a result, being part of this organization is so intense and consuming that most of the members are young – aged less than 30 – without family obligations and thus free to work long hours, flexible to deal with the unexpected and then, forgetting about their private lives. Volunteers rarely last more than a year and a half, and this relatively high turnover allows the gallery to have new ideas from a continual stream of fresh blood.

Since its founding, the Liu Dao art collective has been exhibited widely, including at the Louis Vuitton Maison Gallery at One Central Macau for the *Raining Stars* exhibition in 2010,[11] at Art Stage Singapore in 2012 and at Tally Beck Contemporary gallery in New York for *Sin City – Impressions of Shanghai: New Work by island6.*[12]

7.4 CREATING AN ARTWORK

The creation process of every single artwork at island6 can be compared to that used in the movie industry. When a spectator watches a movie, he witnesses the final result performed by the actors, even though many more people have worked on it, including technicians, scriptwriters, producers, art directors and so on. These contributors are only credited at the end of the movie. It is a similar process with an island6 production: members of the collective work on the artwork throughout its creation, from the very

FIGURE 7.1 **Charleston Craze**
Source: http://island6.org/LiuDao387.html

beginning to the final product, but the work is credited only with the name of the collective as a whole, Liu Dao.

"Charleston Craze" is an example of one of Liu Dao's art works, and one of my favorites, maybe because it is the first one I truly participated in throughout each stage of production.

Charleston Craze is an LED display with a teakwood frame made by Liu Dao for the exhibition *Goddamned Shanghai* at the island6 Arts Center from December 2011 to March 2012 curated by Jack Mur and Loo Ching Ling (Figure 7.1).

The first part of the creation of this artwork is the same for the entire *Goddamned Shanghai* collection which is the research and curating part of the exhibition. For this exhibition, the collective explored the Shanghai of the 1930s using various means of information. What came out of the extensive research was the economically booming city-atmosphere attracting adventurous travelers and the sensuality of dance halls and opium, melting into each other. Then, as the collective soaks up the sensational opulence of the thirties, the creation process follows.

What is really new at island6 is that in addition to the collaborative approach in which all volunteers work together on every artwork, every piece is also entirely unique and made in the gallery's workshop space. For Charleston Craze, the performance was made in the Arts Center, in the middle of other pieces of art, at night, after the gallery was closed. Once the green background was installed, a dance teacher Zhang Tian Yi 张天伦, member of the collective, began to dance to a famous Charleston song, wearing a breathtaking qipao, a traditional Chinese dress. As she enjoyed herself, the Liu Dao collective encircled and guided her and the 1930s sensation was filmed by the high-resolution camera.

This was then converted into LED and put by the technicians' nimble fingers into a teakwood frame highlighting the contrast between pure and natural Chinese material coexisting with the modernity and the brightness of the LED display portraying a scene from the past.

Once the artwork is ready to astonish the visitors, one or two members of the collective write a "blurb" giving a description of what feeling it is meant to convey in the watcher. Below is the official description for the Charleston Craze artwork:

> When the sun goes down the crowded Bund and lights come out of every trendy place, Shanghai becomes another city. While you are waiting for me in the cabaret, drinking your favorite cocktail in the middle of the shuffling feet and the hot smoke of desire, I am putting on my flashing jewels and my sexiest red qipao. The one of finest silk you loved to fondle during so many nights. You know you just can't resist my Charleston craze. I am dancing, swinging, swaying, everybody's looking at me but I don't care, I ain't misbehaving, I'm just having fun. I can keep going forever, from here to Blood Alley, playground of soldiers and sailors. But I know that whatever happens tonight, I'll be with you in the end.

I had the pleasure of being asked to write the Charleston Craze blurb, and maybe this explains why I love this artwork so much; it shows how deeply I have been involved in the process and also in the gallery.

7.5 INTERVIEW WITH THOMAS CHARVÉRIAT

Thomas Charvériat, founder and owner of island6, is an artist and curator born in Paris (1974), who lives and works in Shanghai.

After attending the School of Visual Arts in New York and receiving his Bachelor of Fine Arts in photography in 1998, Thomas Charvériat studied at Columbia University getting a Master's of Fine Arts in sculpture in 2000. Later, he moved to Barcelona where he obtained a Master's in Digital Arts with honors from the Audiovisual Institute (Pompeu Fabra University).

He specializes in curating exhibitions that promote the use of interactivity in art.

As an artist, Thomas creates animatronics installations with GPS, SMS, video, sound, electronic data and humor that interact with the viewer. Simplicity and elegance are combined to create a multisensorial experience of surprise and playfulness.

In 2006, Thomas Charvériat founded island6 Arts Center in Shanghai, where he is currently the director.

How did you get the idea of island6?

The idea of island6 blossomed from the desire to create a platform for the creation and production of contemporary art, open to anybody skilled enough to make art and participate collaboratively in the whole creative process against the backdrop of growing individualism and capitalism in China.

The main goal of this cutting-edge artistic collective was inspired from the working method of the film industry. Unlike common practices in the art world, a movie gives credit to all those who have been involved, from the technician to the producer. It is their different skills, experiences and backgrounds that gave the final work its richness and technical accomplishment.

Since Liu Dao's beginnings, painters, sculptors, photographers, filmmakers, new media artists, software and digital imaging artists, dancers, writers and engineers have all worked together to produce original, intriguing work.

That is the beauty of the island6 collective: for every artwork produced, you can count at least seven or eight people who have participated in creating it. And this is all achieved in a single location: the island6 Arts Center at M50.[13] The collective prides itself on the fact that all artworks are created in the same space: from the very beginning with the filming of videos to the very end in digital editing and physical assembly of the pieces.

How do artists react to the idea of a collective in a country that is getting more and more individualistic?

island6 was initially formed as a response to precisely that. The soaring prices of Chinese artists at Sotheby's and Christie's in the 2000s are already legendary. Chinese art seemed to be headed out to the world in a big way. Big-name artists started their own stables and factories, hiring hundreds of people to work under their name, similar to the Renaissance artists' workshops. In many ways, the bright lights and big money were too alluring to resist. Solo artists really thrived.

But there was a growing number of artists like Liu Dao who realized that some genres of art lend themselves beautifully to collaborative work. New Media Art, with its focus on dialogue, process, a wide variety of media, is perfect for a collective. Indeed some Chinese collectives are making a name for themselves, for example, WAZA the video artists, and Sonart, who make interdisciplinary installations.

Then again, working in a collective is not a new concept to the Chinese, who have close family ties, and are traditionally active participants in their community.

What is your vision about China and more precisely about the Chinese art sector in the coming years?

One has to keep in mind that China, despite being the second economic world power, is still an emerging country. It is still catching up on the years it has spent behind developed countries and it is doing this in a much shorter period of time than others.

This is one reason why we feel that the Chinese market is still developing in its appreciation for contemporary art. China has a long history of its traditional arts (shan shui, calligraphy...)

but this interest has been lost with all the political and economic shifts the country has been through the past 60 years. In today's China, there are many talented artists but we've noticed that they are mostly appreciated and collected abroad. At the moment, many Chinese people may prefer to buy expensive goods to show off to others, a means of saving face or MIANZI (面子), which is why the luxury sector is booming here. However, buying art requires more immersion, experience and discernment than the purchase of a branded bag. Many young Chinese have caught up with developed countries in terms of financial prowess, but are still developing their appreciation for culture. It might take a long time to change local habits and awaken interest in contemporary art, but once it happens, the art sector will surely take off in a big way. Already at art fairs we see more locals in attendance and asking questions about the art; some Chinese collectors have started to put together sophisticated collections. We've started noticing that art in China can be seen as a way to be taken more seriously, yet we are still lacking much of the artistic appreciation that is widely present in Australia, France or even Japan.

What are the links between art and luxury? How do they differ or complete each other?

Art and luxury are linked by many means. They both stand for an appreciation of its value, beauty and quality. Both also serve as an economic distinguisher, separating those who own art and/or luxury in a higher social-economic cast.

However, whereas art is produced in limited or unique editions, luxury goods are produced in large quantities, for the sole purpose of being sold. Moreover, the purchase of an artwork is very different from that of a luxury good – art collectors require a certain taste, which stems only from education and exposure to art. This is what we see here in China. China has become the world's biggest luxury goods market because people are so wealthy, but while they can buy the most expensive clothes or cars, Chinese have yet to grasp the meaning of cultural wealth, which is pretty much Art.

Of course, luxury and art have worked closely for a long time. Big luxury houses such as Louis Vuitton and Dries Van Noten are great supporters of the arts – which is great for art communities around the world! (Dries Van Noten for James Reeve; LV cultural houses . . .). Seeing as art collectors are luxury goods consumers as well, it creates a deeper connection between both closely tied worlds.

Art is quite different from Luxury. How can we distinguish two artists or two oil paintings? Both will have the best material and make their best effort at every single stage of the production process to deliver a perfect result. But it doesn't matter how hard you might work, art relies on taste, which is subjective. If a wealthy housewife doesn't like these red Louboutin pumps, she can still opt for the camel boots. In art it is different; pieces are unique or limited to a few editions and either you love them or you continue on your way.

Yet, since luxury clients are the ones who in general buy art, a new approach has to be made. As said before, in China there are no rules, hence creativity is encouraged and clients experiment with a new approach.

The island6 Arts Center took the challenge to make a difference playing the innovation card using technology such as LED and interactive interfaces. Innovation is also very keen to luxury brand that wants to stand out.

Similar to a luxury brand, the island6 art collective keeps trying to make a name for itself in the art sector. Yet art cannot rely on a simple advertisement on a crowded corner and it is by participating in worldwide art fairs such as Art Stage Singapore, Scope Basel or Art Asia Miami that island6 is targeting sophisticated tastes around the globe. The effort is matched by partnerships with local galleries in cities such Beijing, Bangkok, Singapore, Geneva and New York. VIP previews, selected dinners and elegant happenings are at the core of island6 luxurious direction. The collective also tries to stand out by setting high prices, and reflecting the innovation and technological process used for the unique result which cannot be seen anywhere else.

island6 presents a unique combination of multicultural environment, cultural filter and a small taste of luxury in an ever-changing Chinese reality.

What can the luxury industry learn from this?

Well, the future of this industry in the years to come will be in Asia and more specifically in China. The relevant players in this industry will need to be tuned to what is going on in the Chinese artistic milieu, or to ignore that, and one day wake up and discover that your brand is no longer prized by the market.

7.6 CONCLUSION

Even though buying art is not yet a Chinese common habit, the luxury market there is literally booming, and the arts market is taking off. China is proving to be a blank page for new forms of expression and experimentation. island6 is such an example, it provides in fact a strong model for how the art can take benefits of China's rapid growth in the luxury sector by experimenting new ways of management.

ACKNOWLEDGMENTS

Thanks to my dear friend Chris.

NOTES

1. CIA – The World Factbook (2012). East & Southeast Asia: China, retrieved 8 February 2012 from https://www.cia.gov/library/publications/the-world-factbook/geos/ch.html.
2. Forbes (2011). Record Number of Millionaires, by Luisa Kroll, retrieved 1 June 2012 from http://www.forbes.com/sites/luisakroll/2011/05/31/record-number-of-millionaires/.
3. Hurun Report (2011). Shanghai Wealth Report 2011, retrieved 1 June 2012 from http://www.hurun.net/hurun/listreleaseen552.aspx.
4. China Daily (2012). New Year luxury spending overseas hits $7.2b, 2 February 2012.
5. The Economist (2011). China's luxury boom, 17 February 2011.
6. Idem.
7. Lancel (2011). Cela n'est pas une oeuvre d'art, c'est une déclaration d'amour, Le magazine de la French légèreté by Lancel, 2, p. 79.

8. Wilson, E. (2011). "McQueen: The Final Count, New York Times", retrieved 1 June 2012 from http://runway.blogs.nytimes.com/2011/08/08/mcqueen-the-final-count/.
9. Munter, U. and Bollmann, P. (2012). *Focus Asia insights into the Wemhoner Collection*, Kerber Verlag.
10. Rolf A. Kluenter, D. C. (2007). *Eurasia One*. Shanghai: FoldPress & Timezone8 Publications.
11. Dao, L. (n.d.). *Raining Stars*. Retrieved from http://www.island6.org: http://www.island6.org/RainingStars_info.html.
12. Beck, T. (2012, January). *Sin City – Impressions of Shanghai*. Retrieved from http://tallybeckcontemporary.com/: http://tallybeckcontemporary.com/sin-city.
13. Jie, W. (2010, March 11). "M50 Plans New M50 Art Hub", *Shanghai Daily*, 1.

8

LUXURY SHOPPING PLACES IN CHINA

Joanna Chen

8.1 INTRODUCTION

As recently as one decade ago, there was no stand-alone luxury brand store in mainland China. At that time, wearing a Rolex watch meant luxury, and such luxury consumers were called "Bao Fa Hu" (new rich in short period). With the reform and opening up of Chinese society, more people became rich and broadened their horizons through foreign travel. They started to change their way of life and their demands for luxury products like bags, watches, cosmetics, cars, clothes and so on increased rapidly. To cater to the needs of these local customers, luxury brands and top auto companies, mainly from Europe, set up their shops and factories in mainland China. From then on, high-end brands have been playing a critical role in mainland luxury world.

While many people are convinced that luxury is reserved exclusively for the rich and consider it a waste of money, others aspire to a luxurious lifestyle, a lifestyle that distinguishes them from other people through a display of wealth and social status. For example, in an attempt to reach the same level as those rich people, the middle class in China may consume luxury beyond their income in order to feel that they belong to a certain elite group. Due to urbanization and the ever-rising number of middle classes, the demand for luxury in China has grown rapidly in recent years, in accordance with Goldman Sachs' prediction that China will consume about 30 percent of the world's total luxury goods in 2015 as the world's top luxury brands market.[1]

8.2 LUXURY SHOPPING PLACES

China's economy has grown remarkably over the past 30 years, and alongside this booming economy has come urbanization. Cities like Guangzhou and Shenzhen have followed in the footsteps of Shanghai and Beijing, and built up their power to have more luxury brands within the city. At the very beginning, brands could only find high-level hotels to set up their shops, since, at that time, there was no other place suitable for sale and display of luxury goods. The first shopping mall (as defined by the ICSC) opened in Guangzhou in 1997, positioned for the mass market. It was not until 2002, in Shanghai, that a shopping mall for luxury goods was opened; Plaza66 along Nanjing Xi road. Luxury aficionados could now find luxury goods in the city center without having to go abroad. Following this model, more cities joined the renovation in the center area of the city. Gradually, several luxury shopping places, similar to the shopping avenues in European countries, became well-established in first-tier or capital cities in mainland China where they could provide most luxury goods as well as the dedicated environment and customer service.

8.3 THE TOP FIVE CITIES WITH LUXURY BUSINESS IN CHINA[2]

According to Jones Lang LaSalle's report in July 2011, the high-end luxury shopping streets in Europe (Figure 8.1) include London's Bond Street and Sloane Street, Paris' Champs-Élysées and Avenue Montaigne, Moscow's Stoleshinkov Lane and Tverskaya Street, Milan's Via Monte Napoleone, all of which are characterized by soaring rents. A similar phenomenon can be found in New York's Madison Avenue and Fifth Avenue, Beverly Hills' Rodeo Drive, and in Asia, HK's Guangdong Dao, Singapore's Orchard Road and Tokyo's Ginza. Due to the soaring rents and real-estate prices squeezing out small players, most luxury goods stores along those luxury streets are managed by large corporations with considerable investment in store image.

China is currently experiencing the same as those well-developed markets have done over the past years. The successive positive performance of luxury brands in certain cities is quite outstanding and is drawing great attention from the luxury headquarters overseas. Among these cities, Shanghai undoubtedly ranks No. 1 in luxury sales. With Expo2010, two new luxury shopping places appeared, in addition to the existing Nangjing Xi Road and the Bund, giving Shanghai four luxury places at present. These places provide world-famous luxury products and dedicated cuisine from all countries, while, at same time, creating an elegant shopping environment not only for Shanghai customers, but also for customers from the whole country.

Beijing comes after Shanghai in terms of luxury sales. Over the past five years, and especially around the period of the Olympics in 2008, the capital of China has developed its luxury business. There are now three luxury shopping places in Beijing, two of them set up after 2007 and comparing the sales with those places in Shanghai, only Xinkong mall could achieve the same level.

Hangzhou, the capital city of Zhejiang province, ranking No. 3 in luxury business, has seen a two-digit increase in its GDP annually for the past 18 years; we can only imagine how strong the purchasing power of Zhejiang province is becoming. Top brands like Hermès, Chanel, Louis Vuitton, Gucci and Armani have situated their flagship stores in this area to serve the local consumers. Hangzhou Plaza is just one of the luxury shopping places. Another two are currently being set up.

Ranking four and five respectively, Guangzhou and Shenzhen, both situated in southern China, not far away from Hong Kong, launched out in the luxury business earlier with an active economy. Customer demand is strong, and while most of them enjoy visiting HK to buy luxury goods, this cannot stop the aficionados from creating a luxury lifestyle for the city.

8.4 LUXURY SHOPPING PLACES IN SOUTH CHINA

This part introduces the luxury places in south China including Shanghai, Hangzhou, Guangzhou and Shenzhen.

8.4.1 Shanghai

8.4.1.1 Place 1: Nanjing Xi Road

Nanjing Xi Road was the first area dedicated to luxury shopping. Plaza 66 opened in 2002, followed by Westgate mall, Sogo city plaza, Citic and Golden Eagle. In ten years, this area has become the most famous luxury place in China, maybe even in the world, bringing together almost all the luxury brands present in the China market. LVMH has located its Branch office in this area, dealing with the whole business in mainland China.

8.4.1.2 Place 2: The Bund

For a century, the Bund has been the symbol and pride of Shanghai. With its European and early-twentieth-century Russian architecture, the Bund is as splendid a place as anywhere in the world. Now, many attractive new constructions have been erected in addition

FIGURE 8.1 **Luxury shopping area along Nangjing Xi road, Shanghai**

to the historical buildings and they have become the home of luxury brands like Cartier, Zegna, and hotels like Peninsula. Recently, many small villas have been built in the area, where high-end restaurants have also been established to match the high retail environment turning the Bund into a glittering and luxurious setting.

8.4.1.3 Place 3: Xintiandi area

Xintiandi, the hottest new shopping and entertainment district in Shanghai developed in 2001 by Shui On Land, is made up of an area of reconstituted traditional shikumen (stone gate) houses in narrow alleys, which have been transformed into some of the city's finest clubs, restaurants and boutiques. The successful redevelopment of this historical area had served as a role model for many other city developments, not just in China, but across Asia. Before 2010, this district could not be defined as luxury since it was largely a lifestyle center for foreigners, high-income local consumers and tourists. Later on, several high-rise buildings on Huaihai Road, just near Xintiandi, upgraded their brand mix. LV, Tiffany and Coach, for example, set up their first or second flagship stores in the area turning it into a real place for luxury and leisure. It is also heard that Hermès will renovate an old house near the place and open the flagship of China in 2013 if the progress continues to go according to plan.

8.4.1.4 Place 4: Lujiazhui area

The opening of the IFC mall in 2010 transformed the world-famous Lujiazhui district, with its high-end brands, Ritz Carlton hotel and two office towers, into another luxury shopping area, similar to that of Nanjing Xi Road and earning it the nickname of the Shanghai "Rodeo drive". Lujiazhui includes the Oriental Pearl TV tower, skyscrapers with global banks, other malls and department store like Super Brand mall, Yaohan and Times Square.

8.4.2 Hangzhou

8.4.2.1 Place 1: Hangzhou tower

In recent years, people from the city have started to drive their fast cars to Hangzhou tower for a weekend's luxury shopping, seemingly unconcerned about the expense of the trip or the price of the luxury goods. Formed by four buildings, connected by pedestrian sky bridges, Hangzhou tower gathers together almost all luxury brands with the exception of Hermès, its annual sales reaching €600 million in 2011.

8.4.2.2 Place 2: The Lakeside area

West Lake, a fresh-water lake with its famous sight-seeing attractions set in a naturally beautiful area, used to be the favorite retreat for emperors in ancient times. It can now add a new attraction in the form of the luxury business in this area. Hangzhou's Lakeside Luxury Brand Street (hereafter referred to as "the Lakeside" in this article) is one of the city's high-end districts. Differentiating from the business models in most second-tier cities, the Lakeside adopted the high-end business concept like Milan's Via Monte Napoleone shopping district. Hermès, Gucci, Louis Vitton, Armani and Zegna have set up stand-alone flagship stores in this area, and high-level hotels like Hyatt, Watch boutiques, and restaurants have created an area both for luxury goods and a luxury lifestyle experience.

8.4.3 Guangzhou

8.4.3.1 Place 1: La Perle

La Perle is a retail complex situated in Guangzhou's Huan Shi Dong Road. The area is surrounded by several notable landmarks, including the Garden Hotel, Bai Yun Hotel, Friendship Store and Guangzhou World Trade Centre. La Perle provides a platform for the world's top luxury brands, such as Louis Vuitton, Hermès, Gucci,

Dior and so on, making it a premiere shopping place offering an innovative lifestyle mix.

8.4.3.2 Place 2: Tianhe district

The Tianhe district was the birthplace of the first shopping mall in China – Tianhe City, which opened in 1997. A new member has now joined this area, establishing a luxury landmark for Guangzhou city after ten year's development by Swire group. Taikoo Hui, which is linked to the city's metro system, combines business and cultural elements. It features a five-level shopping mall with top luxury brands, two Grade-A office towers and a five-star hotel with serviced apartments.

8.4.4 Shenzhen

8.4.4.1 Place 1: The Mix city area

Located in Luohu district, the Mix city has become the "new landmark" of the city. The 188,000 square meter retail arcade started its operations in 2004, before a small number of retail places and a five-star hotel were added in phase two. Inside the mall, we can find most luxury brands apart from Hermès and Chanel. Gucci set up an amazing two-story glass box in front of the main entrance of the mall which has become an attraction for tourists as well as local citizens to take photos with the Gucci store in the background.

8.4.4.2 Place 2: The Overseas Chinese town area

Overseas Chinese town is located in Dameisha, Shenzhen consisting of two theme parks for resort and high-end residential flats and villas.

Yi Tian Plaza is in the center of Overseas Chinese town, near to the seashore of Shenzhen bay, surrounding the several five-star hotels and the well-known playground-paradise of Happy Valley. It has several luxury brands like Burberry, Armani and so on, a dedicated designed supermarket and restaurants which can provide shopping, leisure and entertainment to the tourist and local consumers.

8.5 LUXURY SHOPPING PLACES IN NORTH CHINA

8.5.1 Beijing

8.5.1.1 Place 1: World trade center

With phase three becoming operational in 2010, the China World Trade Center complex, including phase one and two, now covers 1,100,000 square meters, making it one of the largest Central Business Districts (CBDs) in Beijing. The initial two phases of the world trade center constituted the first luxury shopping place in Beijing prior to the opening of Xinkong for business. Now, the phase-three tower, the tallest skyscraper in Beijing at 330 m, has given a new lease of life to the classic commercial district. It features office accommodation, a five-star hotel at the top of the building, as well as retail and entertainment venues. A cinema, bookstore-Page One, newly designed Ole supermarket together with Joyce multi-brands store, a coming 7,000 square meter Louis Vuitton store, and many other top luxury flagship stores make this place a site for exquisite products, as well as a lifestyle experience.

8.5.1.2 Place 2: Xinkong Place

Xinkong Place, which opened on April 2007 just before the 2008 Beijing Olympic Games, is a one-stop shopping center, grouping the world's top products, department stores and international cuisine. Located in Beijing CBD Huamao Business Circle along Changan Avenue East, with a constructed area of around 180,000 square meters, Xinkong Place brings together almost all categories, from soft goods to hard goods. It is said that the annual sales of Chanel there rank among the top three in mainland China. Nearby are two super-luxury hotels – the Ritz-Carlton and Marriott, and three Grade-A office towers. The region attracts investment from many world-class syndicates and groups providing the CBD with a strong customer flow to support the ideal and enjoyable luxury shopping place.

8.5.1.3 Place 3: Sanlitun place

Sanlitun place is situated very close to the embassy district of Beijing. Night life began to develop with the arrival of bars and pubs, and later on, an open-style mall, supposedly inspired by Beijing's traditional Hutong architecture, was developed by Swire group.

The ultra-modern, low-density Village Sanlitun is made up of 17 innovative buildings where luxury retail in the city includes cinema and numerous restaurants and art shops including the very popular Apple flagship store and Adidas flagship store in the south part.

The more luxurious side of The Village is the north part, fully opened in 2011. Many stores such as Emporio Armani, Escada as well as high-fashion brands D-square, Pierre Balmain are present. It is a swanky place, just like Shanghai's Xintiadi, for people to enjoy shopping and just stroll around.

8.6 THE KEY CHARACTERISTICS OF LUXURY SHOPPING PLACES

As the cities described above are ranked top five in luxury business in China, they might share certain characteristics relating to the successful creation of more than one luxury shopping place within the city.

8.6.1 Population

According to the sixth population census taken at the end of 2010, China's population surpassed 1.34 billion, with about a third living along China's coast. Of the five cities mentioned above, Shanghai, Guangzhou and Shenzhen are along coastal area.

Shanghai's total population was over 23 million as of 2010, while that of Beijing had risen to 19.6 million. Guangzhou is the most populous city in Guangdong Province, home to 12.7 million permanent residents, followed by Shenzhen at 10.4 million, and

Hangzhou with a registered population of 8.7 million people.[3] The government census did not reveal the size of the floating population of these three cities although this is probably not insignificant.

With the exception of Hangzhou, the populations of the five cities are above ten million. Other cities in China, like Shenyang, Chendu, Chongqin and Tianjin, also have a population above ten million. Despite being in-land, these cities are currently developing their luxury business at an amazing pace.

8.6.2 Transportation

Taking transportation into consideration, Beijing and Shanghai have a very strong network of transport links within the city and with other cities or abroad. They both have two airports, a high-speed train and more than ten metro lines. Guangzhou and Shenzhen are not as convenient as the two big cities of China; however, the metro lines have been well developed in the past years. Hangzhou again is an exception, not even having its own airport.

8.6.3 GDP

In 2011, Shanghai, Beijing, Guangzhou and Shenzhen were ranked top four in the country, exceeding 1 trillion Yuan. Shanghai's total GDP grew to 1.92 trillion Yuan (US$297 billion) with GDP per capita of 82,560 Yuan (US$12,784), standing in the No. 1 position – Hangzhou is No. 8.[4]

The above data shows that the top-ranking cities are almost same as the list of top luxury cities.

8.6.4 Tourism

There is a popular saying: "Above there is heaven, below there are Hangzhou and Suzhou." and the explorer Marco Polo highly praised Hangzhou when he arrived in the town in the 13th century, describing it as "the most beautiful and elegant city in the world". Hangzhou's natural scenery attracts hundreds of thousands of tourists to its West Lake area each year to enjoy the placid lake, Lingyin temple and lakeside teahouses. The total number of tourists to Hangzhou exceeds 65 million.[5]

In Guangzhou and Shenzhen, due to the flourishing business environment and artificial sightseeing, the number of tourists in 2010 was estimated at 127 million and 770 million respectively.[6]

According to the latest statistics, the number of tourists visiting Beijing was more than 200 million in 2011, while Shanghai's figures were 15 percent higher, a 2.9 percent increment compared to the year of the Shanghai Expo.[7]

Although the number of tourists may not lead directly to the creation of the city's luxury business, it should certainly have some influence.

8.7 CONCLUSION

From 2008, the financial crisis has spread over the whole world. However, luxury consumption is keeping firm with rapid growth in China. According to Bain & co, luxury sales in China are still soaring with more than a ten percent increase compared to those of Japan and Europe where business has slowed down with an eight percent decrease.

It cannot be denied that China is becoming an attractive emerging market for many luxury brands.

NOTES

1. Jing Daily (2010),.China "Saves the Day" For Struggling Luxury Industry, retrieved 21 January 2010.
2. People's daily online (2010). Top 10 most luxurious cities in China's mainland, retrieved 29 January 2010.
3. Statistics Bureau (2011). The Report II of the sixth national population census, retrieved 29 April 2011.
4. Suec.cn (2011). List of top 50 cities' GDP in 2011, retrieved 1 June 2012 from www.suec.cn/development/competition/economy.

5. China Investment Advising Network (2011). Investment and forecasting of tourism 2012–2016, retrieved 1 June 2012 from www.ocn.com.cn.
6. China Investment Advising Network (2011). Investment and forecasting of tourism 2012–2016, retrieved 1 June 2012 from www.ocn.com.cn.
7. China Investment Advising Network (2011). Investment and forecasting of tourism 2012–2016, retrieved 1 June 2012 from www.ocn.com.cn.

9

PERSPECTIVES ON LUXURY OPERATIONS IN CHINA

Yves R. Lucky and Francesco Giliberti Birindelli

9.1 INTRODUCTION

Luxury operations in China can be challenging. This chapter first tackles the financial implications of luxury development in Asia and then presents in-depth the issue of licensing. It finishes by presenting two perspectives on what is next in the Chinese luxury market.

9.2 LUXURY BUSINESS FINANCIALS: FROM ASIA TO CHINA

The luxury business as a whole is formed by and includes several sub-sectors, such as fashion, wines and spirits, watches, accessories, perfumes and fragrances, jewelry and so on.

The principle actors in these sectors have come from Italy and France, and if we extend the arena to include all brands, groups and competitors we can find that almost all actors of the luxury world come from (predominantly) Europe or (to a lesser extent) North America.

Notwithstanding the above observation, it is commonly recognized that "The" luxury business is becoming increasingly Asian.

But how can this be possible?

To answer this question, we must look at each of the four phases of the luxury business:

1. Trademark and creation, sampling and prototyping
2. Sourcing, industrialization and manufacturing
3. Wholesale distribution, commercial, customer care and logistics
4. Retail distribution.

The first three business lines are typically carried out in the country or countries in which the brands were initially established. For the vast majority of these, as mentioned earlier, this concerns Europe and North America. Only in the fourth business line, retail distribution, does Asia take its place of honor.

To understand the reasons behind the retail success of the luxury business in Asia, some background information is needed.

The luxury business and brand recognition is fairly recent. Its worldwide popularity[1] only started in the 1970s and 1980s thanks to the success of certain French and Italian brands.

Suddenly these brands have started to have a surprising power over the most-developed economic Asian culture: the Japanese customer base.

Over 30 years, Japanese clients (both in their home countries and worldwide) have proved to be the best-selling clients for luxury items and they have satisfied their thirst for brand recognition by shopping and showing Western brands.

Japanese taste however has shown to be not the only success behind the luxury business in the Asian region.

Two exceptional case stories that confirm the trend set by Japan in the luxury sector are Hong Kong and South Korea.

Hong Kong, with its peculiar status (a territory under administrative control of the United Kingdom until 1997 and being part of the People's Republic of China afterwards) and advantageous customs and tax rules, has, despite its limited territory and population, frequently beaten the worldwide "sale per-square-foot competition" of luxury goods. South Korea, on the other hand, with its giant city, Seoul, has multiplied its sales in luxury products tenfold over the last decade.

To the examples of Hong Kong and South Korea, we can add the case of the "Dragon", the incredible expansion of the

Chinese market and the desire by Chinese clients for luxury products.

In 2010 almost 50 percent of the luxury business sales were generated by Asian clients, buying in Asia or in international destinations, such as Milan, Paris and London.

Among these Asian luxury fans, increasing interest is being showed by customers from the People's Republic of China (including the remarkable presence of Hong Kong).

This can be easily explained by both internal and external factors.

9.2.1 Internal factors

1. China is not alone! It is part of the Asian region that is, by far, the most successful region worldwide for the luxury sector.
2. People's Republic of China was a virgin territory; until the late 1980s this communist state did not even encompass private law in its legal system, and aspirations of individuals had no concrete opportunity for expression.
3. Starting from early 2000, the Chinese economy has been driving world development and has shown to be the strongest overall; The Chinese trend of new millionaires cannot be beaten by any other country.

9.2.2 External factors

1. Western markets have been exploited over the past 40 years by the luxury players and have now very limited range of increase. Western luxury *maisons* are now consistently investing to attract Chinese customers.
2. Historical luxury regions such as Japan, Europe and North America are in recession! Luxury competitors do not have a positive insight on the future of these markets for their products.
3. The Chinese bull is running fast! The number of new millionaires in China is not comparable with the rest of the world and potential targets are multiplying on a daily basis.
4. Cost of retail: the cost of taking over a location, refurnishing and running a store in China cannot be compared with that in

Western locations. Milan, Paris or New York, for example, can cost 10 to 20 times more than in Shanghai or Beijing

The above explains how the Chinese Dragon is pushing hard to break out of its borders and Western luxury businesses are pushing hard to break into the Chinese market. Of course the result is a booming luxury business.

9.3 LICENSING IN ASIA

Over the past 10 years, the licensing business has shown particularly strong development in China: development looks set to expand. The Hong Kong International Licensing Show, an annual event that hosts the Asian Licensing Conference, represented more than 500 world-famous brands in its 2012 edition, attracting local and overseas exhibitors. During the event, the Premier Asian Licensing Awards recognize the outstanding achievements of successful licensing players throughout Asia.

Asian companies and specifically Chinese companies are increasingly on the lookout for good licensing deals. The tremendous opportunities provided by the growth of the Chinese domestic market means that Chinese companies can introduce a famous brand very rapidly and with a high chance of success. Many export-trading companies tend to diversify their activities by turning toward import–export businesses rather than just export. The main reason for this shift is the slow growth of the United States and European markets in recent years and the gloomy outlook for the near future.

Growth in the Asian market, by contrast, is not only strong, but seems very promising for the years to come. This represents a good opportunity indeed for many powerful trading companies to invest part of their cash in new projects including the introduction of famous foreign brands into their homeland market.

After a test period including a not-always-easy import activity, the trend appears to be a licensing agreement. The Chinese company obtains the right to produce locally and market the product or range of products against a determined amount of royalties, often set as a percentage of the total yearly turnover.

9.3.1 The brands market

The world market for brands and licenses is constantly growing and represents a very interesting economic field. Brands are constantly being sold, and brand ownership may change often completely unbeknown to the majority of consumers. Brands are in fact held as any other assets, either by individuals or by companies, as part of their balance sheet.

In some countries, like Switzerland, brands can even be depreciated following precise accounting procedures allowing the company to purchase a brand to deduct fiscal amounts every year! This, however, is not the case in most countries.

We should therefore keep in mind that brands are treated as assets that can be bought and sold with often considerable profits.

In some cases the Chinese company will start with an import activity. If the results are promising, it can turn to a license agreement for a determined period of time and then, at any time after an agreement with the owner, finally proceed with the actual purchasing of the brand.

A brand can either be licensed or purchased for a specific geographical area and for a specific product category. Most countries have ratified the Madrid agreement and therefore accept to follow the rules indicated by the WIPO (World Intellectual Property Organization).[2] Each brand is classified according to numbered classes and can be held totally or partially, class by class or even product by product within each class.

9.3.2 Licensing deals

Up to the end of the 1990s and the beginning of 2000, most licensing deals were signed by Hong Kong- or Taiwan-based businesses with specific geographical clauses covering mainland China.

As an example, a Taiwan-based company started to license the world-famous French brand Pierre Cardin in the early 1990s for domestic electrical appliances and electronics. After penetrating the mainland Chinese market, it then signed a deal to acquire the brand not only for Asia but for the whole world becoming therefore a part-owner of a very famous brand.

Nowadays things have changed as a great number of China-based companies have reached a substantial level of wealth and can easily afford to sign a licensing contract requesting as territory the whole of the Chinese market or more.

Hong Kong however remains an interesting place to establish a company that owns a brand or simply licenses it for tax reasons. The products included in a contract can vary from one category to a whole class.

For example, if the Chinese licensee requests a license for writing instruments (pens, pencils, fountain pens, roller balls etc.), the licensor, the owner of the rights as stated in the WIPO class 16 stationery, will indicate in the contract specifically that only the writing instruments are subject to the agreement, leaving out all the other possible products included in the class 16.

In fact, the terms of every license can vary significantly depending on each deal as *each licensing agreement is nothing but a contract.*

Here are the main points generally and most frequently found in a standard contract:

9.3.2.1 Trademark concession

The Licensor authorizes the Licensee to bear the trademark under specific conditions for a given line of products manufactured and/or marketed by the Licensee on Licensor's design.

9.3.2.2 Artistic direction

The artistic direction of the products and their packaging belongs to the Licensor only, either for what concerns the original designs and colors, or the material to be employed which shall be co-operatively decided.

Upon request, the Licensor can create new designs and shall submit his drawings to the Licensee.

Samples of the licensed merchandise are in general submitted to the Licensor before any marketing takes place.

9.3.2.3 Territory and marketing area

This point indicates the exact geographical area covered by the agreement.

9.3.2.4 Duration

Each agreement is concluded for a given duration. A date can be set before which the parties will negotiate possible renewal terms.

9.3.2.5 Royalties

In exchange for the rights granted, the Licensee shall pay a royalty or a percentage to the Licensor on the net sales of the products included in the agreement.

In general, all royalties are net of all taxes, duties, withholding taxes and so on from the Licensee's country which shall be paid by the Licensee.

9.3.2.6 Advertising

Most frequently the Licensee submits all advertising plans for approval – be they in spoken, printed, electronic or written form.

At the start of each year, the Licensee also submits to the Licensor his promotional schedule (advertising, sponsoring, trade-shows, etc.).

9.3.2.7 Exclusivity

The Licensor indicates if the drawings and models are exclusive and also states that the Licensee does not have the right to market the same models without the licensed trademark (that is, the Licensee is forbidden to sell the same products without the brand).

9.3.2.8 Auditing

In most cases the Licensee will provide a certificate from his auditor – Certified Public Accountant, certifying the accuracy of the sales reports. The Licensor can also be authorized to have the Licensee's sales audited by any independent accountant.

9.3.2.9 Counterfeiting, termination of agreement and applicable law

The Licensee should always inform the Licensor in case of evidence of counterfeiting.

In most cases the agreement can be terminated by a simple registered letter if the Licensee does not pay the royalties on time.

The applicable law or arbitration in case of conflict (Licensee's or Licensor's country) must be indicated in the contract.

9.3.3 Master license versus punctual license

One aspect that readers may find hard to understand at first is the fact that a licensing agreement can be for an extremely punctual operation. For example, a license can be obtained for as short a period of time as a single promotion.

Every year the figures of premium products distributed by mail-order companies or internet-sales companies are growing, reaching several billions of dollars in each developed country. Exact figures are available from the national associations acting in the field of premiums and promotions such as the Advertising Specialty Institute and Promotional Products Association International in the United States, and the European Promotional Products Industry (EPPI) in Europe.

Basically, every time a mail order or Internet company needs to link its sales to a gift, the search for the ideal gift leads the company to either look for an appropriate brand for the gift by itself, or ask for the service of an expert premium/promotion company.

In most circumstances the deal is done with an expert premium company. The premium company already has contact with the owners of the trademark rights of several brands and therefore makes it easier for the customer's buying and marketing team to select the ideal gift item with the most appropriate brand.

Consequently, it is often the premium company that signs a temporary license with the owner of the trademark: an agreement that is valid for a single operation (a "one-shot" agreement).

The agreement will be based on the possibility of turning the gift item into a famous branded product bearing a famous trademark, for a certain quantity of pieces, and for a certain geographical area and period of time (some promotions can last one week, one month, one season or up to one year). Against the use of the trademark, the premium company will pay an established amount of royalties to the company holding the trademark.

In some cases, the premium company can hold an open license to develop several deals within a product category and an area, but in most cases the agreement will be signed for each single promotion.

The amounts of money involved in such deals are rather large because the quantities involved are often very high.

9.3.4 Fashion, luxury brands and punctual licensing

Although many famous luxury brands do not easily accept to license their trademark, the number of world-famous brands willing to proceed seems to be growing. An Internet search will identify hundreds of offers linked to a branded or designer gift every month!

9.3.5 What is next?

This section presents the opinions of two Chinese luxury experts on the next challenges facing companies in the Chinese luxury market: Chloe Reuter from ReuterPR and Mier Ai from HEARST Magazines China.

Dealing with HNWI by Chloe Reuter[3]

Within modern history, China is known for its rapid development and speed – and the Chinese luxury market is no different. Not only are Chinese luxury consumers growing in numbers, but, at a certain level, their preferences towards luxury are becoming increasingly sophisticated. Art collections, private jets, luxury yachts, private education and customized luxury travel trips are just a few examples of China's maturing and diversifying market.

Sophisticated HNWIs are straying away from "mainstream" and overexposed luxury goods, such as the classic Louis Vuitton bag. The China Market Research group notes that "rich people are getting richer, and want more exclusiveness and self-indulgence", opting away from commonplace luxury goods.[4] The need for exclusiveness and uniqueness may be one reason why Chinese wealthy are turning to art collecting. Just five years ago, only a handful of art collectors were in the Chinese scene, but now there is a booming growth in the art market and those with money are keen to buy and collect art.

Despite the rapid growth in the Chinese luxury market, and the tremendous opportunity for continued expansion, companies should keep in mind that China's cultural and historical background is very influential in business. The concept of "guanxi", roughly translated as "relationship". is especially important in the luxury market. Luxury brands should establish one-on-one relationships with their clients, focusing on unique experiences and education in order to thrive. Another influential factor is an increasing appetite for luxury with "Chinese characteristics". Within the recent history of luxury goods in China, there has been little tradition of homegrown Chinese luxury brands – but this is all changing. Many Chinese now proudly buy "made in China" goods. Hermes launched the Chinese brand "Shang Xia" in 2010, which can be described as a "renaissance" of Chinese culture. Each part of the design process is headed by a Chinese team, making it a wholly Chinese brand.

In 2011, China became the world's second-largest consumer of luxury goods.[5] The challenge now is for brands to create a meaningful dialogue, engaging and developing relationships with more discerning luxury consumers. The key to success in the Chinese luxury market is to recognize the uniqueness of the Chinese consumer and adapt accordingly.

Looking for talent by Mier Ai[6]

Trying to forecast luxury consumption in China will always be a challenging task, and one should understand that no matter how well-studied and analyzed it may be, the result can be taken only as a reference of growth of a trend.

Let's start with the key features of the Chinese luxury market and consumers. First of all, China has a similar landscape to that of Europe. Consumer behavior is widely affected by different cultural backgrounds, climates and living standards. The various stages of economy, commercial and environment development also adds to the complexity of understanding regional differences.

The second key feature is often addressed to me from the clients' side. The luxury consumers of China are generally much younger than those

(Continued)

of Western markets. These are groups of well-educated and sophisticated customers, with media-consumption habits formatted with very strong personality. They seek emotional links with personality, profession and style, rather than chasing traditional "BIG" brands.

The third feature, which is evolving dynamically day by day, if not hour by hour, is that the influence factors and drivers of China's domestic luxury market come from integrated campaigns. The power of individual media campaigns is no longer relevant since the potential target consumers can only be contacted and attracted using multi-platform, cross-media offers. Not only because the consumers are widely spread across media platforms, but also because they are constantly being bombarded with information.

Weibo, the equivalent of Twitter in China (Twitter is banned in China), had a registered user-base which grew from zero to 250 million within 12 months for just one of the operators – Sina. Almost 88 percent of our international clients set up and actively manage their accounts. By May 2012, our top 60 clients had forwarded more than one million tweets on monthly basis and could generate in excess of 400,000 comments. Monitoring the daily performance of Weibo has suddenly become an important part of the marketing staff's responsibility for all luxury brands.

This brings perhaps the ultimate challenge for the Chinese luxury market – talent. I had the privilege to ask over 20 top luxury-industry executives responsible for China market the question: "what do you see as the biggest challenge for your business in China in the next three to five years?" The most frequently mentioned word among the answers is "talent". The need for talented employees is enormous. Not only because brands compete with each other for experienced junior and senior staff, but because the fast-growing market itself creates high temptation for skillful executives to seek opportunities among different industries.

NOTES

1. By "popularity" I mean the recognition of brands in customers' (consumers) perception. The focus of the purchase started to shift from the purchase to satisfy a need and/or a purchase to acquire high quality products to the purchase of a good for its brand, for the need for public recognition and for the scope of belonging to a specific social class by using coded habits (dressing, drinking, wearing and so on).

2. See www.wipo.org.
3. Founder and Managing Director, ReuterPR.
4. Reuters, *Louis Vuitton so Last Season for China's Super Chic*, 7 June 2012.
5. Hurun, *The Chinese Millionaire Wealth Report* 2012.
6. Managing Director, HEARST Magazines China.

10

LUXURY CONSUMER TRIBES IN ASIA: INSIGHTS FROM SOUTH KOREA

Bernard Cova and Tae Youn Kim

10.1 INTRODUCTION

As a professional or student in the luxury and fashion management industry, you are probably most familiar with the term "tribe" when it is used to describe an ancient, primitive, outdated system of human social organization based on close kinship ties and close geographical proximity. Further, you may think that today tribes only exist in far-flung corners of the world, in isolated communities, barely touched by the modern world. The study of tribes, surely, is the domain of the anthropologist and documentary film-makers for the *Discovery* or *National Geographic* television channel. What do tribes have to do with luxury brands? And what can you learn from a tribal marketing approach? These are the questions that we seek to address in this chapter. More specifically the aims of our chapter are to:

- encourage you to think of consumers as tribes and understand the luxury marketing and management implications of doing so;
- show how a tribal marketing approach can be implemented for luxury brands by drawing on a series of investigations on Asian luxury tribes.

10.2 CONSUMER TRIBES AND LUXURY GOODS

10.2.1 Consumer tribes and brand communities

Many of you will be familiar with the long-running television and film franchise *Star Trek*. In the original television series whenever the Starship Enterprise came across a new species somewhere in the galaxy, Dr McCoy or "Bones" would turn to Captain Kirk or Jim and remark that this was indeed life, but of a different kind. In a similar vein, the tribes that we are concerned with are not the tribes of anthropological study that we began this chapter with: they are quite different; they are everywhere; yet previously we did not have the tools, techniques or opportunities to identify and understand them. To put it another way, as marketing academics and practitioners we were suffering from myopia; we couldn't see them.

Our understanding of tribes takes its inspiration from the work of an eminent French sociologist called Michel Maffesoli. In a landmark book, *The Time of the Tribes*,[1] he reinforced the argument that the fundamental building blocks of human life are found in the multiple social groups that we all belong to, knowingly or not, throughout the course of our everyday lives. These "little masses", or *tribes* as Maffesoli calls them, are central to our everyday experience and to who we are, our identity. This is especially true of the tribes that we knowingly and actively participate in. And this is where our tribes differ from anthropological tribes; throughout the course of our lives and as who we are, as our identity develops and changes, we can belong to and participate in many little tribes. Our tribal affiliation is no longer limited to the one big tribe that, once-upon-a-time, we were born into and that determined what we could do, be or become.

The tribes we are interested in, though, are naturally occurring groups where: tribe members identify with one another (or alternatively they can be "activated" and encouraged to be linked together by social media or marketing activities); they have shared experiences and emotions; and they are capable of engaging in collective social action; that is, together members of the tribe can "do" things that they would be incapable of doing outside of the collective. A tribe could form around any leisure-based activity, interest, hobby or passion. If you are passionate about surfing, traveling, a TV show, snowboarding, running, reading books, a band or singer, knitting, fine wine, a film-star, music, international politics, fossil-hunting or fishing, the rise of social media via the Internet means that you can search for and find other like-minded devotees and *voilà* you will have the basis of a tribe. However, when a tribe forms around one specific company or one of its brands then we can say we have a brand community.[2] Thus, brand community stands for any group of people who possess a common interest in a specific brand and create a parallel social universe rife with its own myths, values, rituals, vocabulary and hierarchy.[3] We have identified three main features of a tribe:[4] collective identification – shared experiences; passions and emotions; and the ability to engage in collection action. Similarly, brand communities exhibit three key features too: consciousness of kind or the feeling that you are connected to other like-minded consumers through the brand; shared rituals and traditions that help the community to cohere around a brand; and a sense of moral responsibility, duty and obligation to other people in the brand community.

Cases of consumer tribes are numerous across industries (see Table 10.1) and include snowboarders, roller skaters, climbers, opera lovers and so on. Cases of brand communities range (see Table 10.2) from Apple enthusiasts to AFOL (Adults Fans of Lego). One paradigmatic example involved groups of bikers and Harley Davidson devotees gathered inside the Harley Owners Group – HOG.[5]

TABLE 10.1 **Famous consumer tribes studied in marketing**

Consumer tribe	Industry
River Rafters	Sports
Skaters	Sports
Ravers	Music
Salsa dancers	Music and dance
Goths	Music and fashion
Couch surfers	Hospitality

TABLE 10.2 **Famous brand communities studied in marketing**

Brand community	Industry
Hoggers – Harley-Davidson owners	Motorbikes
Saab owners	Cars
Star Trek fans	Movies/TV series
Apple enthusiasts	Computers
Ducatists – Ducati Fans	Motorbikes
Hummer owners	Cars

10.2.2 Dealing with brand communities

The reason why these groups have become interesting for branding is the strong affiliations that arise among the group members to specific brands chosen by the group. Group members tend to be very loyal to some chosen brands, which make them a target group for many marketers; hence a clear relation exists between brand loyalty and brand communities. It has been shown[6] that the success of a brand increasingly relies on the existence of a community of totally captive and loyal fans who co-create the value of that brand through their many different practices.[7] Furthermore, the HOGs example and other success stories, such as Lego, Mercedes, Mini, Saab, Star Trek and Star Wars, have buttressed the positive aspects of brand communities in marketing managers' minds, leading many firms to make (or to consider making) significant investments in building and facilitating brand communities.

Developing brand communities is today considered a central topic of brand management. It is not a matter of attempting to directly influence consumers, but of providing them support in interacting with each other through activities of their community, which, in turn increases their level of engagement and loyalty.[8] It has been shown[9] that participation in brand fests led to a significant increase in overall feelings of integration into the Jeep brand community, and positive feelings about the product category and brand. The example of Ducati,[10] led by Federico Minoli, selected by new shareholders in the late 1990s to lead the company's recovery efforts, allows us to show the way to manage a brand community. The tribal management model that Minoli created exceeded all expectations, and today Ducati is not only the darling of the European motorcycle industry but also a cult brand with a growing number of followers called Ducatists (see http://www.ducatisti.co.uk/). Its new management model can be schematically described as a complete erasure of the traditional division, postulated in most economic theory, between customers and producers. In this new scenario, employees and consumers have the same status with regard to a brand community, that is, they are indistinguishable insofar as they belong to the same tribe. On one hand, employees consume brand products. On the other, consumers can be transformed into producers of events, ideas and even brand accessories. Ducati, for example, no longer has a Marketing Director but a Community Manager in charge of developing the community both internally and externally. The end result is that hiring becomes an act of co-optation. The cornerstone of this edifice is everyone's shared passion for the brand. This religiously inspired model is based on the idea that passion erases all boundaries. Categories like consumers or staff members' age, socioeconomic status or nationality no longer matter. The only prerequisite for participation is feeling the passion. There is no room in the community for anyone who is not a Ducati enthusiast (Table 10.3).

In this tribal model, the role and function of commercial offerings are to strengthen community links and foster a sense of tribal

TABLE 10.3 **Tribal management model at Ducati**

Old Management model	New Tribal management model
Recruit	Co-opt
Employee	Member of the tribe
Client	Member of the tribe
Customer–Company Relationship	Customer–Customer Relationship
Communicating with Customers	Sharing emotions
Marketing activities	Rituals
Factory	Cult Place
Keeping people out	Bringing members in
Discipline	Passion
CEO	Shaman

belonging and membership or "we-ness". Linking value therefore has two distinct yet complimentary meanings: for consumers it is the value (the fun, pleasure, satisfaction, usefulness, sociality etc.) inherent communal relations, however ephemeral, fostered by the tribe or brand community; while for the company it is the value its products/services/brands have for the construction, development or maintenance of these communal relations.[11] Linking value is rarely embedded intentionally in the value proposition of a company's products/services, but the greater the contribution of a product or service to the development and strengthening of the tribal bond, the greater its linking value will be. From a company perspective, linking value has to be produced and engineered into the product or service offering and companies are beginning to invest significant resources into this process. However, companies cannot produce linking value without the support of the members of the tribe or brand community who "work" very hard to produce it.[12] Consumers are both creators and users of linking value.

Companies as diverse as Innocent (a drinks and food company specializing in smoothies) and Jeep (the American 4 × 4 company) host tribal events called brand festivals.[13] At these "brand fests" consumers of their products have the opportunity to interact and develop relationships with each other and with the company. At these events it is consumers who create the community through their participation in the "brand fest" with the company facilitating this process. Consumers can also create linking value that is then attached to the brand or the product, which is consequently perceived as more valuable. New products emerge as a tribal product: the more consumers participate in the new product development process, the more they perceive the product's value, because they regard it as "their" product, from both the individual and the tribal point of view.

10.2.3 Tribes and luxury?

The most intriguing element in this social phenomenon is that consumer tribes seldom relate to fashion goods or luxury brands (Table 10.1). The vast majority of case studies used to highlight the relevance of the tribal marketing approach, together with recommendations on how to implement it, revolve around brands delivering niche products such as cars, motorbikes, cult movies, software, video games, entertainment and sports. Indeed, it is difficult to find a tribe of Gucci lovers, a tribe of Hermès devotees and so on. It seems that luxury consumption does not fit well with the tribal phenomenon in Western societies.[14] Exceptions are groupings of young, urban affluent consumers such as the Stockholm Brats[15] who live their lives in the fast lane, and frequent the trendiest nightclubs in Stockholm. The Stockholm Brats clearly differentiate themselves from the "ordinary Swedes" who lack sophistication, and instead search for inspiration from imagined soul-mates around the globe. This global lifestyle is to a large degree made up of the consumption of different global luxury brands such as Möet & Chandon, Gucci and Prada. Knowing which brands are appropriate at a certain time is an important part of the sub-cultural capital. In this case, the key to stylishness lies not in objectification, that is, in just buying and having the right luxury brands, but in embodying the consumption of goods in precisely the right manner.

The questions at the heart of luxury branding conversations today are related to communities and tribes.[16] Some interesting experiments have already been carried out on this subject, such as that undertaken by Diesel on the 55DSL brand:[17] 55DSL was started as an experimental line oriented toward the street culture and the emerging fashion trends among young consumers influenced by the culture of skateboarding and extreme sports, later extended to other cultures of consumption, in particular to those of gamers and several music-related subcultures. 55DSL focused on the importance of building a bridge with communities of gamers and with communities of young music fans.

It is interesting to see how luxury brands adopt social media while, at the same time, trying to balance their exclusive appeal with the social masses. Do social media make luxury brands too accessible and diminish the brand value and perception of affluence? Burberry, Gucci and Chanel are three brands that have received massive attention for their three million+ Facebook communities. Burberry has launched its own social networking site, the *Art of the Trench*, November 2009, with the hope of creating an exclusive brand community.[18] Burberry filters users – giving a smaller segment of users a more personalized experience with the brand and isolating customers who are more likely to become long-term customers. By raising the barrier, Burberry is increasing engagement with those individuals who might not even be customers yet. Or they may be a customer for a bottle of fragrance or for eyewear. These are the customers who need the brand experience, who need to feel the brand. Burberry has organized the *Art of the Trench* website in such a way as to facilitate consumers' "self-exposure",[19] hence the personal marketing with each and every one of them. Burberry has relied on each individual's existential need for recognition, based on the notion that "I exist if I am seen", that is, *Essere est percepi*, a dictum put forward by Georges Berkeley, England's renowned philosopher of immateriality. In short, the brand community that Burberry has generated and consolidated on its *Art of the Trench* website seems to have assembled a host of anonymous extroverts who decide to display intimate details about themselves because they want to be heard and have the sense that they exist, without necessarily entering into conversation or interaction with anyone else. As such, this site does not entirely satisfy predefined canons for a brand community.[20] This is very similar to the Facebook strategy of many luxury brands. Twenty percent of prestige Facebook pages, including those of many of the iconic luxury leaders, do not allow fans to post on the brand wall, suggesting the industry still largely sees the platform as a one-way communication vehicle.[21]

10.3 LUXURY CONSUMER TRIBES IN ASIA

However, in Asia, the emergent luxury consumption appears to be a tribal one. In Seoul, for example, people form clubs and organize many evening gatherings in order to share their passion toward luxury brands. In addition, these luxury tribes let their members know about luxury events such as private sales and fashion shows. This unique phenomenon provides new avenues to the marketing of luxury brands in Asian countries which will be detailed here under.

10.3.1 Luxury in Asia – the Seoul case

Seoul in Korea has become the second-biggest luxury goods market after Japan, ahead of Shanghai and Hong Kong. Consulting company McKinsey estimates the size of Korean luxury goods market, with Seoul as the center, to be about 4.5 billion dollars: It currently has 4 percent of the global luxury goods market, while luxury goods spending among households in Korea is 5 percent of income, compared to 4 percent in Japan. It is predicted that the Korean luxury goods market will continue to increase for at least three to five years,[22] so, as one of the countries with the most potential of the global luxury goods market, the case of Korea is significant. Vincent Bernard, Seoul regional director of "Christian Dior Couture Korea", said "Korea is 15 years ahead of Brazil and Dubai", and he also remarked that "If it could settle down in Korea, the effect will spread to the whole Asian market".[23]

Luxury addiction is not solely a Korean phenomenon. The tendency can be found all over Asia. Nevertheless, the obsession in Korea seems outstanding. Korean people love luxury items to such an extent that there is a second-hand market for Chanel and other brand-name paper shopping bags.[24] Such transactions are easily found on second-hand online shopping sites, where brand-name paper bags are traded for as much as $30. What is striking here is that Korean people actually spend money on mere paper shopping bags if they are branded Burberry or Louis Vuitton. Korea has become the model of other Asian countries in areas like music, movie, fashion and so on, so Korean luxury goods consumption situation may provide implications for marketing strategies of global luxury brands when the targets are other Asian countries.

The rapid development of information technology in Korea has brought about a lot of changes to the consumption environment, such as the increasing use of online shopping malls and activation of consumer online communities. The development of Internet led to the emergence of spontaneous communities in which consumers could exchange information and opinions about certain brands or goods, breaking away from the company-driven brand homepages and communities of the past. Consumer enthusiast-oriented, self-born, spontaneous online communities are now actively emerging with the themes of fashion, automotive and restaurant in

Korea. Online communities with common interests like the latest fashion style, celebrities' appearance, luxury brands, luxury fashion, skin care and plastic surgery show a good number of members and a high participation rate. These communities use names such as "Luxury Mania", "Luxury Brand", "Luxury Style-Lovers Club" or "Luxury Fashion Leader". "Luxury Fashion Leader" is an online community with more than 306,000 members that developed spontaneously around the shared passion for luxury fashion brands. These online communities are interested in the international fashion designers brands such as Michael Kors and Marc Jacobs, and high luxury brands like Hermès as well as Louis Vuitton, Christian Dior, Chanel, Prada, Bottega Veneta, Gucci, Salvatore Ferragamo, Lanvin or Givenchy. In these luxury online communities, male membership is growing fast.

The atmosphere of spontaneous participation, especially in online luxury brands communities, appears in the form of posting pictures of one's luxury collection. Members, who transcend different financial and social backgrounds, come together for the same interest in, and enthusiasm for luxury brands and luxury fashion. They participate autonomously by posting photos of luxury goods which they purchased or received as a gift, or by posting photos of themselves wearing luxury brands clothes, bags or accessories. Through comments on the posted photos, they exchange information about price, purchasing place, sales and new products, as well as posting emotional reactions (envy, admiration and enthusiasm), evaluations, opinions, feelings and purchase experience along with the digital pictures of themselves posing with the luxury brands items. Some members would post invitations for special events like private sales or fashion shows held by luxury companies to invite other members.

This interest in sharing information about luxury goods purchases is found not only among regular and intermittent luxury brands consumers, but also among other enthusiasts, such as college students, who, despite not being able to afford luxury goods, still have an interest in luxury brands and fashion trends. In other words, the collective enthusiasm for luxury brands expressed through online community activities extends beyond consumers or devotees of luxury brands to those who have just a simple interest in luxury. It shows that a bond of sympathy could be built between luxury goods consumers and enthusiasts, regardless of their financial or social position, and on the basis of this bond of sympathy, a kind of united community could appear. In this way, luxury brands consumer and enthusiast communities can be called a kind of "consumer tribe" in Korea.

10.3.2 Sharing luxury emotions through online posting

In Korea, current luxury brand consumers and enthusiasts share their passion, emotion and imagination about luxury consumption mainly through the posting of photos in which they strike a pose wearing their luxury goods.

The bulletin boards where these pictures are posted form a sort of stage. A stage on which community members who gathered under the main theme of luxury brand become actors of the play as posting members,[25] and/or as the audience members who look at the photos and respond to them. For the people who just have a simple interest in luxury brands, these online community bulletin boards may become imaginary shop windows, and foster their dreams of luxury goods. Through the bulletin board as a stage or imaginary shop window, members could bring imaginative values of the luxury brands and goods. By expressing and sharing their feelings and emotions about the pictures through comments, they generate an intimate participation which arouses the communal empathy.

Through this process of intimate participation and empathy, a preference may be formed for luxury goods which are given imaginative values by these pictures. What is more, the motivation to buy aroused by the simple interest in luxuries, can lead to actual purchases. In fact, luxury goods are spiritualized with their own images and symbolized as a lofty and privileged image by history, logo, design and quality. In this context, the aesthetic elements and symbols which luxuries possess as "imaged object"[26] are continuously and repeatedly delivered by posted pictures. The pictures of luxury goods being worn by the consumer which are consistently uploaded (or posted) in online communities may visually stimulate sensual and aesthetic emotions. Thus, the members of these luxury consumption tribes can develop aesthetic sympathy and share symbolized meanings and experiences.

10.3.3 Sharing luxury emotions through offline events

So, in the context of Goffman's viewpoint of social life as a theater,[27] luxury companies could develop strategies in order to help people experience collective play with luxury brand items and share photos in online communities in the way presented above. Furthermore, consideration is needed to let people share not only the consumption experience, but also "those of an immaterial, spiritual and sensuous level, such as refined preference, aesthetic feeling, refined beauty, perfectness, sophistication, which is produced by the luxury brand".[28] Along with the consuming action of luxury brands, an emphasis on the importance of appearance and dress is needed, as well as the creation of an atmosphere in which high quality life, refined preference and high-class lifestyle could be exalted. For this, through "re-enchantment" of luxury brands, consumers and enthusiasts should consider luxury items as something with which they could experience a better life, and which could satisfy their desires of life condition and quality improvement in various styles.

When a friendly propensity for luxury brand and goods is developed and luxury consumption becomes something related to their lifestyle, people will add totemic "fetishism"[29] to luxury goods in their everyday life and they could become, consciously or unconsciously, assimilated to luxury lifestyle. That is, it could be proposed that luxury goods have religious value – sacred and transcendental – which could bring people together. Indeed, luxury consumers and enthusiasts who meet in online communities wish to make new relationships and have a tendency to bond with each other under the shared passion for luxury brands and lifestyle.

This religious value of luxury brands is particularly at play in offline events and gatherings organized around luxury items. Korean luxury consumers and enthusiasts like to participate in events such as fashion shows, luxury brand private sales, opening parties of new luxury brand boutique, wine-tasting events).

Special events related to luxury brands such as exclusive membership club parties, luxury fashion brand launching parties, new product-introductory parties of luxury brands could sustain "people's desire to share". In other words, emotional, pleasurable, relational and religious values included in luxury goods could be the elements for neo-tribalism in Asian countries. This is clearly related to the "party culture" which can now be found frequently in Korean or Japanese consumption culture but rarely in other Asian countries. This "party culture" could be an important factor for establishing a strategic plan of advancing into Asian luxury market through the co-creation of parties with tribes of luxury enthusiasts.

10.3.4 Partying with Asian luxury tribes

Moët & Chandon, the world's largest Champagne house which entered Korea in 1999, has, since 2004, been actively promoting its Magnum bottle (1,500 ml) which could be shared by several people. Moët & Chandon developed this marketing strategy in order to attract young Koreans who are familiar with club and party culture, and who would go to bars or clubs in a group of four or five together with young Korean ladies who pursued a high-classed, fancy and refined lifestyle. As a result of its double-sized-bottle strategy, the annual sales volume increased in average by 49 percent from 2004 to 2007, and was 76 percent up in 2007 compared with the previous year. This result highlights the paramount importance for luxury brands to support Korean luxury tribes' parties.

To Korean consumers, luxury consumption has a meaning of pursuing "life here and now" and present pleasure or Carpe Diem, and it can be said that luxury goods and consuming behavior also have a value as entertainment in current Korean consumption culture. Accordingly, it could be proposed that the pursuit of the value as entertainment in luxury brand could be reflected in strategic luxury brand-side event. Luxury brands such as Louis Vuitton, Chanel, Christian Dior, Gucci and so on hold parties for their VIPs in Korea. Motorola, BMW and Dolce & Gabbana co-hosted new product-introductory parties for luxury consumers in 2006 as a marketing strategy. These represent typical brandfests[30] as discussed above.

In addition, it seems that some luxury brands like Hermès have already offered "present pleasurable experience" to luxury consumers or enthusiasts. Hermès opened its flagship shop "Maison Hermès" in Seoul in 2010 after Paris, New York and Tokyo. "Maison Hermès" has a museum, gallery, fashion boutique, cafeteria and sample room where Hermès exhibits different items (furniture, handicraft, etc.) and showcases the works of rising Korean artists in this shop (e.g. the *Soirée Paris Mon Ami*, September 2011). People learn new styling tips and take part in a photo shoot! Thus luxury consumers, enthusiasts or the public can get closer not only to Hermès itself as a luxury brand through the museum in "Maison Hermès" but also to art and creative culture.

In Seoul and Tokyo, this kind of flagship shop has actually become a trendy boutique while cementing the status of a luxury brand. "10 Corso Como", founded in 1990 by gallery owner and publisher Carla Sozzani, is another typical example. "10 Corso Como" is a multifunctional boutique dedicated to art, fashion, design, music and cuisine which opened in Seoul in 2008 after Milan and Tokyo. As a multi-brand shop and multi-complex, luxury consumers or fashion devotees can purchase various selected items of luxury or designer fashion brands, look around the bookstore and eat the Italian food with authentic ingredients or drink a glass of wine in a single location.

Based on these examples of leisure-oriented shops created by luxury brands or designer brands, one could think that multifunctional boutiques which offer a place to rest after shopping, a place to meet friends, eat or drink, would be a good solution for gathering luxury consumers and enthusiasts and making them familiar with luxury brands. Such a luxury brand shop where people could experience and enjoy leisure and art would contribute to the successful settlement of luxury brands, their infiltration into daily life, and increase the consumer's appetite for luxury brands.

10.4 CONCLUSION

What people do with brands has always been considered a source of value for them. Moreover, this phenomenon has accelerated over the past decade due to the rising power of consumer tribes backed by the development of the Internet and social media. It has been advocated that the success of a brand increasingly relies on the existence of a community of totally captive and loyal fans who co-create the value of that brand through their many different practices. However, this tribal phenomenon seldom appears around a luxury brand in Western countries in contrast to Asian countries and especially Korea where the emergence of luxury tribes has opened new avenues to generate tribal marketing strategies. Indeed, through the online posting and commenting on photos in which they pose wearing luxury items and through the organizing of luxury parties, Asian consumers spontaneously build and develop luxury consumption tribes. This unique way of setting up tribes around luxury consumption opens new perspectives for the marketing of luxury brands based on the co-creation of images and events with luxury enthusiasts.

NOTES

1. Maffesoli, M. (1996). *The Time of the Tribes*. Sage: London.
2. Muniz, A. M. Jr and O'Guinn, T. C. (2001). Brand Community, *Journal of Consumer Research*, 27(March), 412–432.
3. Wipperfürth, A. (2005). *Brand Hijack: Marketing without Marketing*. New York: Portfolio.
4. Cova, B. and Cova, V. (2002). Tribal Marketing: The Tribalisation of Society and its Impact on the Conduct of Marketing, *European Journal of Marketing*, 36(5/6), 595–620.
5. Schouten, J. W. and McAlexander, J. H. (1995). Subcultures of Consumption: An Ethnography of the New Bikers, *Journal of Consumer Research*, 22(June), 43–61.
6. Veloutsou, C. and Moutinho, L. (2009). Brand Relationships through Brand Reputation and Brand Tribalism, *Journal of Business Research*, 62(3), 314–322.
7. Schau, H. J., Muniz, A. M. Jr and Arnould, E. J. (2009). How Brand Community Practices Create Value, *Journal of Marketing*, 73(5), 30–51.
8. Algesheimer, R., Dholakia, U. M. and Hermann, A. (2005). The Social Influence of Brand Community: Evidence from European Car Clubs, *Journal of Marketing*, 69(3), 19–34.
9. McAlexander, J. H., Schouten, J. W. and Koenig, H. F. (2002). Building Brand Community, *Journal of Marketing*, 66(January), 38–54.
10. Sawhney, M., Verona, G. and Prandelli, E. (2005). Collaborating to Create: The Internet as a Platform for Customer Engagement

in Product Innovation, *Journal of Interactive Marketing*, 19(4), 4–17.

11. Cova, B. (1997), Community and Consumption: Towards a Definition of the Linking Value of Products or Services, *European Journal of Marketing*, 31(3/4), 297–316.
12. Cova, B. and Dalli, D. (2009). Working Consumers: The Next Step in Marketing Theory?, *Marketing Theory*, 9(3), 315–339.
13. McAlexander, J. H. and Schouten, J. W. (1998). Brandfests: Servicescapes for the Cultivation of Brand Equity, in Sherry, J. F. (ed.), *Servicescapes: The Concept of Place in Contemporary Markets*, pp. 377–401. Lincolnwood, IL: NTC Business Books.
14. Kapferer, J. N. and Bastien, V. (2009). *The Luxury Strategy: Break the Rules of Marketing to Build Luxury Brands*. London: Kogan Page.
15. Ostberg, J. (2007). The Linking Value of Subcultural Capital: Constructing the Stockholm Brat Enclave, in Cova, B., Kozinets, R. V. and Shankar, A. (eds), *Consumer Tribes*, pp. 93–106. Oxford: Butterworth-Heinemann.
16. Tynan, C., McKechnie, S. and Chhuon, C. (2010). Co-Creating Value for Luxury Brands, *Journal of Business Research*, 63(11), 1156–1163.
17. Di Maria, E. and Finotto, V. (2008). Communities of Consumption and Made in Italy, *Industry and Innovation*, 15(2), 179–197.
18. Tokatli, N. (2012). Old Firms, New Tricks and the Quest for Profits: Burberry's Journey from Success to Failure and Back to Success Again, *Journal of Economic Geography*, 12(1), 55–57.
19. Cova, B. and Pace, S. (2006). Brand Community of Convenience Products: New forms of Customer Empowerment – the Case my Nutella The Community, *European Journal of Marketing*, 40(9/10), 1087–1105.
20. Muniz, A.M. Jr and O'Guinn, T. C. (2001). Brand Community, *Journal of Consumer Research*, 27(March), 412–432.
21. http://www.business2community.com/social-media/the-top-10-luxury-brands-with-the-highest-facebook-iq-038023.
22. http://csi.mckinsey.com/Home/Knowledge_by_region/Asia/South_Korea/Korealuxury.aspx.
23. Corée, La nouvel eldorado des marques luxe, *Le Figaro*, 2011. 8. 6.
24. One Example of How Much Koreans Love Luxury, *The Wall Street Journal – Korea Real Time*, 2011.8.17.

25. Maffesoli, M. (1993). *La contemplation du monde: figure du style communautaire* [The Contemplation of the World: Face of Communal Style]. Paris: Grasset.
26. Maffesoli M. (1996). *Éloge de la raison sensible* [Praise of Sensible Reason]. Paris: Grasset.
27. Goffman, E. (1959). *Presentation of Self in Everyday Life.* New York: Doubleday Anchor Books.
28. Roux, E. and Lipovetsky, G. (2003). *Le luxe éternel: de l'âge du sacré au temps des marques* [The Eternal Luxury]. Paris: Gallimard.
29. Durkheim, E. (1990). *Les formes élémentaires de la vie religieuse: le système totémique en Australie* [The Elementary Forms of Religious Life], 2nd edn Paris: Quadrige/PUF.
30. McAlexander, J. H. and Schouten, J. W. (1998). Brandfests: Servicescapes for the Cultivation of Brand Equity, in Sherry, J. F. (ed.), *Servicescapes: The Concept of Place in Contemporary Markets,* pp. 377–401. Lincolnwood, IL: NTC Business Books.

11

LUXURY IN RUSSIA AND IN COUNTRIES OF EASTERN EUROPE

Laurent Lecamp

11.1 INTRODUCTION

When it comes to the countries of Eastern Europe we automatically think about Russia, the largest of them all, with its vast territory, its nine time zones, the link between Europe and Asia and the unique behavior there which makes the country so unusual. This country has such an influence, both politically and economically, on its neighbors (including those of the former communist bloc) that there is a need to understand it better before considering its relationship with the world of luxury.

11.2 RUSSIA: A COUNTRY WITH A HUGE POTENTIAL

Time magazine presented a scathing article[1] on 18 July 2011 about Russia being a post-imperial state lacking both vision and influence; a state plagued by corruption at all levels, preventing initiative and undermining any chances of success.

Russia is certainly a country whose human resources are much diminished. The 142 million Russians living in Russia (plus 20 million abroad) represent only 2 percent of the world population. They are also more likely to leave the motherland (Родина-Мать) in order to try their luck elsewhere. According to the Russian weekly *New Times*,[2] over the past three years 1.25 million nationals have decided to leave everything behind in what is the largest wave of emigration since the revolution of 1917. This is all the more disturbing because most of the candidates are very highly qualified. So where is Russia going? And what if Russia were in fact going in the right direction?

Russia is first and foremost the story of a bold people that has always held its head high. What if the future of the world were in Russia's hands? We know little about the country but Russia is the second-largest oil producer (after Saudi Arabia). Russia is estimated to hold between 7.5 and 15 percent of world oil deposits, 25–40 percent of world gas deposits and 25 percent of coal deposits.[3]

The country is not far behind for gemstones either. Russia has encouraged diamond mining of which 96 percent is controlled by Alrosa, the state-owned company supplying about a quarter of the world's diamonds and producing more of the precious stones than De Beers, historically the dominant miner and marketer of the gems.[4]

As far as agriculture is concerned, Russia could become the breadbasket of the world if global warming continues to take its course. The country is currently a major importer of agricultural commodities (one of the biggest in the world) with a trade deficit of $23.5 billion in foodstuffs for 2008. However, a rise in the earth's temperature caused by global warming would enable the development of farming on the vast plains available (some 16 billion km^2). A study published by the Center for Global Development in 2007[5] states that output per hectare could be increased sixfold in the plains of the Urals and Siberia by the end of the century and this does not take into account the potential arable land which would become an important source of income.

Russia is in fact a rich country but its wealth is very poorly distributed. Moscow returned as the world capital for billionaires in 2011 (according to *Forbes* magazine's annual ranking of the world's richest people), a rank it had lost following the collapse of the commodities market in 2008. In 2011 there were 79 billionaires living in Moscow against 58 in New York. In 2010, Russia had 62 billionaires (compared to 32 in 2009). And in 2012... Moscow is still the city number 1 in the world for billionaires.[6]

While it is true that a handful of billionaires are not the market, it is clear that the number of millionaires is growing again and the "nouveaux riches" are very fond of luxury goods.

When in September 2007, Vladimir Putin said that officials of the Russian state had to work "like a Swiss watch", he might have added that they all had to wear one as well! This appears to be what was understood if one considers the number of Swiss watches strapped to the wrists of the Russian political class. The watch became an essential luxury object. Was Patriarch Kirill, head of the Orthodox Church, not singled out by the Russian press for having a Swiss watch air brushed from a picture of him? The photo editor was guilty of negligence because he had failed to remove the reflection of the watch on the table.[7] The story might have ended there had the Russian media not taken the opportunity to remind the public that the patriarch maintained a very special relationship with Swiss watches. During one of his visits to Kiev in July 2009, which aimed at bringing the Slavs closer, the Patriarch was unable to turn people's attention away from his Breguet worth over $60,000 which he wore set in a beautiful crocodile leather strap.[8]

This enthusiasm for Swiss watches is probably due to a virus straight from the Kremlin, a new type of virus that sometimes spreads from the heart.

Vladimir Putin, during a visit in August 2009 in Tuva (southern Siberia, bordering Mongolia), offered his Blancpain (worth $10,500) to the son of a shepherd, an event immortalized by photographers on a background of the Russian landscape.

The experience was not lost on a worker in a munitions factory in Tula. The city, located south of the Russian capital, received a visit from Vladimir Putin who made a speech on the economic situation in September 2009. He acknowledged that times were difficult for the average Russian. A worker then shouted: "Vladimir Vladimirovich, could you give me something to remember you by?" Although embarrassed, Vladimir Putin first said that he had nothing on him until the worker had the presence of mind to ask "your watch perhaps?" In a gesture of generosity and solidarity, the country's leader had no choice but to give him his Blancpain (once again) for whom the watch represented a year's work ($6,000).[9]

My intention, through these examples, is absolutely not to criticize the political leadership, but rather to show the importance that luxury goods may have for key decision-makers. Many countries are working along the same lines, primarily China. The RTS Swiss television show "Mise au Point" on 22 January 2012 pointed to the fact that almost all Chinese civil servants were wearing Swiss watches, different brands according to their rank. This is all the more striking because the annual salary of the civil servants is, officially, no more than a few thousand dollars. These very same officials have made, unwittingly, a great deal of publicity for Swiss watches, so much so, that one Swiss watch in two sold in the world today is to a Chinese person and this is only the beginning.

11.3 BRAND AND OBJECT RECOGNITION

Let us return to Russia. Whatever their level, state officials like luxury goods and Swiss watch manufacturers are the first to benefit from this. Indeed, but what watches, or more precisely, which brands are coveted? Mainly Rolex, Patek Philippe, or Omega? Or can other lesser-known brands expect to benefit from their game?

The important thing is to understand that the watch is a sign of recognition at two levels. Brand recognition first, but also object recognition.

What difference does it make?

Recognition by the brand means that we seek to acquire a single, luxury object whose brand already has an aura. Rolex is a prime example. The brand has achieved a truly exceptional level of recognition which is unusual in the field of watch making.

For the Russian market, I saw during my meetings with collectors and local watch enthusiasts, that the Ulysse Nardin brand is hugely popular. It was a long process for the brand, but the results are convincing. Owning a Swiss Ulysse Nardin watch in Russia is a sign of social recognition.

Other brands will have a special aura too such as Blancpain, as we saw above. These brands have names that are very select in High Society, their design and movement (although "manufactured") are not the main reason behind a purchase.

Let us now consider the second sign of recognition, recognition by the object and with it, its price. This is a very important point because the main interest in the watch as such lies in its design and its movement rather than in its brand name. The brand De Witt is a perfect example because in the pre-crisis boom years it achieved high sales in Russia. The deputy mayor of Moscow in 2009 wore a top-of the range article listed at $1 million but at other times he was more reasonable, wearing a Greubel & Forsey Double Tourbillon 30 worth a more modest $360,000.

Many of my private clients told me that they were looking for a watch with extraordinary horological complications and an unusual design in order to attract attention: "I am what I wear." Retailers the world over jumped with joy when they saw a Russian customer come into their shop, thinking they had hit the jackpot and sell complications that very few collectors can actually understand.

This used to be true but it is no longer the case for two reasons: Firstly, the Russian clients discovered luxury relatively late, only after the communist regime collapsed in 1991. So there was an inevitable "catch-up effect", a true buying spree of luxury items. Once satisfied, the Russian clientele became more demanding and was soon better informed. Contrary to much popular belief, the Russian customer is a connoisseur who has learned from past mistakes. Brands at times appearing from nowhere sold extraordinary products (on paper) at sky-high prices without any form of after-sales service. Let's get it right, new brands are not alone in having succumbed to the temptation of producing anything and everything at surreal prices.

I particularly remember a well-known brand that had produced a $500,000 watch (listed price), sold to a Russian customer in a Swiss retailer. Barely two weeks after the purchase, the customer had to return the article to the shop because it had stopped working. The horological complication, a Tourbillon one, did not live up to expectations.

Never mind, the watch was sent back to the maker for repair, a repair requiring two years' work! The reason given was that it was a very special complication and that only a few watchmakers were able to do the work. In fact, the watch was manufactured by an outsourced manufacturer who had neither the time nor the expertise to restore the movement he himself had designed.

This is the kind of problem that Russian clients have often faced; it also corresponded to a strong desire to own unique, exceptional and very expensive products. While in the Middle East the client often requests a plausible discount, in Russia for several years, it was essentially the most extravagant price that mattered. I also remember one of my Russian clients who, seeing the collection of watches that I suggested, asked: "Which is the most expensive watch?"

This reflex still exists in Russia but it is gradually disappearing, being replaced by sound product knowledge. The price is not an issue if the perceived value is real and felt by the customer. S/he must understand the product and even if s/he is willing to pay the price, s/he will compare it on different markets to get the best deal. This is why many Russian buyers do not buy watches in Russia because the taxes are very (too) high. Prices in Russia are on average more than 40 percent higher than prices in Switzerland which is the reference market. Why buy the same watch 40 percent more expensively?

As we are dealing with purchaser's behavior in Russia, it is important to insist on one aspect, the attitude of Russian buyers. Russian buyers, contrary to popular belief, are not grumpy or rude. On the contrary. When we make the effort to speak Russian (which is the least we can do if we want to dialogue with them – Russians over 40 years old speak very little English), we realize that we have much to learn from them. Once their confidence is gained, we can develop a lasting relationship. The image of the Russian buyer as a rude person is much more a stereotype than a reality. It is time that brands understand that point.

Let us return to an important point that we mentioned above – tax. Russia, like many countries in Eastern and Central Europe, has a level of tax that can sometimes deter potential buyers. This is particularly the case when the tax payable is added to the retail price. However, if tax is included in the retail price which is close to that of other countries (in order to remain competitive), then the customers can buy the article in their own country.

This is all very well. However, let us take an example of a young country, Croatia, where we have recently seen a rise in taxes. A gold watch, for example, will be imported by a Croatian retailer who will have to pay a 5 percent import tariff, a 30 percent tax on luxury goods (gold) and to cap it all, a 25 percent VAT levy will be added. In other words, if the dealer grants a 15 percent discount to its customers (on a retail price similar to that of its European neighbors), there will be virtually no profit. This raises the question of how to pay the employees' wages, the rent for the shop and all the other overheads. This pattern of taxation (we could also mention the example of Hungary with 27 percent VAT since 1 January 2012 – against 25 percent in 2011 – the highest rate in the European Union) is extremely counterproductive and explains the extraordinary development of two main trends, the counterfeit market and the development of what is commonly known as the black market.

11.4 COUNTERFEIT AND BLACK MARKET

Counterfeiting affects all areas of the economy in some countries and sometimes has extremely serious repercussions.

Let us consider the example of Russia again. The Waito crime-infringement report, published in 2011,[10] shows that Russia holds the record for aircraft accidents in the world with 8.6 crashes per million flights in 2007, 13 times the world average. The reason for this is the use of parts of dubious origin. A similar problem can be found for other products. For example, two-thirds of alcohol consumed in Russia comes from illicit distilleries, while 10 percent of drugs consumed in Russia may be fake or unlicensed. The luxury industry is likewise affected, and one can find all types of counterfeit products.

It is common to find replicas of top-of-the-range watches which sometimes even include a certain level of radioactivity! It is especially difficult to fight against this crime as the criminal networks operating in the shadows are constantly evolving. This massive counterfeiting of certain watch brands can also help explain why some Russian customers refuse to buy these brands. This is because not only will the original model on the wrist not be guaranteed (unless you buy it abroad), but increasingly, they will see the same product on the wrists of too many other people, which actually devalues the brand and contravenes the will to stand out.

Personally, I have always been surprised by my Russian clients insisting on having a range of certificates and other guarantee cards for their timepieces, with a view ultimately to ensure that the purchased product is a "real" brand product and not a replica.

The black market is the second consequence of high levels of tax.

Indeed, if the products continue to be taxed and if VAT is at record levels in some markets, it makes sense that buyers and retailers will seek to buy their products through means other than traditional channels. Who could blame them? The black market is a logical response to governments that think that raising taxes is the only way to solve the country's economic problems.

Recently, I met a dealer in Switzerland from a Central European country who had come to find some watches "under the table". To avoid having to pay import tariffs, taxes on luxury goods and the high level of VAT, he had simply taken a plane to acquire a special model (of around 20,000 Swiss francs). This watch was then sold without a trace in his bookkeeping. Is this act reprehensible or merely a backup solution for retailers who feel stifled in an increasingly oppressive fiscal environment? Personally, I would never act that way, as by doing so one breaks the rules and decisions developed by states and makes it much more complicated for the end customers to get an after-sales service. How do you want to officially send the watch back for repairs (from your country to Switzerland, for example) if the watch never officially entered your country? Customs regularly control shipments and can keep watches in a safe until the situation has been cleared (if it can be).

Consequently, the end customers risk waiting a very long time for the watch to be returned, which sometimes never happens.

Currently it is possible to find almost every product of most of the brands on the black market. While it is certainly more difficult to find the very latest models of a brand, in the months following the launch it becomes easier, especially in times of economic downturn. Obviously, a brand cannot predict its level of sales and will have to take the risk that some of its production will be sold at lower prices.

What is surprising is that sometimes exceptional timepieces at a listed price of several hundreds of thousands of euro and sometimes even a million euro can be bought on the black market at 30, 40 or 50 percent below the initial price! Some retailers feel the need to sell almost any brand at any price because of the excessive taxation policies in some countries.

The general public is largely unaware of this situation so some retailers, up to their necks in taxes to pay and obliged to provide their customers with a discount (the economic crisis is biting here), have little choice but to buy on a thriving black market. This type of shopping can be done for a single item or in bulk. Although the models for sale are not among the most recent ones, a little patience is needed to access them. Lastly, there is always the opportunity (even if a rare one) to buy models from some agents or distributors of brands that are occasionally delighted to let some pieces go at highly competitive prices. But this is a short-term solution as brands can decide to stop collaboration with agents or distributors acting this way.

Moreover the brands can decide to reduce the production of some models to keep their values high. Less discount will also be given by retailers as products are more difficult to be found (both on the market and the black market). Of course the brand has to take the risk to produce less and reduce its turnover in order to maintain the value of the brand. But this is a really wise decision based on a long-term strategy.

In fact, the situation in the watch-making industry is not among the most flourishing at present. Although export statistics from Switzerland show ever higher figures month after month, it is relevant to see where these timepieces are going. It is estimated that currently one Swiss watch in two in the world is sold to an Asian, and given that the countries of Central Europe and Eastern Europe are not among the favorite destinations of Asian customers, this means that these countries have only themselves to rely on to overcome their situation. Ukraine is a very good example of one of the countries that have long been able to rely on local customers to increase its business. Moreover, the state capital Kiev was the first city to launch a luxury concept, hard as it may seem to believe!

One of the largest networks of local retailers, Noblesse, opened the Deluxe shop in 2008 in central Kiev. The concept? A large area of several hundred square meters, window-free and always closed to the public. Or rather, open only on request. A true temple of luxury, bringing together the finest timepieces and jewelry. If you are a buyer of more than $100,000 in jewelry and watches every year in the Noblesse sales network (about 20 shops in Ukraine, under various names), the Deluxe shop will open just for you, giving you the opportunity to try a rare piece that you like and that you would like to buy. Your personal salesperson will be assigned by your side, a bar made available and staff will treat you to what you want – exceptional treatment for exceptional customers. A few years after the opening fanfare of this shop, it is now clear that the customers have fled. Political change in Ukraine, the economic crisis, and too much uncertainty have led to a drastic reduction in purchases of top-of-the-market pieces. This does not mean that the money has gone but it is being hoarded and will remain so as long as the future remains uncertain. Many brands are complaining about this situation but they should recognize that the market is saturated, that is to say, there are too many brands on a market that cannot absorb them and it is now the time to approach consumers in new ways.

Ukrainian, Russian or other countries' customers need to feel reassured during these difficult months by seeing the products in the press, on the television or on posters and billboards. Brands need to get used to the idea that they should not spend their communication budgets solely on the Chinese market. Those who continue to make the effort to communicate in countries currently affected by economic woes will undoubtedly be the winners in the aftermath. Communication does not only mean showing its products in particular media, it also means visiting the shops more regularly and encouraging them to organize more varied events with their private clients. This means being very creative and providing them with something new, something that they would never have had access to previously, even if they had been willing to pay for it. It is through differentiation and innovation that brands can win the hearts of their consumers. Very recently, a Ukrainian client asked me which brands had "another" story to tell rather than those traditionally told by the press. By "another" I realized very quickly that he wanted something new, a story untold; a story that stands out, one full of emotion. This emotion can be passed on in the story to be told, the ambassadors of the brand, or simply by the person who will explain the product to the customer and who will succeed in conveying his passion.

With the economic crisis, customers are becoming more demanding and need to become the fans of a product, not mere consumers or buyers. There is a genuine desire, especially in the Eastern and Central European countries, to stand out and make a statement about what you wear and why you wear it. It is the job of the luxury brands to get as close as possible to these "fans" to gain their loyalty by explaining who they are, what they are and what the brand brings them.

Some countries try to sustain the luxury market by not increasing tax thresholds on luxury goods whose sales could subsequently plunge and in fact lead to the disappearance of many retailers. The increasing mobility of populations, which previously could not travel, makes markets porous and buyers pay increasing attention to price differentials.

A small country, Slovakia, has understood that high levels of taxation make little sense. If you buy a watch in, say, Bratislava (the capital city) you know that VAT is levied at 20 percent and that there is no luxury goods tax. This is useful because it helps especially in keeping jobs, and local customers continue to buy locally. This example is very relative because the country numbers only 5.5 million inhabitants. The fact remains that purchasing power is retained domestically. A retailer in Bratislava recently told me that he had been able to retain customers, in spite of the economic crisis, not only because his government had not raised taxes (generally leading to an increase in retail prices and therefore a loss of competitiveness), but also because he had made much more effort with regard to his customers. The discounts reach a maximum of 10 percent (whereas some competitors go up to 25, 35 or even 40%) because this is the way future is built. Indeed, the retailer has chosen to work only with very carefully selected independent brands (such as Cyrus or Corum) in the main shop. This allows him to avoid giving higher discounts because these brands are very qualitative; they have a selective network (often exclusive) and are not found in all cities. This exclusive selection of brands ensures a higher level of profitability and gives confidence to the end user, even with a low discount, who is aware of the "value for money" given.

11.5 SHOULD LUXURY BE BOUGHT AT A DISCOUNT?

The low discount given may seem incidental of course, but an incredible experience springs to mind remarkable enough to want to write about it here. The incident took place two years ago in Riga, Latvia, when I was visiting a new retailer who held exclusive rights for a particular brand of luxury telephones (from €4,000 upwards).

He opened a sales outlet in the heart of the city dedicated to the brand. My local contact, like most of his clientele, is Russian and he asked me to come into his shop and pretend to be a customer.

He wanted me to observe one of his salespersons, someone special. I went into the shop and pretended to take an interest in the telephones on display. I put all kinds of questions to the salesperson who mastered his subject in every way, even going so far as to explaining the quality of the leather used for the telephone case (its origin, the quality of the skin and so on). But this was nothing compared to what I was going to witness in the shop which I will describe below.

A Russian customer entered the shop with two very attractive, expensively dressed women. He bowed briefly to the salesperson who was chatting with me and begged him to show him the latest limited-edition telephones. The salesperson apologized and asked if he could serve the customer. To which I replied "yes, of course", not intending to buy anything myself but mainly wanting to see the work of this outstanding salesperson. Then the show began. The Russian customer pretended to know everything about the telephone while being surprised in turn by the extent of the knowledge of the salesperson. He continually gave highly relevant and interesting information and, in doing so, he not only described the product but rather sought to arouse the customer's emotions. True to form, he did not fail to look at the two young women to involve them in the sales process.

There is no worse sales blunder than not to pay attention to the company of the prospective buyer as they are often very involved in the purchasing decision, even if they remain silent and withdrawn.

The salesperson aroused the curiosity of the Russian client by giving a series of anecdotes about the brand, little "nothings" that allow one to "shine" in society. Indeed, what better than to know everything about one's product (and more) in order to impress one's friends? Then suddenly, the client enquired about the price of the limited-edition telephone that he had chosen. The salesperson gave him the price; in return he was asked what discount he could give. Without even blinking, the salesperson said he could not give a reduction but he could offer a "gift" in the form of a leather wallet designed by the brand. The client refused by saying he could find the brand in many other countries and he was sure he could get at least 20 percent off. He also showed his own telephone and explained that he had obtained a 20 percent discount when he had bought it. This was the moment chosen for the salesperson's final blow: "If you cannot afford to buy this telephone at the price offered, you can return in a few months' time once you have saved some money". I held back a smile at the coolness of the salesperson who was standing up to a Russian customer; he was being very friendly, both in tone and in manner implying that the price was probably too high for him. Not thinking twice about it, the client looked surreptitiously toward his two mistresses and not to lose face, he looked at the salesman in the eye and said, "I'll take three!"

This remarkable story does not end there because three months later I learned that this client had returned to the shop and had asked to speak to the same salesperson. Without negotiating the price, he bought some more new telephones as gifts.

We may wonder why he did that. As far as I am concerned, there is in this example the user's guide as to what should be done in the luxury industry. Extraordinary products, expertise and a unique quality at a set price. In our example, there is a very interesting point to remember. The product does not derive its value from the discount given but rather from the lack of discount. This is precisely what the salesperson allowed himself to tell the Russian customer when delivering the three telephones: "When would you feel more pride, when you purchase a product at a reduced price or at the listed price? We can afford luxury or we can't, that is the way it is." It is true that this example may seem unusual but we are used to seeing luxury devalued by asking for discounts and this is nonsensical. A "small" discount, between five and ten percent maximum can be acceptable with regular, loyal customers but sometimes it is better to give gifts, specific objects such as a "watch winder" for automatic watches for example, rather than discounts.

This example is all the more interesting as it happened in a mono-brand shop, a trend that is growing endlessly. Go to the main cities (Paris, Geneva, London, New-York or Hong-Kong) and observe the increasing numbers of mono-brand shops.

Why do we see a growing number of mono-brand shops everywhere in the world? Basically because they can control their prices, their discounts (officially they do not give any), learn about their customers' tastes and of course increase their reputation. It is worth noting that many mono-brand shops are not profitable but brands still think that it is necessary to have them as standard-bearers. This tendency is so true that the big luxury retail groups are now looking for new watch brands to replace those which have chosen to start their own shops; the luxury market is changing. Brands want to control their sales once again, even if this is not always profitable and even in countries considered as "poor".

Does this necessarily mean that the consumer is better catered for? In the countries of what is known as Eastern and Central Europe, it is common knowledge that the customer likes to have choice in a shop unless s/he knows exactly what type of product and brand s/he wants to buy. S/he likes to compare. A Monaco-based retailer told me that his client countries of Eastern and Central Europe liked to come into his shop to handle, feel and scrutinize various products. This fact seems to go against the principle of opening mono-brand shops which, by definition, offer only products of one brand. It is true that the mono-brand shop is highly profitable and quite justified for very established brands. Others, however, have understood that their interest lies in the multi-brand shop because it provides access to a wider customer base, customers that do not come initially to see the brand in the shops but who are interested and who may eventually become a consumer.

The customer, however, is not always as free as he thinks, so caution is needed. Almost all the countries of Eastern and Central European left behind them a very eventful past. The collapse of the communist regimes, war, political change and numerous other factors have made the rebuilding of these countries problematic. In most of them, average wages remain low and there is a genuine desire to increase the standard of living. This has not been left unnoticed by some luxury brands which openly offer to pay commissions to salespersons if they push their brands in the shop. These commissions can range from a few dollars to a few hundred or even a few thousand at times. They can be formally agreed with the shops that pay the commissions to salespersons or directly to them in cash. In this context, it is naturally no longer the law of "the winner takes it all" but the "strongest or richest" who wins. It is also particularly unfair that consumers can be influenced by salespersons promoting a brand over another given the commission they will receive from the brand without the intrinsic quality of the product, its history or innovative features being the decisive sales arguments.

Furthermore, contrary to popular belief, with the exception of a few brands, the consumers do not really know what they want and can be easily influenced. It is important to be clear, although I must admit that in many countries of Eastern and Central Europe where I have traveled, I have dealt with these problems. With the current economic difficulties, many brands are struggling to survive and it is true to say that they are willing to make some departures from the rules and take any necessary measures to maintain or even increase their sales. This practice is especially unfair as it can marginalize the small luxury brands, those whose passion is their driver but which do not necessarily have the requisite resources for their development. I strongly advise those in that position to monitor retailers and visit them as often as possible so that a more "emotional" relationship grows, sometimes allowing the money to be relegated to the background. Honesty and hard work always end up paying, even if it takes a long time.

It is worth mentioning here that as a counterweight to the financial argument, some great stories of friendships can be developed with retailers in Eastern and Central Europe which can be stronger than in other regions of the world. It is precisely for this reason that I especially like working in these countries because, in contrast to popular belief, the contacts are very friendly as is the widespread notion of sharing. Luxury is also about developing sincere long-lasting relationships. Whatever the brand, whatever the name, luxury is more than just about products.

ACKNOWLEDGMENTS

The author thanks Malcolm Parker for translating the chapter from French to English.

NOTES

1. Time Magazine (2011). "Why young entrepreneurs are fleeing Russia", by Simon Shuster, 18 July 2011.

2. New Times (2011), «Отъезд с отягчающими, обстоятельства ми» retrieved, 23 March 2011 from http://www.newtimes.ru/articles/detail/39135?sphrase_id=832744.
3. Sources: International Energy Agency (2012). Statistics available online at www.iea.org; CIA World Factbook – www.cia.gov/library/publications/the-world-factbook/geos/rs.html.
4. The Telegraph (2011). "Russian diamond giant Alrosa confirms plans to float", by Garry White, 18 March 2011.
5. See Cline, W. R. (2007). Global Warming and Agriculture, Peterson Institute.
6. Forbes (2012). "Moscow beats New York-London in list of billionaire cities", retrieved 16 March 2012 from http://www.forbes.com/sites/calebmelby/2012/03/16/moscow-beats-new-york-london-in-list-of- billionaire-cities/.
7. New York Times (2012). "USD 30,000 watch vanished up church's leader's sleeve" by Michael Schwirtz, 5 April 2012; Russia Beyond The Headlines (2012), "Patriarch Kirill's missing watch raises heated debate on the Internet" by Marina Darmodas,; 7 April 2012.
8. KOMPROMAT.RU (2012), "Как на сайте РПЦ зачищали фотографии с часами Патриарха Кирилла", 5 April 2012.
9. The Telegraph (2009). "Vladimir Putin hands over watch to cheeky metalworker", by Andrew Osborn, 15 September 2009.
10. WAITO report 2011 (World Anti-Illicit Traffic Organization), waito-foundation.org.

12

LUXURY IN INDIA: SEDUCTION BY HYPNOTIC SUBTLETY

Sandeep Vij

12.1 THE WHIFF OF LUXURY

The allure of luxury intensifies if ownership is restricted at one end and the thirst to possess is unadulterated and lusty at the other.

The super-rich can afford the luxury they desire. But what adds greatly to the desirability is not being able to get it. Genuine rarity and unattainability has a particularly powerful persuasive appeal.

To be and to remain exclusive, the price of admission must be high. Entry to the club must be restricted to a few, but desired by many. The greater the barrier to access, the more magnetic the offering.

This emotional gratification derived from 'exclusivity' that provides a deep-seated need to feel worthy is made available through varied means – fine art, fine wine, a luxury jet, that unattainable watch, language and knowledge, to name but a few.

In every economy there is a super elite – the most affluent one or two percent of the population. Of course, in a wealthy country, the size of this elite is far larger than in a poor country. However, given the universal desire to be the blue sheep, people around the world find their own way to stand out. Culture, social order, political ideology and economic potency, all play a role in molding what defines exclusivity. And as people and economies alter, these forces continuously mutate, forming newer constituents and expression.

12.2 THE ENGLISH CLUB

When India attained her independence from the British at the stroke of the midnight hour on 15th August 1947, free India's first Prime Minister Jawaharlal Nehru made his "tryst with destiny" speech in English. Millions of mesmerized Indians applauded the speech. Millions of Indians sensed the fervor and excitement of the moment. Yet to the millions of spellbound Indians, this historic well-crafted speech was incomprehensible.

Perhaps the reason Prime Minister Nehru chose to address a mass Indian audience in English rather than in Hindi, the language of the masses, was to demonstrate that he belonged to an elite white club, a club so exclusive that few could enter but most coveted. Distanced from the masses, yet connected.

The English language had become the admission ticket to enter the luxurious world of taste, intellect and power. English-speaking Intelligentsia lived in their own cocooned world, away from the masses. The English language had become a dominant symbol of a superior tribe, bestowing on the user the characteristics of a superior natural leader.

Perhaps Jawaharlal Nehru was, by opting for the Queen's language, declaring that New India had a distinguished, learned and worthy leader.

Even today one does come across an 'up market' anglicized lady condescendingly shrieking at the 'lowly disoriented blue-collar worker' and admonishing him with a volley of rapid-fire English, which he doesn't comprehend ... while he stares at her in bewilderment and rapt awe. She uses this 'exclusive' weapon to 'show him his place' by showing him her place.

During the 1980s and 1990s, Indians who had had the opportunity to travel overseas, even for a short time, very quickly adopted a well-defined foreign English accent. Some managed this rather extraordinary feat simply by going overseas for a holiday! An English accent became a symbol of membership of the revered 'Indian foreign-returned tribe' blessed by exposure to a largely inaccessible world.

With the rapid spread of English across India, particularly in the last decade, the Queen's Language has begun to lose its upper-class pomposity. It is ironical that the symbol of elitism has been flattened by the more unifying and egalitarian 'Hinglish" – a language both attractive to the masses and fashionable for the upper class. Once scoffed at by the English-speaking elite, Hindi and Bollywood music have now become not just acceptable, but trendy. Most discotheques and parties gyrate to the beat of Bollywood music, occasionally shifting to English music, but very quickly returning to the common denominator – Bollywood Hindi music. The garnish of English music on the Hindi music main dish is perhaps a subtle way to suggest the existence of their fading English edge. Just in case.

The 'English foreign accent' is fading and being replaced by a growing self-confidence and a strengthened sense of identity. British and Americana, and what they represent, finally seem to be losing their grip on us as a Nation and as a People.

Today, the English language finds itself on the cusp of mass luxury – the chasm between exclusive and ordinary – as it finds its way into the belly of India, the process of democratization is well on its way.

12.3 THE LUSTER OF EDUCATION

The caste system in India is governed by a series of Hindu texts known as the Vedas which dictate one's position in society. Under the Indian Caste System, the penniless Brahmin – the reservoir and guardian of knowledge – was on top of our social heap. Priests and scholars are classified as Brahmins, and members of this caste, who were gifted to understand the will of the Gods, traditionally wielded tremendous power over Indian society. Membership of this privileged and influential class was restricted by birth and subsequently by knowledge. The acquisition of this knowledge was increasingly confined to Brahmins. The Brahmin symbolized mind over matter – a combination of knowledge and austerity – a virtue that was difficult to attain and consequently considered attractive.

During the age of innocence (the 1950s and early 1960s) wealth and its brazen display was not prized. Even among the haves, the awkwardness of flaunting it was high. Materialistic exhibitionism was scorned and consequently kept under check. Perhaps this was due to social sensitivity toward the glaring poverty all around. Perhaps The Indian Caste System and Mahatma Gandhi, the Father of India, and his ideals had a role to play in shaping this view.

As the nation progressed, albeit very slowly, and her people evolved, the unfounded idealism and impracticality of abstinence became clearer to people. Consequently, asceticism as a virtue reduced and the practicality of education increased. The role of caste began to diminish and education as the common thread that bound together a pan-Indian elite group began to grow stronger.

The lust to possess inanimate objects of desire was at that time not developed. We as people were content to live in a continuous state of denial. And the absence of choice did aid the process of self-discipline and denial. Perhaps this absence of choice made the notion of asceticism easy to accept and flaunt.

Given the framework, hunger for exclusivity was quelled not through material acquisitiveness but via education and profession and an image of refinement that was associated with it.

12.4 MONEY AND ITS ACQUISITIVE POWER – THE NEW SOCIAL ORDER

The mid to late 1980s (the era of Prime Minister Rajiv Gandhi) gave birth to a generation untouched by the idealism of the struggle for freedom. At 40, Rajiv Gandhi, the youngest Prime Minister of India, was believed to be progressive, decisive, articulate and well-educated. He was at home in the world of high technology and was an antithesis to the much maligned politician archetype. And, much to the glee of the starved Indian, one of his primary goals was to propel India into the 21st century.

India and Indians saw Rajiv Gandhi through the prism of their own needs and an overall sense of un-met optimism began to simmer. For the first time there was a growing realization that self-interest was a decent enough cause.

The liberalization policies of the 1990s freed Indians from the pretense of any notion of restraint, the professed bias for the poor was over, material wants were severed from any notion of guilt, and consumerism was sanctified.

The new social order – money and its manifestations – raised its attractive head, and briskly spread through the lifeblood of Indian society.

Aristocracy of wealth began to replace the aristocracy of education and profession that had replaced the aristocracy of birth.

In India, life's food processor was in full churn, mixing together all the key influences – social, economic and cultural – resulting in an environment that was unfamiliar in content and unprecedented in magnitude.

The first onslaught came in the form of mass-consumer offerings – cars, fashion, toiletries, entertainment, consumer electronics, two wheelers, alcohol, packaged food and so on. In the beginning, we Indians behaved like kids in a candy store, our eyes darting hungrily at each new temptation. Asceticism and self-denial was happily brushed aside. Hedonistic consumerism was suddenly exciting and guilt free.

Following this mass consumerism came a second wave: the slicing and splintering of each category into slivers – gaps in the market that marketers spotted and attempted to make mainstream.

The third wave, a consequence of the second wave, was an effort to create a luxury industry. However, most luxury and badge brands were slow to take off. Success had probably more to do with the inherent value of the product offering and the fit-with-Indian needs, values and lifestyles rather than with the badge of foreign-ness. For many entrants it had a sobering effect – a realization that the market could not be skimmed, but had to be patiently developed. The impatient either withdrew or broad based and were sacrificed on the altar of so-called mass luxury.

12.5 REFINEMENT AND MONEY – A HEADY COCKTAIL

With money and its acquisitive power becoming more egalitarian, genuine rarity began to diminish. The exclusivity of the luxury Club started to be sullied by unwelcome interlopers, albeit superbly disguised with their Gucci and Fendi. In order to survive and to remain exclusive, the Club needed to find newer ways to select its members. In other words, the 'stronger, blue-bloodied' members of the luxury Club needed to be continuously vigilant and find newer ways to keep membership lean and restricted at the supply end and the thirst to possess strong-at-the-demand end. They understood that availability and access would destroy their Club.

One solution to keeping membership lean was to prescribe that money and its acquisitive power must be appropriately bundled (and cloaked) with the subtle edge of refinement. Such an attitude suggests that the overt display of money and its power is passé. The power of money should now be displayed with understatement and elegance.

Approved targets for the spending of wealth are the likes of literary festivals, classical music, art and photography. The imposing forts of Purana Quila in Delhi, or the palaces of Jaipur provide an appropriate setting for the wealthy to come in their private jets and their Bentleys and discuss the deeper meaning of the color red. The deeper and more accomplished members of this exclusive club would help curate literary and art sections.

In a poor country like India, where the notion of creating and hoarding personal wealth has been hugely appealing for a long while, the idea of philanthropy and the ability and strength to give selflessly without any expectation does indeed place one in rarified stratosphere and is therefore rare and alluring.

Conscious Capitalism, performance with purpose and philanthropy are today powerful notions in these corridors of well-heeled elegance.

We do, for the sake of India, hope that the tribe of philanthropists grows out of its rarefied space.

12.6 THE CHASM BETWEEN EXCLUSIVE AND ORDINARY

In their yearning to keep the party going, a number of upscale brands that genetically need to continuously focus and concentrate, surrender to the greed gene, weaken and are ultimately sacrificed on the altar of growth.

In the Indian automotive market, BMW and Mercedes seem to have relinquished their top-of-the-pile vantage position and have begun to vie for the 'mass luxury market'. And with the relentless downward pressure on price, the number of BMWs and Mercedes on the road has started to swell, much to the delight of the marketing team who are experiencing the animated excitement of the wannabes. A brand that draws on accessibility and price to grow suggests that it has every intention of vacating the luxury set. That Mercedes has begun to drop prices and has launched the Maybach suggests its intention. The sheen of BMW and Mercedes has started to fade. The short term once again trumps the long. The King is dead. Long Live the King.

This act of hara-kiri is unfortunately a universal trait. The developed world is speckled with examples of this slow process of self-immolation.

In fashion, Burberry and Gucci, for example, have become almost 'affordable luxuries'. Gucci in the 1980s began to indiscriminately license its brand, albeit to exclusive stores, and by doing so, compromised its allure in the mind of the luxury consumer. Burberry also increased access and availability, with similar results. Tiffany is another example of a luxury brand which vacillates between retaining a small, loyal band of up-scale devotees who feel unique, special and worthy versus a larger number of customers. In the late 1990s, Tiffany started making affordable jewelry. Expectedly and much to the delight of the Management, it pulled in customers in droves. Unfortunately it also drove away Tiffany's loyal upper-crust aficionados.

Very quickly it adopted a strategy to make amends to its luxury customers, by creating distinct sectors within the store – one for the rich and another for the relatively 'poor'.

This is a solution that has been adopted by most luxury brands that have surrendered to the greed gene. After swinging precariously between anxiety and greed, and after much deliberation, they arrive at similar strategic paths – create distinct spaces for the two segments or sporadically launch the 'limited edition'.

As its name suggests, the appeal of the limited edition is in its being scarce and precious and consequently enticing. This practice of releasing limited editions was started as a way of stimulating a consumer's desire to stand out. Today, however limited editions are everywhere: limited-edition McDonald's Happy Meal, limited-edition black-painted Toyota Innova, limited-edition Sony Audio, limited-edition Beatles book, limited-edition Lenovas and so on. Marketers, united in their collective desire to milk the brand, have unwittingly killed the goose that laid the golden egg.

The shadow-of-a-slowdown is obviously at its zenith, where fear swiftly overtakes common sense. Research informs us that the real top-end of the luxury consumer is not unduly affected by the recession as much as one might think. Rather than lose focus, luxury brands should in fact sharpen their focus and give absolute attention to the consumer on top of the heap – the 20 percent that accounts for 80 percent of the sales. Unfortunately fear causes most managers to freeze and then overreact, rather than assess and then react.

Uncertainty directs and drives human beings to focus on the here and now. Tomorrow is unknown and marketers are staring at the one thing they can see, which is what is in front of them: today. The adage "in the long run we are all dead" does seem to support short-term gains against the unknown ghost of the dreaded long term. It does seem ironical, but during uncertain times, brand marketers should be leading consumers, not adding to their insecurity, by giving them mixed signals. Consumers must be given confidence that they can be secure because they are guaranteed by a brand they can trust.

The obviousness of this oxymoron – if many can acquire what was once rare and precious, how can it retain an enigmatic magical magnetism? – does seem like such an obvious thing not to do. However, as Sherlock Holmes remarked, "the world is full of obvious things that nobody by chance ever observes."

12.7 THE INDIAN LUXURY INDUSTRY

All signs indicate that the desire to be exclusive is insidiously, silently and gradually but surely engulfing us, that sooner than later the Indian luxury market will mature into an industry. High disposable income, shifting consumer mindset, growing confidence and optimism and the positive Indian economic climate are slowly but surely reaching the critical mass needed to attain profitability.

At a time when the world seems to be announcing the demise of print media (*Philip Meyer in* The Vanishing Newspaper *predicts that the last reader will recycle the last newspaper in 2040*) it seems curious that a number of glossy high-brow lifestyle luxury magazines are being launched in India.

The Luxury Marketing Council Worldwide has established a Chapter in India.

Its mission is to aid luxury brands interested in India with inputs on markets and consumer insight.

Accordingly to the CII–AT Kearney report titled 'India Luxury Review 2011', the luxury market in India witnessed robust growth of 20 percent over the past year and is estimated to have reached US$ 5.75 billion in 2010.

Among marketers, doubt and uncertainty is slowly but surely evaporating and giving way to a new wave of optimism and confidence. Consumers are moving up the nirvana path and decidedly adopting exclusivity as a reason to be. The diffusion theory and effect has begun to permeate the idea of luxury to tier-two cities of India. Seeping into cities like Bangalore, Chennai, Pune, Chandigarh, Ahmedabad, Ludhiana and so on.

The CII–AT Kearney report throws up an interesting insight into the difference between the composition of luxury market in India compared to that in South East Asia. While jewelry dominates the Indian luxury product market, apparel and accessories form the largest segment – over 60 percent – of the South East Asian luxury market.

Another salient difference is in the audience composition. Unlike India where luxury consumption is limited to the affluent – traditionally wealthy families, businessmen or successful professionals – the South East Asian luxury consumer is relatively more egalitarian – it cuts across age, profession and social-class boundaries.

The Indian consumer is still grappling with his relationship with luxury. Most consumers have an external, flaunting, consumption motivation compared to a more elegant, internalized, self-indulgent inspiration. And given Indians' previous affinity of scorning materialistic exhibitionism, an internalized drive could hasten the Darwinian process of evolution.

With the West's attitude toward inappropriate spending and with frugality becoming a virtue even among the wealthy, the spotlight is optimistically turning eastwards – with China and India at the very center of this optimism. Perhaps this hopefulness and cheer is itself laced with a bit of excessive optimism.

India is at a nascent stage and to say that several challenges exist, would be an understatement. Marketers are keenly observing and pushing the experimentation bar with cautious optimism.

The luxury market in contemporary India is in its puberty, which is a time that separates the men from the boys. Ambition, lust and confidence are transforming us as a nation. What will turn us into men will be the democratization of lasting prosperity.

The whiff of the emerging Indian luxury industry is getting stronger.

12.8 LUXURY BRANDING = (RULES OF BRANDING)^N

The fundamental intent of positioning any brand is to create a distinct feeling, a distinct idea; a distinct emotion that characterizes the product in the consumer's mind. The operative word is 'distinct'. The question that keeps marketers awake, in a world where brand differentiation is being blurred, is how does a brand create distinctiveness?

Now think about luxury brands for whom the primary reason to be is to help magnify the halo. Transfer unique fame, recognition, appeal, self-expression, self-worth, deep emotional reward, irrational aura and mystique and transcend any rational justification – it is brand power at its purest. To create a successful luxury brand, all rules, tenets, processes and practices of branding have to be magnified a hundred times and religiously pursued.

Bill Bernbach stated that *"The magic is in the product"* and that *"Advertising doesn't create a product advantage. It can only convey it"*.[1] For luxury branding, this tenet must be repeated every morning – it is a necessary condition to succeed. The product must itself be articulate in its ability to communicate its value. The magnificence of quality must shine through the sheen of the "brand" coating. Brand power along with powerful product oratory must create the awe, the mystique, the circle of light. Many luxury marketers believe that advertising agencies are mass-brand gurus but when it comes to luxury products they unwittingly employ the same rules with dismal results. To embellish a product truth or a consumer benefit, advertising gurus search for an 'idea' that could bring it alive in the mind of their target. However, in doing so in luxury branding, very often, the idea that has a noble intention manages to draw attention to the idea rather than what it intended to help shine.

More often than not, luxury possesses a strain of senselessness – an enigmatic aura and mystique. To seduce this 'irrationality' a heightened emotional drama must be created – charmingly seducing the irrational part of the mind. The product must be articulate, however communicating its usefulness and its rational details must be implied – left to superior intellect and sense – and presented with reassuring, unassuming confidence.

12.9 LUXURY MAGNETISM NOT LUXURY MARKETING

Inherent in our understanding of the word Marketing is the notion of reaching out. And reaching out is against the fundamental principle of luxury where rarity and unattainability are the appeal. Marketing has a crass, vulgar, almost offensive air about it. It implies that the marketer's need to sell is stronger than the consumer's desire to possess. In the orthodox market model, when price falls, demand rises. With luxury, the reverse should occur.

Perhaps the term Luxury Marketing should be replaced with "Luxury Magnetism" – the skill of subtly drawing-in consumers by creating a craving, a subconscious pull for the luxury product.

12.9.1 The power of story telling

An effective way to cloak a brand with meaning and mystique is through engaging storytelling. A story does build authenticity, build powerful connections, set identity and insidiously work its way into your heart. Telling a story does build on the distinctiveness and supports the evolution of value. Most luxury brands do have a person behind them. And building empathy with the backstory of the human brand and the mythologies and legends that help build that human brand is a powerful wedge and an integral part of marketing strategies for luxury brands.

12.9.2 Eye of the buzz

Another way to strengthen the magnetism of a brand is by creating a buzz, and positioning oneself at its center. Buzz drives brands. However, it drives some brands much more than others. To succeed, luxury brands must be in the eye of the buzz – peer-group appreciation. Recognition and recommendation is the force multiplier to the halo of fame, an absence of which an avalanche of covetousness can never be delivered.

Unrehearsed customer evangelism is what generates the wind in the sails and attracts like-minded devotees. Ensuring customer delight is often more valuable and effective than enticing new customers. Once the point of peer enthusiasm has been reached, the sails automatically tip to the wind, effortlessly pulling in new brand missionaries, creating a brand epidemic. At this point, the essential marketing ingredient is a subtle mix of seduction via creativity and originality liberally doused with hypnotic subtlety.

Large marketing budget is not the success driver. In fact, it may be damaging. People become aware of luxury brands through animated conversations. The nature of luxury (very akin to cool) is often subtle, and certainly more contagious than mass consumer markets.

12.10 SOCIAL CREATIVITY

The digital democratization of technology and information that is effortlessly pushing ahead the hyper connectedness of our world, is transforming marketing communications. The Consumer today is flushed with self-expression and getting more blasé, experimental and difficult to influence. Consumers expect their brands to be honest, transparent, participative and engaging, and in return brands will be rewarded with their attention and money. And like everything else, this reality is far more amplified in luxury branding.

We have only just begun to understand that the interruptive, top-down model of communication is clearly no longer working. Only brands that understand influence and influence-cascades will be able to create swarms of fans and reap the rewards. The key is to think about turning people into media and getting them to talk about your brand.

Given that luxury brands are built through conversations, as per DDB Group, the power of social creativity must be leveraged through ideas that create a social reaction, ideas that people will want to participate in, ideas that ripple through social groups and social networks and create influence.

We must experiment with the power of Creativity that gives people social capital, which encourages participation, play and passing-on; Creativity that connects people to people, not just people to brands, and which turns people into advocates and brand communities.

In today's world, the notion of communication touch points/360 degrees has become an outdated idea. Intrinsic in the idea of 360 degrees is that the role of communication is to bombard the consumer from every possible direction. For luxury brands the philosophy and operating framework urges us not to surround the 'victim' but to create a six-degree effect. Where the idea enables and encourages consumers to participate, play and pass on the content thus creating an influence cascade.

12.11 AMPLIFIED CUSTOMER INTIMACY

The relationship between consumers and luxury brands is far more intimate than with other brands, and it is this interactive relationship that provides the added value. It is this unique connection that effectively differentiates a luxury brand from mass-market competitors.

For a luxury brand to succeed, every single act – from endorsements, personalization, high-touch and retailing, to public relations, events, direct marketing and brand placements – needs to be innovated upon, and delicately amplified. Unrelenting focus must be the guiding canon.

There are very few Indian marketers who have negotiated this path. And when they do they will need somebody who is capable of handling these unique issues rather than allowing past experiences and knowledge cloud the path.

NOTE

1. Levenson, B. (1988), *Bill Bernbach's Book: A History of the Advertising That Changed the History of Advertising* (New York: Random House USA Inc.), 220 p.

13

POLO AS A VEHICLE FOR COMMUNICATING LUXURY

Ivan Coste-Manière, Anna Hoarau and Cedric Laforge

13.1 INTRODUCTION: LUXURY BRANDS AND SPORTS

Sports have always been a privileged tool or vector exploited by most brands in order to communicate their image, looking for notoriety, awareness and visibility. When used in the right configuration, sport, synonymous with dynamism, physical prowess, aesthetics and health, seems to represent a real opportunity for brands to promote their goods and services, and to create a buzz, with one of the biggest effective reaches and one of the biggest audiences.

Regarding luxury brands, the choice of the sport has to be precisely oriented, in resonance with uniqueness and exclusivity, both values defining the essence of luxury. One of the biggest challenges of luxury brands is also to be able to stay tuned and to demonstrate innovation and originality. While luxury brand strategies have traditionally focused on golf and sailing, the recent trend is clearly focusing on a "new-old sport" – polo.

Polo has always been "associated with royals and it was the game of kings. It is very fast and it is very sexy", says Andrew Murray, polo manager at Asprey, the UK luxury goods group which has been involved in polo by sponsoring teams and tournaments since 2007 and developing professional polo lines of clothing and accessories. Andrew Murray adds, "polo is becoming more commercially viable because the game has developed. It used to be amateur, but it's now much more professional. Players fly in from around the world and the game is drawing more commercial interest. The days of it being an amateur game for the gentry are changing."[1]

Golf, sailing and polo have in common the fact that they generally attract wealthy and potential luxury consumers. These sports are obviously linked to elitism because they basically require an important financial investment for the players due to the cost of equipment, registration fees, training and tournament organization. Strongly associated in mind with prestige and superior status, this range of sports activities represents efficient marketing channels for luxury brands.

For luxury brands, diverse ways exist to partner with sport: the positioning and building of their brand around a particular sport, the creation of a special collection specific to the practice of a sport with ergonomic considerations, the sponsoring of sporting cups, events or competitions, the selection of professional sportsmen or women as emblems of the brand, or even the participation in winning prizes.

For example, TAG Heuer, the Monegasque watch-making brand revolutionary for having introduced the first automatic as well as the first square-cased chronograph, launched the first special watch for professional golfers in 2005 and logically chose the famous professional golfer Tiger Woods as ambassador. Limited to 8,000 copies, this watch was priced at €1050. The system presents a patented clasp located in the head of the watch so as not to interfere with the golfer's swing, weighs significantly lighter than watches in general, and possesses an incredible shock-absorbing capacity, 45 times greater than that received by the watch during a swing.[2]

Another example of association between sport and luxury trademark is the collaboration between Omega and sailing. The Swiss luxury watchmaker known as "the first watch on the moon" in 1969 thanks to the NASA's choice has been designing a tailor-made watch for sailing, promoted by Dean Barker, the legendary New Zealand yachtsman.

Without going into any further detail, we can clearly conclude that the watch industry has always been at the forefront of this type of sports-celebrities communication activity, as a catalyst in the innovation carburant, reaching the most refined target customers within even the smallest emerging international destinations.

13.2 POLO: MORE THAN AN OPPORTUNITY FOR LUXURY BRANDS – A REAL PASSION

Presently, only a few luxury brands have perceived polo's niche. Ralph Lauren has been best known since 1970 for his Polo-Ralph Lauren clothing brand and whose logo showed a polo player for the first time in the fashion industry.

The proactive involvement of luxury brand in this sport usually comes directly from the founder himself, not by a pure business opportunity but by a real and true passion, a kind of Dancing Queen.

Yves Piaget, Chairman of the eponymous brand has always nurtured a passion for horses. Vice-Chairman of the Swiss Equestrian Federation, Chairman for 20 years of the Geneva International Show jumping World Cup, and patron of the Avenches National Equestrian Institute, it is no surprise that he created the Polo line among Piaget's collections, officially launched in 1979 and revisited since 2002. "I've always found a great many similarities between the nobility of the horse and that of our products",[3] says Yves Piaget, sponsor of the World Polo Championship in the United States, partner to tournaments in Europe and India, and owner of his own polo team for several years.

Piaget developed a special line for professional polo subtly mixing technicality and elegance. This line comprises among others the Polo Tourbillon Relatif model launched in 2006 and the Polo Chronograph which houses the first mechanical chronograph movement.

Backes & Strauss chose another approach in sponsoring Polo

In November 2011, Backes & Strauss started sponsoring the British Polo Day in Singapore and later in other emerging countries such as Dubai and India. The British Polo days in emerging countries are a very good example of a successful marketing strategy between one of the most luxurious British timepiece manufacturers and the sport of Kings. Backes & Strauss managed to use polo as a vector of communication but in a different way compared to that of other luxury polo sponsors (Figure 13.1).

(Continued)

FIGURE 13.1 **Backes & Strauss Clock during the British Polo Day in Singapore**

The British Polo days represent for Backes & Strauss the perfect opportunity to celebrate its British identity, to share its creativity and highlight its vision of what a luxury timepiece is for the brand.

In Singapore, Backes & Strauss sponsored the team of Eton, a team with deep British roots.

The brand even created a special watch for the British Polo day of Singapore – the Regent Fancy Canary – crafted in 18 kt white gold, hand-set with the finest diamonds – a perfect fit for this Royal sporting event (Figure 13.2).

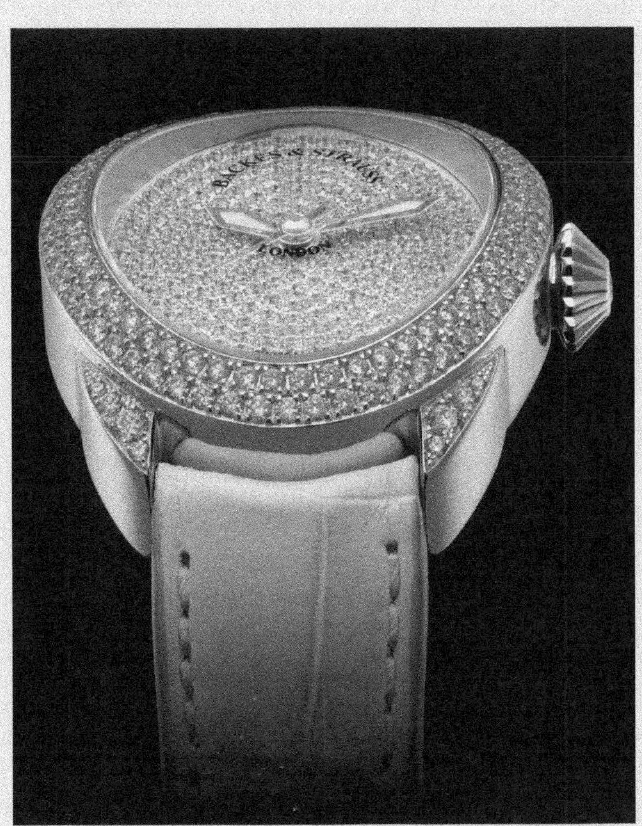

FIGURE 13.2 **Backes & Strauss Regent Fancy Canary**

Another company with significant investment in Polo is Hackett London. Owned by Richemont group until June 2005, Hackett London, the British Gentlemen's luxury clothing company founded in 1979 started getting involved in polo in 1987. Approached by two army officers who were looking for sponsorship, Hackett launched the same year the Hackett polo shirt and formed the Hackett Polo Team playing out of Guards Polo Club. Still involved in polo today with teams in the United Kingdom, Spain and France, Hackett is also the official sponsor of the British Army Polo

Team since 2006 as well as of the Rundle Cup, the long-standing and hard fought annual polo match between The Army and The Navy.

13.3 POLO: FROM A HISTORICAL POINT OF VIEW

In order to better understand the emerging craze for polo, it is important to remember some of its history and the rules of the game.

Originally a training exercise for elite troops, polo was invented by the Persians around the 4th century B.C, and over time grew into Persia's national sport, then being enjoyed exclusively by the nobility, both men and women. This oldest team equestrian sport was introduced to India by the Muslim conquerors during the 12th century. There, it acquired the majority of its present characteristics. "Polo" for example comes from the Hindu word "pulu", which is linked to the type of wood used to make the mallets to strike the ball. Jaïpur Polo Club has always been one of the most prestigious jewels and is still so today.

Europe was initiated to polo thanks to the plantation owners and the officials of the British army in India. The first European Polo Club was launched in 1859 in the United Kingdom, a country that highly influenced the establishment of polo in Spain and Argentina among others.

Incorporated in the Olympic Games from 1900 until 1936, polo is no longer included. Nevertheless, the International Olympic Committee might reconsider its comeback to the Games, probably as entertainment sport.

> In general, polo is a sport that pits two teams of four players against each other, made up of a captain and three players, who can be professional polo players or not. The matches are divided into chukkers (between four and eight depending on the competitive level) and are played on fields that are double the size of a football ground. Due to the different game levels of the participants, they all play with a handicap, a scale that reflects their skills in the game. The sum of the players' handicaps gives the handicap of the team, which is the factor that determines if

the team can participate at a certain level of competition (high, medium or low).[4]

13.4 POLO: MORE THAN A SPORT, AN EXTENSIVE LUXURY ENTERTAINMENT

The attraction and seducing effect of Polo are related to its remarkable nature, its highly selected social surroundings and the strong traditional aspect that it evokes.

It can widely be considered as a competitive, aesthetic and fascinating sport spectacle, maybe worldwide, which is definitely not the case for all other existing sports. It combines social and cultural attributes, and is particularly known for its social events, contests and contexts.

"Consumers of luxury brands are used to being pampered", says de Souza of Tiger Sports Marketing.[5] This often leads brands to embellish the sport with other entertainment such as fashion shows, cocktails, live concerts and inviting famous celebrities to provide a truly memorable luxury experience.

Cartier, for instance, has been a loyal supporter of polo for more than 25 years, starting at Palm Beach in 1983, and two years later founding the Cartier International Polo Cup, one of the most exclusive events within the English sporting agenda. Prince Charles and his sons are among the players each year, and Queen Elizabeth herself presents the trophy to the winning team. This kind of event is the perfect opportunity for brands to unveil a new brand product.[6]

13.5 POLO: A HIGH INVESTMENT

Top-level polo is expensive to support and relies on sponsors and wealthy players. It costs between $80,000 and $160,000 a year to sponsor a low-level team, while a medium-level team costs $390,000–$770,000. At the top of the sport, the cost of sponsoring a team can reach between $1.6m and $3.9m a year.[7]

According to Jérôme Lambert, chief executive of Jaeger-LeCoultre (the Swiss watchmaker whose famous Reverso watch had been developed in 1931 for British polo-players in India), polo's various sponsors invest up to €20m a year in the sport.

Polo requires high financial investments and consequently arouses the passion of people with a high standard of living and business groups looking for a marketing occasion focused on a very specific target.

13.6 POLO: A PRIVILEGED AUDIENCE AND HIGH-END AFFINITY

"Polo, till a few years ago, was a virgin sport. Those who played were the ones who watched. Now, the audience has grown and changed",[8] notes Anjani Kasliwal, group director of S Kumars Nationwide that owns Reid & Taylor, sponsor of the 103-year-old Indian Open polo tournament for the past eight years.

The public associated with Polo clearly differs in terms of its financial level, its particular habits and its social network. It can be divided into two categories: the polo player and the polo spectator, who can be an occasional, seasonal or a team supporter. The first group represents the target of companies for specific polo equipment while the second group is the target for many sponsors' marketing strategies.

Noblesse involved, a brand at the top of the luxury pyramid must lend its support to events that directly address its consumers. The fact that luxury brands have turned to polo comes naturally. "For all brands, polo is pukka when it comes to forging links with retailers and customers."[9]

The Cavalry Cup for instance, held in Delhi on the Jaipur Polo Grounds, represents a lasting legacy of the days of the Maharaja. The event took place on 13 March 2011, in partnership with Cartier, who made a unique and customized trophy in the form of a mallet especially for the occasion.

Polo is currently a successful tool for companies, via sponsorship agreements, to market their image and achieve visibility and notoriety in the sport-social polo events. The biggest polo tournaments offer sponsors valuable exposure to an affluent clientele as well as sought-after product associations.

Therefore, lots of luxury international brands, mainly concerning automotive, watches, jewelry, alcohol and ready-to-wear fashion sectors take the opportunity to associate with polo, including Mercedes, Audi, Jaguar, Lexus, Rolex, Piaget, Cartier, Jaeger Le Coultre, Hermés, La Martina, Santa Maria Polo, Veuve Clicquot, Chivas, Perrier-Jouët, Johnnie Walker, Chivite, Armani and Harrods, among others.

As a result, the polo market is turning out to be increasingly conditioned by those business groups which integrate a diversification of their sponsorship strategies.

On the other hand, polo has an incredible impact on the mass media because it attracts an audience including consumers for luxury products and celebrities or famous public figures. This therefore puts more pressure on companies that finance the tournaments. Maybe polo could today be considered one of the very few opportunities to redefine the VIP world, much more than F1 which is increasingly shifting to a bigger audience, reducing its enhanced affinity.

13.7 POLO: A BOOMING NUMBER OF PLAYERS, MEMBERS AND SPECTATORS

One more collateral effect is the growing number of polo players enrolled in the Federation of International Polo which represents national polo associations in all corners of the world. The number of member countries of the federation demonstrates a huge coverage of this new-old sport.[10] In France, the French Polo Federation has seen its number of players trebled from 333 player-members in 2000 to 954 in 2010.[11]

What is more, the number of children and women polo players is growing noticeably and is synonymous with pertinent emerging markets.

Although the most significant polo events take place in England, Argentina, Spain and the United States, recently, the booming implication of emerging countries such as Mexico, India, Switzerland, France and the United Arab Emirates clearly depicts the incredible success of this sport in a global perspective and consequently the huge interest in polo from the corporate world.

Argentina is undoubtedly home to one of the most famous polo competitions worldwide; the Argentina Polo Open, which takes place from November to December brings together world-class players and wealthy visitors. Ralph Lauren, Rolex and La Martina are among several international luxury names supporting the Argentinean event.[12] Richard Mille is even using polo during its tremendous presentations for the SIHH in Geneva, and La Martina is co-branding with Porsche, or Ferrari or Baldessarini, far from the brands currently existing at Nike, Puma or Adidas.

For the first time, the British Polo Day took place in Singapore on November 2011 at the Singapore Polo Club. Sponsored by some British luxury brands including Backes & Strauss jewelry, the event celebrated the 125th anniversary of the club, and at the same time the precious heritage of the polo game and the historical relationships between the United Kingdom and Singapore.

On November 2011, Bentley luxury carmaker, in partnership with Veuve Clicquot champagne and Breitling watchmaker also organized an exclusive Polo tournament at the Val de Vie Wine and Polo Estate in Paarl, Western Cape, South Africa. At the end of the competition which had brought together four sponsored teams, players and guests were invited to enjoy an opening ceremony and a cocktail party.

Moreover, Romania, following in the footsteps of Hungary, Russia and Poland, hosted a major polo tournament in March 2011, the Carpathian Snow Polo European Championship, with a main prize of €100,000 expected over 20,000 tourists to attend the event, the first major polo competition ever to take place in Romania.

In addition to the TAG Heuer Precision Golf Tournament which takes places at the upmarket DLF Golf and Country Club in Gurgaon on the outskirts of New Delhi, TAG Heuer is also the official timekeeper for the Indian Polo Association, seen as a heritage sport in India.[13] We have been lucky enough for the last six years to meet some of our friends there, from all around India.

13.8 POLO: ALSO A SPORT TO LISTEN TO

Polo is not only a question of physical performance; it is part of a pure and singular ambience connected with spirit and symbols, being luxurious by essence. Released on the occasion of the 5th Open de France de Polo held at Apremont in June 2005, the album

Polo Club house lounge music was composed by Cecil Maury for the movie *The Wedding Gallant*. This documentary, dedicated to Patrick Guerrand-Hermes, heir to a luxury industry and passionate for polo, presents music inspired by the universe of polo, tinted with elegance and aestheticism.

13.9 POLO: THE SPORT TO DRESS

Polo also leads, drives and orients how to dress. According to the online Vogue magazine, in 2011, "the dress must of course take center stage. With Henley or the Cartier Polo in mind, it's easy to be overcome by the preppy attraction of Ralph Lauren or Tommy Hilfiger. Summer is upon us, and suddenly fashion has moved its attention to the great outdoors. Horse racing, polo, regattas, outdoor operas, motor festivals, suddenly after just getting to grips with summer office-dressing we are forced to address outdoor occasion wear for the season. From top to toe, here's how to do it."[14]

13.10 POLO AND ITS SURPRISING INTERPRETATIONS

Polo is definitely not a static sport and it has given rise to reinterpretations that are somewhat innovative or even surprising and original. Recently, Louis Vuitton in association with polo bike-players Hengst and Barbier has come out with a new product: the stylized polo bike. This sport, a modernization and reinvention of regular polo is played on bicycles instead of horses, and on a hard-court instead of grass.[15]

Another surprising and real sport is elephant polo. The concept remains the same as for equestrian-based polo, but with bigger animals, more jockeys and longer mallets. The King's Cup Elephant Polo event is held annually in the Golden Triangle region of Thailand and is considered one of the favorite local high-society tournaments. Luxury watchmaker Audemars Piguet is one of the sponsors and has also been exhibiting a competing team.[16]

Polo is also becoming more and more popular in China, thanks in part to the Snow Polo World Cup event hosted by the Tianjin Golden Polo Club. "With club membership costing between

$60,000 and $1.6 million, the complex and its posh events are testament to China's ability to reinvent old school style. The luxury of the club not only reflects China's growing love of horses – it suggests the exponential growth of Chinese cities as villa-style residential complexes crop up around town."[17]

Polo and Luxury Advertising by Hervé Pommier and Hervé Temmerman[18]

Rolex has been involved in equestrian sport since 1957. Excelling in this sport demands a perfect control of timing, precision and grace both from the horseman and his watch, states the brand's official website.

When talking of grace and elegance, Rolex links its feminine models such as the Oyster Perpetual Datejust to the most-talented horsewomen on the planet. Ambassadors, whose equestrian qualities reinforce this aspiration to excellence that is inherent within the brand.

Méredith Michaels-Beerbaum and her Datejust, Zara Phillips and her Lady-Datejust, Isabell Werth and her Lady-Datejust Pearlmaster, are the ultimate symbols of femininity[19].

As for the horsemen?

The male is asked to show less grace and more physical prowess. In this respect, Polo lends itself as much to this game as Formula One.

The association of Rolex and its model Datejust, with its mainly Argentinian world of Polo, is the perfect illustration.

The use of the image of Gonzalo Pieres Jr,[20] international Polo champion and winner of the Argentinian Triple Crown Tournament, Handicap: 10, gives us an idea of the level of excellence of people owning these objects. However, the essence of this relationship is to be found in the association between Rolex and the oldest of Polo competitions, the Argentinian Open.[21]

This association is communicated via two images showing polo players before their public.[22] The first image in black and white, has obviously been taken during the 20th century, while the second, in colour, is more modern. Together, they tell a story of continuity and a passion shared by the Argentinian Polo Association and Rolex, down through time.

Luxury brands that use the sport of Polo as a communications platform use the usual codes and associations of luxury brands within a sporting environment.

The absence of a clear differentiation between brands (whether intentional or not) is one of the key aspects of this type of communication;

the same personality could be used by two different competitor brands – Tiger Woods, as used by Tag Heuer to Rolex – without this appearing to pose the slightest problem.

The association of a product with an international personality is fairly recurrent and the feeling of "going round in circles" in terms of communication style is fairly apparent for anybody reading a magazine used by luxury brands.

Actor or spectator?

The polo player is obviously the target for suppliers.

Suppliers, players and prestigious spectators are a well-identified target for investment banks, such as the Zurich bank, Julius Bär, which doesn't hesitate to compare its knowledge to the professionalism of specialist bootmakers.

Spectators, on the other hand, are a specific target for the majority of luxury-brand communication strategies and no matter if this public increases in size and becomes more democratic. VIPs will always be separated from small time players...

With this in mind, the meticulous staging of a rigorous selection of Polo match spectators brings a touch of modernity to the sport. It's not yet at the same level for Audi, but the video reports of New Audi International Polo Series could show the way for a renewal in terms of form and tone.[23]

By creating a select and celebrity-oriented environment, made up of young fashion leaders, favorite actors and actresses, Audi will inevitably create the desire to share these exceptional "Polo" moments, among an affluent, young and mixed public.

Brand Content – the communications future for Polo and luxury brands?

13.11 CONCLUSION

More than 2,000 years on, polo continues to feed the sphere of the wealthy and the influential. Yet it has also become a globally recognized sport, seducing serious luxury and fashion sponsorship and investment. The exceptional skill of the players relies on their symbiotic relationship with the horse, crucial to achieving high levels of performance. Polo seems to be everlasting...which is also one of the key driving forces of global luxury.

More than a sport, polo also corresponds closely to a luxury standard of living worldwide. "Polo is a lifestyle, not just a sport. What was built is a concept of a brand that people come in and ask for. For that naturalness, for that realness, it's about unfashionable fashion, it's about elements of style", says David Lauren, senior vice-president of advertising, marketing and corporate communication, and son of Ralph.[24]

By the way, the brand leads polo to its paroxysm with the Polo Modern Reserve fragrance. Combining notes of Fresh-cut Basil, Vetyver-Leather and Humidor Wood, this perfume fits "the personality of traditionalist who appreciates luxury living in the country with a passion for Polo sport. Polo Modern Reserve is for the guy who loves life and values the importance of his heritage."[25]

The Polo Modern Reserve bottle, inspired by the classic gentleman's flask with distinctive green glass from original Polo fragrance with the gold cap and bold Polo Pony, refers its content to the power of heritage, classicism, authenticity and country-living lifestyle.

Finally, luxury brands allow polo to be developed. "[Sponsoring polo] was the opportunity to support a great sport that we believe is very much within the realm of our brand's culture. Our patronage is substantial enough to make an influential contribution to the development of the sport", says Arnaud Bamberger, executive chairman of Cartier UK, one of the sport's most significant sponsors group involved in polo for almost 30 years.[26]

Moreover, within the latest surveys dealing with the top 50 most-searched luxury brands published by luxurysociety.com in 2012, we can notice that in the United States, Russia and China, the two preferred and searched brands are commonly automotive brands with BMW and Audi taking the lead. Consequently, it is not surprising for such brands to create a thrill around polo, because polo attracts luxury brands which retroactively attract through their brand image and personality-loyal consumers. It is clearly a win-win strategy for polo clubs and luxury brands to create a partnership.

Nevertheless, some dampers can appear. Cartier Company decided to end its long-running sponsorship of the International Day at Guards Polo Club in Argentina, which will have to find a new sponsor for the 2012 event. It seems that Cartier considers that the event has become too celebrity-focused and no longer attracts the clientele with which it wished to be associated. Once again, the definitive hunt for an almost established balance between affinity and audience.

Another damper is the return of investment. "The skill, speed and endurance needed in polo make it for me an exciting sport to be involved in",[27] says Richard Mille, the Swiss watchmaker. However, the benefits gained from polo do not compensate the sums spent on it. It must be considered as a long-term bet on an everlasting awareness building. "But then it wouldn't truly be a luxury product without some sacrifices."[28] The most important thing is to be able, at any moment, to sacrifice what we are for what we could become, is it not? If polo represents a certain financial sacrifice for luxury brands, it also epitomizes an incontrovertible stepping-stone.

NOTES

1. Davoudi, S. (22 July 2011). Glamour and exclusivity help fund games of kings. Retrieved from http://www.ft.com.
2. Calmejane, J.-L. (April 2005). La Professional Golf Watch de Tag Heuer. Retrieved from http://luxe-magazine.com.
3. The legendary Piaget Polo (18 September 2008). Retrieved from http://journal.hautehorlogerie.org.
4. www.pololand.org.
5. Shah, G. (28 April 2008). Luxury Brands bet on sport to market products. *The wall street journal.* Retrieved from http://www.livemint.com.
6. Feradov, A., Cartier Cavalry Polo Cup. Retrieved from http://www.internationallife.tv/.
7. Feradov, A., Cartier Cavalry Polo Cup. Retrieved from http://www.internationallife.tv/.
8. Polo, probably the most luxurious sport equestrian,(30 November 2011). *Business of luxury.* Retrieved from http://www.cpp-luxury.com.
9. Luxury brands team up with polo (19 September 2008). Retrieved from http://journal.hautehorlogerie.org.
10. www.fippolo.com/.
11. www.francepolo.com/.

12. Feradov, A., Cartier Cavalry Polo Cup. Retrieved from http://www.internationallife.tv/.
13. Shah, G. (28 April 2008). Luxury Brands bet on sport to market products. *The Wall Street Journal.* Retrieved from http://www.livemint.com.
14. Macalister-Smith, T. (27 May 2011). Summer Dressing. Retrieved from http://www.vogue.co.uk/news.
15. Louis Vuitton Polo Bike Adds Style to the Sport (12 January 2012). Retrieved from http://www.justluxe.com/.
16. Adams, A. *Audemars Piguet Watches and The Rare Sport Of Elephant Polo.* Retrieved from http://www.luxist.com/.
17. Tianjin aims to rule in polo and urban development (12 March 2012). Retrieved from http://red-luxury.com/.
18. Sup de Création/SKEMA Business School.
19. http://www.rolex.com/fr#/world-of-rolex/sports-and-culture/equestrian.
20. Advertising on Polo Quarterly (PQ) http://www.pqinternational.com/.
21. The tournament takes place since 1893 at Campo Argentino de Polo in Palermo, a neighborhood of Buenos Aires.
22. Source PQ.
23. New Audi Polo International Series http://www.hurlinghammedia.com/.
24. Copping, N. (23 July 2010). Polo gives life to global fashion empire. *Financial Times.* Retrieved from http://www.ft.com.
25. Sharma, R. T. (5 December 2010). Polo's luxury rides. Retrieved from http://economictimes. times.com.
26. Feradov, A., Cartier Cavalry Polo Cup. Retrieved from http://www.internationallife.tv/.
27. Feradov, A., Cartier Cavalry Polo Cup. Retrieved from http://www.internationallife.tv/.
28. Feradov, A., Cartier Cavalry Polo Cup. Retrieved from http://www.internationallife.tv/.

14

MIMESIS AND THE NEXUS OF LUXURY INDUSTRY IN INDIA

Mukta Ramchandani

14.1 INTRODUCTION

The proverb "First deserve, then desire" is not one that may comfortably be applied to the communication of brands in the luxury industry. As the world revolves around the spectrum of luxury industry and the consumers worldwide, we can relate how the communication of brands has been playing around, against this proverb. Many modes of communication are prevalent in the luxury and fashion industry, but there are certain hidden elements that strategically form the concrete stimuli of the luxury consumption.

The middle-class population in India is forecast to grow from 50 million in 2007 to 583 million by 2025 and more than 23 million of them will be among the country's wealthiest inhabitants. Potential luxury customers in India always want to stand out from the crowd.[1] In fact, they want to be a step ahead of the crowd and they look up to brands to identify the key trends for them and buy these products before anyone else. This, for members of a particular high-end segment of society, has become a means of displaying their power, image and status leading to hedonism.

14.2 CONCEPTUAL ANATOMY: MIMETIC DESIRE AND ITS INTEGRATION INTO THE LUXURY INDUSTRY

A mimetic desire is observed when a brand is bought without any fulfillment of its functional objectives (like quality, precision, style

FIGURE 14.1 **Process of mimetic desire**

and longevity) but with a sense of fitting in a status by purchasing a brand. That is to say that the desire of something which is possessed by someone else is equivalent to imitating the other person.[2] The premise of mimetic theory is the romantic myth of "divine autonomy", according to which our desires are freely chosen expressions of our individuality. Hence, it is from others that we borrow our desires. Moreover, this desire is provoked by an influencer (model) in order to possess the desired object (Figure 14.1).

The high density of population, word of mouth and looking up to the possessions of the higher class, all act as a major catalyst for the luxury consumer. The mimetic process involves looking up, missing the object and desiring it.

The theory of mimetic desire has been an inherited conceptual part of consumption among Indians. One of the common means of elevating one's social status in India has been to be an early adapter of a luxury product. In the common Indian perception, the luxury product has been identified as inaccessible, expensive, unaffordable or something that is unseen and unheard of. This captivity of luxury products and brands has been easily inflicted in Indian society through the tendency to show off, further leading to the desire of mimicking the early adapters.The primary influence on buying behavior of consumers in India are peer feedback and word of mouth. A luxury consumer in India has not been identified merely by an association with luxury brands or services, but also with the possession of a house, a car or perhaps a foreign education.This is how first impressions are created and form the basis of mimetic desire within the mindset of the Indian luxury consumers.

The major influencers are celebrities or the influencial class that highlights their possessions. For the middle classes it is easy to fall prey to such adoption of luxury brands by percieving them in the media, the big fat Indian weddings, or special events. Luxury has been synonymous with "existing because somebody has created a buzz about it".

Indians are quite easily motivated by brand names even though they may not know much about what the product stands for. The communication disparity here comes from the fact that they have been exposed to the luxury trends by the people surrounding them creating mimetic desire.

14.3 ASYMMETRY IN LUXURY COMMUNICATION

14.3.1 Communication differentiation

Communication is one of the most important elements of the luxury and fashion industry and involves various facets, especially when a brand is global and communication is multicultural. Advertisements in one country or culture could cause offense in another. There are many more elements involved in the communication of luxury brands but many of these facets are contradictory.

> The brand is the primary means by which consumers associate themselves with a luxury company. It is what creates and sustains the attraction and desire for products.[3]

In order for a luxury brand to differentiate itself from the universe of classic consumption goods, communication must aim to do more than just "make sales". Luxury marketing should allow people to dream and aspire. In luxury, one applies the communication strategy in order to create a dream and to recharge a brand's value, not just to sell.[4]

14.3.2 Integrated modes of brand communication and adoption in India

14.3.2.1 Celebrity advertisements and campaigns

In India, celebrities are increasingly used in marketing communication by marketers to lend personality to their products. The activities and movements of these celebrities are closely watched and imitated. Indians claim to be influenced by the local celebrities as they feel a similar aspirational interactivity with them endorsing the luxury brand.

Consumers are more attracted to advertisements if they are admirers of the celebrities featured in the advertisements. Thus, the popularity of brands is correlated with a celebrity's power to influence. The globally appealing celebrities like Shahrukh Khan, Aishwarya Rai and Anil Kapoor, endorsing brands like Tag Heuer, L'Oreal and Canali, respectively, are highly paid and extremely demandable for the Indian market. Famous celebrities are able to attract and retain attention by their mere presence in the advertisements.[5]

14.3.2.2 Newspapers and magazines

Luxury brand communication involves perception, image and aspiration and it is important to educate consumers in a virgin territory like India; the media can make or break the brand image and value to the consumer.[6]

For example, an advertisement for the French brand "Jours Après Lunes" was criticized in Indian newspapers, consequently damaging the reputation of the brand in India.

14.3.2.3 Social media

Social media play an important role in impacting market trends. Photos of consumers displaying their newly purchased Louis Vuitton or Burberry products are shared online and viewed by the consumers' peers creating an involuntary desire for these products.

As an example of the influence of social media, when Hina Rabbani Khar, Pakistan's foreign minister, visited India in 2011 she was spotted with a black Hermès Birkin bag and Roberto Cavalli sunglasses. This immediately became a topic of discussion on twitter.

14.4 LUXURY EXPERIENCE

According to Pine and Gilmore[7] there are four dimensions of luxury experience that are well identified by the brands when they communicate themselves in various regions. These dimensions are based on the involvement and the intensity of the brand's communicational strategy.

14.4.1 Entertainment

Fashion shows and designer boutiques have adopted the entertainment strategic approach to attract the consumer of today. The mall culture has long been associated with the entertainment of the consumer. Nonetheless in India the DLF Emporio and Select Citywalk malls have emerged as the luxury malls in New Delhi where people prefer to shop for brands while being entertained by the concept of designers in their boutiques.

14.4.2 Escapist

This dimension is high on involvement as well as intensity. One example is the Royal tented Taj spas in Jaipur at the Taj hotels and resorts which have recreated the mobile palaces used by the Mughals in the 16th and the 17th centuries.

14.4.3 Aesthetic

This dimension is low on involvement and high on intensity. For example, Hermès, the French fashion house established in 1837, specializing in leather, lifestyle, fragrances, luxury goods, ready-to-wear and so on, launched its local strategies for India. In October 2011, Hermès launched a line of limited-edition saris, an Indian traditional dress, with a starting price of $1800 with an additional blouse priced at $500.[8]

14.4.4 Educational

The educational dimension comes into play when people are actively involved but the intensity is low. For example, Tata Nano, one year before its launch was marketed as the world's smallest car.

Waiting time between registration and delivery was a minimum of six months.

14.5 HIGHLIGHTS AND RATIONALE OF THE CONSUMERS OF LUXURY BRANDS IN INDIA

Being in a mimetic desire-driven society of India, it can be said that what the middle-class mass perceives as a benchmark brings huge sales to the company or to the sector.

According to Credit Rating and Information Services of India Ltd (CRISIL) research report,[9] there are various kinds of Indian consumers at the top of the pyramid that can be categorized as follows:

(a) Inheritors
(b) Self-made
(c) Professionals

14.5.1 Inheritors

These are the traditionally wealthy consumers. They focus on the preservation of their wealth. They buy branded, high-value products and are aware of the emerging trends in luxury markets. They experiment with the newer brands. Wealth is passed on within the extended family and from generation to generation.

14.5.2 Self- made

These are the first-time entrepreneurs. They mimic and follow the spending patterns of the inheritors. Buying branded, high-value products is their means of displaying wealth and status. Their wealth is transferred to the immediate family.

14.5.3 Professionals

These are the consumers who have earned wealth based on their professional and academic merit. They are very passionate about their career and consider wealth to be an outcome of success in their career. Their purchasing pattern is highly dependent on "value for money".

India and the case of Ed Hardy

In India, "hype culture" is used to target customers. Any brand which creates a hype of luxury becomes mass market. For example, after its launch in India in 2007, Ed Hardy by Christian Audigier was perceived as a luxurious brand due to its high prices and worldwide reputation. Urban India was buying Ed Hardy products. It was also being worn by celebrities and their public appearances helped to promote the brand. Youngsters were easily targeted by the brand. By 2008 it became prestigious to wear Ed Hardy. Soon after, Ed Hardy clothes and accessories were seen worn by students in colleges and universities. In New Delhi, where the mimetic desire is highly prevalent, Ed Hardy was commonly spotted among the university or college students. The original Ed Hardy t-shirts, with a starting price of Rs 3500 (€60) had remarkable sales. Counterfeit Ed Hardy products sold for Rs 100 (approximately €2) were also seen in the markets and were being worn by every other person, including low-waged workers in New Delhi, making it a huge mass-market brand by 2010.

14.6 CONCLUSION: WINNING IN INDIA WITH THE COMMUNICATION STRATEGY

The asymmetry between the luxury brand communication in India and other countries has been due to a number of empirical factors including culture. India is an upcoming lucrative destination for luxury brands. The communication strategies should focus on educating the consumer, as this is how the desire for the luxury product will be achieved, rather than by a flamboyant, shallow purchasing motivation. What the Indian consumers crave needs to be dissected and related over and above the barrier of simply mimicking their neighbors, friends or business associates. It is more important for them to know how a luxury brand will help reflect their status in their surroundings instead of just showing off.

We can conclude that luxury brands can be more proactive and more culturally conscious when entering a huge multicultural economy like India, and must not be hindered by the traditional communication process of portraying the brand identity to the connoisseur category. With the lower dependency on making a brand fall prey to a trend, it should strategically be identified as market-driving rather than the market driven. This new step could serve as the launch pad to increase the brand value of catering to the aspirational and admirational luxury and fashion consumers in India.

NOTES

1. McKinsey & Company (2007). The "Bird of Gold":The rise of India's Consumer Market. Retrieved 12 July 2011, from: http://www.mckinsey.com/locations/india/mckinseyonindia/pdf/India_Consumer_Market.pdf.
2. Girard, R. (1996). *The Girard Reader.* St. Louis, MO: Crossroad.
3. Okonkwo, U. (2007). *Luxury Fashion Branding.* London: Palgrave Macmillan.
4. Kapferer, J and Bastien, V. (2009). *The Luxury Strategy.* Philadelphia: Kogan Page Limited.
5. Georgeta, V. (2008), Engineering and Manufacturing Industries, DAAAM International. Vienna.ISSN: 1726-9679. Retrieved 10 November 2011 from: http://www.freepatentsonline.com/article/Annals-DAAAM-Proceedings/225316710.html.
6. IndiaRetailing.com (2011). The rules of consumption, interview with Radha Chadha, retrieved 10 November 2011. From: http://www.indiaretailing.com/Expert-view-consumption.asp.
7. Pine, J. and Gilmore, J. (2011). *The Experience Economy.* Boston, MA: Harvard Business School Press.
8. Sharma, T. (2011), Economic Times. Retrived 9 August 2011 From: http://articles.economictimes.indiatimes.com/2011-08-09/news/29867281_1_hermes-family-sarees-limited-edition.
9. CRISIL (2011). Top of the Pyramid. Retrieved 3 August 2011 from: http://luxurysociety.com/articles/2011/08/understanding-the-indian-ultra-high-net-worth-individual.

15

TESLA MOTORS, THE REINVENTION OF THE LUXURY SPORTS CAR INDUSTRY

Daniela Milosheska

15.1 HISTORY OF TESLA

Since its creation in 2003, Tesla has faced financial, management and technical challenges to become what it is today: an emerging luxury brand in the automotive industry. Much of the company's success is down to its co-founder Elon Musk. Elon Musk is a visionary whose only goal is to make the world a better place to live in. This eminent risk-taker has founded many companies, each and every one of them special and each and every one of them contributing to his primary goal. From founding PayPal to launching the nation's biggest solar-energy supplier Solar City and creating the SpaceX, Elon Musk's life has been one adventure after another. In 2003, Musk was faced with one of his biggest challenges. Together with two other engineers, Martin Eberhard and J. B. Straubel, he created Tesla, a company that produces the world's best electric vehicles. The only question was whether the company would succeed and turn from an unprofitable to a lucrative business. Seven years later, not only has Tesla reached its goals, but it has also surpassed car enthusiasts' expectations and altered the way electric vehicles are viewed today. What started as an American-based car manufacturer with the ambition to create something valuable for the world has become a serious challenger in the automotive industry.

Tesla Motors is an independent company with high-profile investors such as the Google cofounders Sergey Brin and Larry Page, former eBay President Jeff Skoll, Hyatt heir Nick Pritzker, as well as the venture capitalist firms like Fraper Fisher Jurvetson, Capricom Management and the Bay Area Equity Fund managed by JP Morgan Chase. Toyota and Daimler have also acquired stocks in the company.[1] Tesla Motors' goal is to make electric vehicles that will sell as luxury cars but will eventually end up as mass-market vehicles. The essence of the brand is expressed in the words of Elon Musk: "We will not stop until every car in the world is electric." However, due to the cost of materials, the final result was the creation of a semi-luxurious electric car priced at around US$109,000.

Initial funding for the company came from Elon Musk himself who put in a personal investment of $6.3m in 2004. This proved insufficient and a further $20m was injected in 2007 from Musk's personal savings after which he began his quest for potential investors. Tesla's target was Daimler AG, but in order to get this company to invest, Tesla needed to prove that they could provide sustainable battery packs for Daimler's cars. To do this, Tesla needed to buy a Smart car, the problem being that this kind of car was neither manufactured nor distributed in the United States. The solution was to pay someone to buy the car from Mexico and transport it all the way to California. When all of this was done, Tesla had less than four weeks to assemble Daimler's Smart car with Tesla's electric technology and make it efficient for driving. The result was a success. After Daimler's CEO tested the car, he offered Tesla a strategic partnership and an investment of $70m. It seemed like Tesla's moment to shine had finally arrived. Despite the financial crisis in 2008 in the United States, and the closure of its branch in Detroit, Tesla Motors still managed to sell 500 cars. However, to keep Tesla from collapsing, Musk invested his last savings of $40m, bringing his overall investment in Tesla to around $75m by the end of 2009.

15.2 TESLA'S FIRST MODEL: TESLA ROADSTER

In 2009, Tesla hired Franz Von Holzhausen to become the chief designer for the next generation of Tesla's vehicles, the Model S. The aim was to bring back a sense of passion and emotion into the sedan, a car with space for seven passengers. Once again, additional funding was needed for the Model S to be mass-produced. Therefore, Tesla submitted an application for a US-governmental loan from the department of energy, and received $465m. This period of Tesla was followed by extreme controversy and almost every car manufacturer wished Tesla's demise.

Their success was seen as an attack on the conventional vehicle, and the increasingly strong presence of Tesla became a serious threat for other companies (Figure 15.1).

FIGURE 15.1 **Tesla Roadster**

Tesla Motors Facebook Page (2012), retrieved 1 June 2012 from http://www.facebook.com/photo.php?fbid=10150342237782801&set=a.10150342237652801.369075.18790602800&type=3&theater.

Tesla went public in 2010 which made it the first American car manufacturer to go public since the Ford Motor Company in 1956.[2] Although considered unlikely to succeed, Tesla's IPO reached 40 percent in a single day and brought an additional investment of $15m from Toyota. This bold move made Tesla a benchmark for companies such as GM, which followed Tesla's example not only in the introduction of their own electric vehicle but also going public.

In 2010, Tesla opened its first factory in Palo Alto, California. The following year, Tesla sued Top Gear for allegedly showing false information on their TV program when they were given Tesla's Roadster for a test drive. The lawsuit is still in process. 2011 also marked the deliverance of the 1,650th Roadster sold around 50 countries all around the world.[3]

15.3 DRIVER IMAGERY

Tesla's brand is not a conventional luxury vehicle; consequently their target market is very different from that of other manufacturers of luxury vehicles. The high price obviously attracts the wealthy, but other driver profiles are also targeted. The company relies on people's consciousness and their feelings related to the environment, which is at their core for finding future potential customers (see Figure 15.2).

The first profile is the eco-aware and eco-friendly driver who prefers driving a vehicle that respects the environment. This in fact

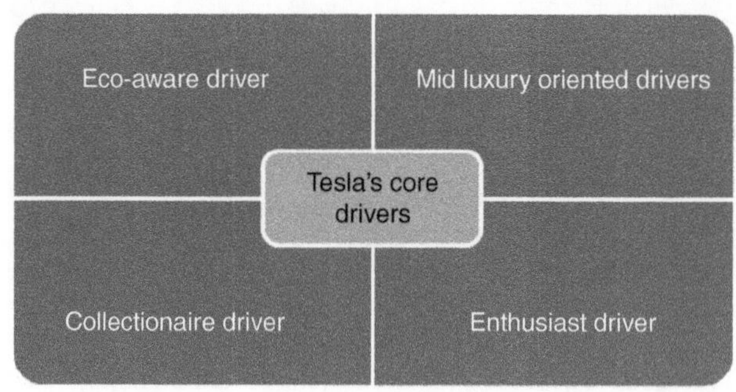

FIGURE 15.2 **Driver imagery of the Tesla brand**

is the profile of someone who already possesses a Tesla or is most likely to possess one in the future. Such drivers believe that Tesla is a blend of two practicalities, great quality performance with an eco-friendly engine.

Mid-luxury-oriented drivers are people who buy vehicles that are at the high-end of the mass-consumption market. Tesla's vehicles can provide a taste of luxury with a more or less reasonable price tag. For the moment, these drivers form the core customers segment of the company.

The collector driver is a profile of people who collect cars just to have the latest vehicles parked in their garage. These people are wealthy individuals, whose passion is speed and comfort while driving. They sometimes buy the cars just to marvel at the impeccable design without even driving them. These people are not the brand's core customers, even though they can be used as a great promotional tool to advertise the car and show just how special it is.

Another driver type is the car-enthusiast driver. These people are usually involved either in the manufacturing process of the vehicle or in the marketing process. People like forum writers, bloggers, public faces and TV commentators are all included in this category. However, there are also those who just want to enjoy the driving even if that means that after 500 km, they should wait for another four hours to recharge the vehicle.

15.4 LUXURY BRAND EQUITY OF TESLA

As Tesla is a very new brand in the automotive industry, the company's luxury brand equity can only be measured through their sales performance in the last three years. However, the admiration for the brand, the affinity to the brand, the perception of the brand innovation, the recent popularity, as well as the price are all contributors to the overall equity of a brand.

By the end of 2008, just a year after the brand's first model was introduced, Tesla reported sales of around $10.9m for 100 cars sold.[4] 2009 was known as the year the company made its first profit of $1m, selling 837 cars, thus generating revenue of $20m.[5] The profit generated might not be much, but what often takes many years for other car manufacturers took only one year for Tesla to establish a brand. In 2010, Tesla delivered a total of 1,400 Roadsters gaining revenue of $28.4m and reporting a loss of $38.5m. In 2011, Tesla sold 1,650 vehicles gaining revenue of $58.2m and a loss of $58.9m.[6] The fact that Tesla reported profits in the second year of production testifies that Tesla has gained enormous admiration and respect for what it does and the way it conducts its business. This demonstrates that although Tesla is a new brand, its luxury brand equity is solid considering it has only been in production for four years. Another interesting fact that supports this is that Switzerland, one of the richest countries in the world has the highest per-capita Tesla ownership of any country.[7]

The other components are going to be explained through Tesla's brand elements as steps for the composition of the luxury brand equity.

15.5 STEPS OF BUILDING TESLA'S LUXURY BRAND EQUITY

Although Tesla is a very young car manufacturer and because of its immaturity, it is almost impossible to show how the brand has developed over the years, it already enjoys a very strong reputation. I will try and explain how the brand has become what it is today and how it can expand even further through the use of various brand elements.

Brand elements can be divided into two parts, the ones that people can see – the physical elements (size, communication, uniqueness, vividness, content and appeal) – and the ones that people cannot see but are the foundation and the most crucial part in forming the brand (brand likeability, brand loyalty and brand confidence).[8] The physical segment is especially important when launching a luxury brand and Tesla is no exception to the rule. This is why the structure of the brand with its brand elements is compared to an iceberg.

Tesla has been described as an attack on mainstream vehicles. When its first model was launched, Tesla was considered to be just another expensive toy for the wealthy, but the identity of the brand focuses on the advantages of electric vehicles over gasoline ones. An important part of this step is the positioning of the brand and defining the brand values. Let us start with the definition of the brand values. One of Tesla's core values is respect for the environment with the electric vehicle's zero emissions. Another thing that Tesla's brand wanted to prove was that electric vehicles could also be much more powerful than gasoline cars as well as more attractive. As Elon Musk suggests, the vehicles they offer have "high sexual appeal that in a sense helps save the world".[9] Where improvements in brand image could be made in the future is in a more futuristic design to their vehicles, and increased exclusivity. This step of the brand is not really formed yet, because there have been some problems regarding the recharging of the vehicles, as well as the distance that they can go to. Considering the fact that it is supposed to portray a solution to the preservation of the environment, Tesla should concentrate on this as their primary goal.

Regarding positioning, Tesla is considered a premium brand, and is treated as such. However, the brand vision and mission is not to remain a premium brand. On the contrary, Tesla is trying to make its brand part of the bargain brands. With the launching of the Model S, Tesla's aim is to produce around 20,000 units to be sold for half the price of its Roadster (around $50,000).[10] In my opinion, Tesla should focus on developing the brand both as a premium and as a bargain. This means that different lines of electric vehicles should be launched in order to maintain Tesla's reputation as a luxury brand and to develop the vision of the company's founders.

The luxury brand imagery for Tesla is created mostly through customer satisfaction, critics' articles, as well as professional bloggers. So far, these cars have been viewed as highly efficient vehicles with zero emission. This is how Tesla is perceived by their customers, as well as by people who have profiled the brand. The crucial segment for shaping the luxury brand imagery of Tesla is the environmental impact of the car. This is the core of Tesla's brand imagery. Brand elements that shape the brand's imagery are brand mantras and audits. Tesla's slogan is "Changing perceptions". This slogan is the DNA of the company, because the company's sole aim is to change people's perception about the electric vehicles versus the gasoline vehicles while at the same time raise their eco-awareness. By demonstrating what EVs can do, Tesla relies on the brand's attributes such as speed and driving pleasure.

Tesla's brand enjoys high level of brand credibility, which leads to the affinity of the brand. With celebrity customers like George Clooney, Leonardo DiCaprio and Arnold Schwarzenegger, people trust Tesla and are willing to buy its cars. A particularly important contribution to Tesla's credibility is the promise that the company makes and manages to keep. Brand credibility also greatly depends on the brand's security. In 2010, after only one customer had reported problems with Tesla's Roadster, Tesla issued a safety recall of all 345 cars manufactured. The company even sent technicians to customers' homes to perform security checks and make any adjustments necessary.

Creating a luxury brand relies on creating a positive emotional response from its potential customers. Positive feelings will enhance admiration for the brand and thus the luxury brand equity and brand credibility. People's feelings are usually spurred from how much they trust the brand. This step is defined through the memorability of a brand, its meaningfulness, likeability, innovation, as well as the brand's transferability and adaptability.

The memorability of Tesla is mostly defined through a word-of-mouth marketing strategy. This is just how the company has been advertising itself from 2008, when the first model was launched, up until 2011. Various forums, blogs and car critics act as catalysts in the process of increasing the brand's memorability, therefore making the brand sustainable in the long run. Even the toughest car critics are impressed by what this brand and its products are doing and its potential in the future.

Another factor that increases the memorability of the brand is its logo: a simple letter T (or a simple word mark) that celebrates the scientist whose initial idea served as basis for Tesla's products. What is extremely helpful for Tesla's brand is the fact that the company is the first electric car brand to have ever gone into mass production. This segment contributes the most to the memorability of the brand and will serve in the future as a powerful tool to increase its brand value (Figure 15.3).

The meaningfulness of Tesla's brand is to demonstrate that an electric car can be twice as efficient as any other sports car that runs on gasoline. This brand element is complemented by the simple notion that the car has zero emission and therefore does not impose any threat to the environment. The only factor that might diminish

FIGURE 15.3 **Tesla's logo**
Source: www.teslamotors.com

Tesla's meaningfulness is that an electric car cannot go long distances. This said, Tesla has already revolutionized and altered this notion by making their batteries last for as far as 400 km with a single charge, and further progress is expected.

The likeability of Tesla's brand cannot be easily evaluated, due to the fact that its vehicles are only three years old. What can be said, however, is that during these three years Tesla has done much more than any other car manufacturer has. Likeability is measured by how many people want to buy Tesla's electric cars and how many customers are satisfied afterwards with the car's performance. The enormous leap from only 100 cars in 2008, to 1,650 cars sold in total by the middle of 2011, demonstrates that at the moment these vehicles represent the latest luxury accessory for the rich and famous.[11] The future predictions of 20,000 units for Tesla's newest model suggest that electric cars will no longer be reserved for the wealthiest.

The perception of the brand innovation is extremely high, considering the fact that Tesla's vehicles are the first electric vehicles to go into mass production. This may be explained by the many technological inventions that are part of the vehicles. Their exterior design bears a close resemblance to that of the Lotus Elise. The reason for this is that Tesla Motors had made a production contract with the Lotus Group.[12] With the upcoming sedan, the Model S, Tesla believes that it has made significant improvements and aims

FIGURE 15.4 **Tesla's newest model: The Model S**
Source: http://www.teslamotors.com/

to continue to do so until its vehicles conquer the hearts and minds of their customers as well as all other car fanatics (Figure 15.4).

From 2003 up until today, almost 70 different patents have been used to protect Tesla's brand, due to the innovative techniques of this new and unexplored industry.[13] In 2010, Tesla Motors obtained its most important patent, for battery charging based on cost and life.[14] This demonstrates that in contrast to most car manufactures, Tesla brand's innovation is found under the hood rather than over it. Tesla is also issuing licenses to brands like Daimler and Toyota to use their electric power components (Figure 15.5).

Tesla is still too young a brand to have its own brand extensions and become transferable. Nevertheless, there are early signs for brand diversification. It already has opened its own shop for Tesla's apparel, key pendants and different car accessories bearing the name of the brand, as well as an online shop.[15] As a producer of electrical components, Tesla has found strategic partners in Daimler and Toyota by producing these components and selling them. In the future, I see Tesla doing almost everything that the other mainstream car manufacturers are doing. My suggestion for a brand extension would be to make their own tournament where they would award a special cup for the most advanced electric vehicle. In this way, they would create a spirit of competition that would help them innovate even more. I also believe that they should only diversify within the field of their own industry

FIGURE 15.5 **Tesla's patents**

Source: http://www.facebook.com/media/set/?set=a.10150265898457801.347106.18790602800&type=1

to avoid the risk of losing the brand's DNA. For instance, when Ferrari launched its own collection of cell phones together with Acer, I think that the brand just went too far. Even though this kind of strategy is profitable and cost effective, there's something called brand's integrity which is compromised here because all that Ferrari needs is a brand of ice cream in their portfolio to destroy and dilute the brand completely. They want to stay the privilege of the wealthy, but their brand extensions are showing that they want to increase their revenues by offering piece of the cake for mass market.

The adaptability of the brand is yet to be proven, because it is new and has not faced any major crisis. Elon Musk saved the company in 2007, when additional funding was secured by his personal savings, but there has been no change in ownership yet, which makes it hard to claim with certainty that the brand can really be adaptable. What Tesla has done throughout the short period of its existence is to alter the common opinion of the superiority of gasoline luxury vehicles over electric luxury vehicles. This achievement, along with the fact that Tesla is the first brand ever to mass-produce electric vehicles, suggests that the brand has a great chance of becoming the leading force on the electric vehicle market.

Another segment that contributes to the luxury brand equity is the base price. The Tesla Roadster, the only vehicle in production, is priced at US$109,000 (not including numerous tax incentives, credits and waivers). This places the Tesla Roadster as a semi-luxury vehicle. Price is therefore not the brand's strong point, mostly because Tesla is planning to downgrade the brand by making it available to the mass market: the price for Tesla's Model S has dropped to around $50,000. This pricing strategy forms an essential part of the marketing strategy as well, but in achieving its goal, Tesla risks losing its present core customers, thus affecting the company badly.

The fourth segment is also closely interrelated to the establishment of the brand's credibility. The relationship that is formed between the brand and its customers is mostly linked to consumers' emotions and the credibility of the brand. As the brand is so new, this special bond with its customers is not yet developed, but the brand is working on establishing a loyal relationship, which will be based on trust and mutual respect. By forming a firm bond with its customers, the brand will gain reliability. This relationship can be formed through implementing the right PR moves, such as maintaining the promised level of quality, creating clubs for existing and potential customers, forming race team for electric cars, movie placements, celebrity endorsements, displaying their cars at popular car shows, auto leases and collaboration with hotels as selling approach.

15.6 COMPETITION

Tesla Motors will face increased indirect competition from other car manufacturers like Nissan, Toyota and GM, even though these companies cannot be direct competitors as Tesla manufactures sports cars and more recently sedans.

Nissan has set up a partnership with Renault to launch its electric vehicle program. Started in 2010, it offers seven models, none of which is a sports car. The price is competitive, around €20,000 per model and the partnership is expecting sales of around 200 vehicles in their first year of production.[16]

Toyota also has plans to launch electric vehicles in 2012. At the moment, it only produces hybrids, the brand's most recognizable model being the Toyota Prius. Toyota has also partnered with Tesla in order to produce longer-distance and more sustainable EVs.[17] However, the company has stated that the production of electric vehicles is not going to be its core business. Toyota is more likely to be a partner, than a direct competitor of Tesla in the long term.

General Motors also brought out an electric hybrid in 2010, called the Chevrolet Volt claiming it was the direct competition of Tesla. However, as the Volt is not even fully electric, and the electric part is limited to a range of around 80 km, it cannot be a competition of Tesla's Roadster, nor of its upcoming model, the Model S. In 2010, GM had reported production of 10,000 vehicles for 2011, out of which only 4,210 were sold.[18]

As Elon Musk declared in a recent interview for GTM TV, "The Tesla Roadster is more a competitor for a car like a Porsche and not a competitor for a car like a Honda Accord. It's like the person who is looking to buying a Roadster would not say should I buy a Roadster or should I buy, you know a Honda Accord, but it's more like I want to buy a great sports car."[19]

15.7 CONCLUSION

The constant increases in gasoline prices, the scarcity of gas resources and the impact of gasoline on the environment make electric vehicles extremely attractive. Consequently, many car companies have decided to add hybrids and electric versions to their portfolios. Some have managed this with style and grace. Tesla is one of those companies which believe in the power of pushing the boundaries a little bit further than other car manufacturers. The fast establishment of the brand and its positioning on the market is a success story and a blueprint for every emerging company that manufactures luxury electric vehicles. This emerging luxury trend is something to watch out for, as it has tendencies to alter the course of the automotive industry, as we know it today.

Several challenges lie ahead for the company, and, being a very young brand, Tesla has not yet had the opportunity to show what it can do. So far, the success that Tesla has achieved stems largely from customers' admiration and the novelty, which is rooted in the DNA of the brand. As electric vehicles become mainstream, Tesla has an early entrant advantage that is not negligible, but will it be enough to face the likes of BMW or Mercedes? Only time will tell.

NOTES

1. Tesla Motors Quarterly Report (2010), retrieved 1 June 2012 from http://ir.teslamotors.com/secfiling.cfm?filingID= 1193125-10-259068&CIK= 1318605.
2. *Wall Street Journal* (2010). Tesla Motors revs up $244 million IPO, retrieved 1 June 2012 from http://www.marketwatch.com/story/tesla-motors-revs-up-244-million-ipo-2010-06-28.
3. Tesla Motors Press Release (2011). Tesla Motors Reports First Quarter 2011 Results, retrieved 1 June 2012 from http://www.teslamotors.com/about/press/releases/tesla-motors-reports-first-quarter-2011-results.
4. Autoblog Green (2008). Remember that guy Oprah leaned on? He bought Tesla Roadster #100, retrieved 1 June 2012 from http://green.autoblog.com/2008/12/11/remember-that-guy-oprah-leaned-on-he-bought-tesla-roadster-100/.
5. CNNMoney (2009). Electric roadster maker making money, retrieved 1 June 2012 from http://money.cnn.com/2009/08/07/technology/tesla_profitability/?postversion= 2009080716.
6. Automotive News (2011). Tesla reports wider 2nd-quarter loss on development costs; Revenues more than double, retrieved 1 June 2012 from http://www.autonews.com/apps/pbcs.dll/article?AID= /20110803/OEM05/308039679/1429.
7. Tesla Motors Facebook Page (2012), retrieved 1 June 2012 from http://www.facebook.com/photo.php?fbid= 1015035016517780 1&set= a.398080447800.166146.18790602800&type= 3&theater.
8. Interbrand (2001). Bank on the Brand, retrieved 1 June 2012 from http://www.brandchannel.com/images/papers/Bankonthe brand.pdf.

9. AdAge (2009). Interview of Elon Musk.
10. *Wall Street Journal* (2011). Interview with Elon Musk, retrieved 1 June 2012 from http://www.marketwatch.com/video/asset/elon-musk-ill-put-a-man-on-mars-in-10-years/CCF1FC62-BB0D-4561-938C-DF0DEFAD15BA#!CCF1FC62-BB0D-4561-938C-DF0DEF AD15BA.
11. Tesla Motors Press Release (2011). Tesla Motors Reports First Quarter 2011 Results, retrieved 1 June 2012 from http://www.teslamotors.com/about/press/releases/tesla-motors-reports-first-quarter-2011-results.
12. Automobile Mag (2010). Tesla Extends Production Contract with Lotus, retrieved 1 June 2012 from http://rumors.automobilemag.com/tesla-extends-production-contract-with-lotus-2822.html.
13. Patent Docs (2012), Tesla Motors Inc. Patent Applications, retrieved 1 June 2012 from http://www.faqs.org/patents/assignee/tesla-motors-inc/.
14. Wall Street Pit (2010).Tesla Motors (TSLA) Receives Patent for Battery Charging Based on Cost and Life, retrieved 1 June 2012 from http://wallstreetpit.com/41880-tesla-motors-tsla-receives-patent-for-battery-charging-based-on-cost-and-life.
15. Tesla Motors website (2012). retrieved 1 June 2012 from http://shop.teslamotors.com/collections/miscellaneous.
16. Wikipedia (2012). Nissan electric vehicles, retrieved 1 June 2012 from http://en.wikipedia.org/wiki/Nissan_electric_vehicles.
17. Toyota corporate website (2012), retrieved 1 June 2012 from http: //www.toyota.com/concept-vehicles/rav4ev.html.
18. Motortrend (2011), GM September 2011 Sales Climb 20 Percent on Back of Chevrolet Cruze, Truck Sales, retrieved 1 June 2012 from http://wot.motortrend.com/gm-september-2011-sales-climb-20-percent-on-back-of-chevrolet-cruze-truck-sales-122569.html.
19. Youtube GTM TV Channel (2010). GTM TV: Elon Musk on the Model X SUV and Tesla's New Batteries, retrieved 1 June 2012 from http://www.youtube.com/watch?v= 9cfHGDoniU0& feature= player_embedded.

16

WHY BUY LUXURY? INSIGHTS FROM CONSUMER RESEARCH

Maureen Morrin

16.1 INTRODUCTION

This article reviews recent consumer research on what drives consumers to purchase (or not to purchase) luxury products. We discuss the various types of psychological processes, situational influences and individual differences that impact the decision to buy luxury goods and highlight a few gaps in the literature worthy of further investigation.

16.2 GROWING INTEREST IN LUXURY MARKETING

The luxury market is large and growing: The global retail luxury goods market was estimated at €180 billion in 2010, up 24 percent from 2006 (Mintel). One driver of this increase in sales is the growing number of middle- and upper-class consumers in rapidly expanding emerging markets such as Brazil, Russia, India and China. The rapid increase in the number of high net-worth individuals in these previously largely untapped markets has grown the market for luxury brands, bringing them within the reach of a greater number of consumers.

Perhaps not surprisingly, interest in luxury marketing is on the rise among businesses, students hoping one day to work in the industry, and academic researchers. Several luxury management and marketing programs have sprung up in recent years at universities worldwide to address growing student interest and demand (for example at Glasgow Caledonian University, New York University, Shanghai University and SKEMA). The luxury market is an interesting phenomenon to study, not least because of its apparent invulnerability to the vicissitudes of the economy. Many luxury marketers, for example, report experiencing little or no negative impact from the recent economic downturn.

Luxury marketing has attracted attention from a growing number of consumer researchers who, in recent years, have published their work in some of the top journals in the field.[1] A number of currently popular theoretical research streams have important implications for luxury marketers. Those regarding self-control,[2] hyperopia,[3] and ego-depletion[4] serve as appropriate contexts for researchers interested in conducting luxury marketing studies and will be discussed in more detail in this chapter.

16.3 DEFINING LUXURY

Several of the textbooks on luxury marketing published recently attempt to conceptualize luxury goods and services and offer advice on how to manage such brands effectively.[5] Definitions of just what constitutes a luxury product can be vague, however, and tend to vary from author to author. A useful definition has been provided by Chevalier and Mazzalovo who suggest that a luxury product must satisfy three criteria: it must have a strong artistic element, it must be the result of craftsmanship and it must have a global brand reputation.[6]

Luxury brands have traditionally been found in certain product categories, such as high-fashion clothing, jewelry, watches, perfumes, cosmetics, handbags and leather goods, wines and spirits, automobiles and hotels. Some authors have attempted to explain the reason for their existence, suggesting that they serve the necessary purpose of recreating social stratification in modern democratic societies, because individuals fundamentally need to know their "place in society".[7] The demand for luxury goods and their function in helping to satisfy this need appears to have existed since at least the Middle Ages. As Freedman states, "However much moralists and advocates of simple and sensible living complain, the flaunting of fashionable and expensive goods is a constant social fact. What changes is the nature of such goods. What provides status and pleasure in one historical period may not carry over into the next... Spices in the Middle Ages were marks of status and success, but they occupy this position no longer, and have not for several centuries."[8]

More recently, marketers have begun to offer more affordable luxury products in order to appeal to an even wider audience. So-called masstige or mass-prestige products are conceived of as luxury brands for the masses, and many have gained widespread acceptance in markets such as Europe and North America. Masstige products are typically offered in categories that do not require large out-of-pocket expenditures, thus making them available to consumers at nearly every socioeconomic level. The availability of masstige offerings has grown to the extent that now even mundane products such as coffee (Starbucks) and quick-serve sandwiches (Panera Bread) offer customers the chance to purchase what many consider to be a luxury product or small indulgence. A similar concept, that of "new luxury" has been coined to refer to products that are of higher quality than most other competitors within a category, but that are not so expensive as to be out of the reach of middle- and upper-middle-class consumers, many of whom have been observed to be trading up to such products.[9] Examples of new luxury brands include Belvedere vodka, Nutro pet food, Mercedes-Benz C-class cars and Kiehl's skin cream. Thus, the concept of just what consitutes a luxury brand from a marketer's point of view would appear to be evolving.

Research suggests, however, that consumers themselves seem to understand what luxury products are, and how they differ from more utilitarian or value brands. Neurological studies have shown that luxury brands activate different areas of the brain compared to value brands.[10] It has also been shown that exposure to logos for brands such as Mercedes-Benz and Porsche tend to activate areas of the brain that are associated with self-reflection and self-relevant processing. More utilitarian brands such as Toyota and Opel, in contrast, activate an area of the brain associated with moral judgment and cognitive control.[11] This stream of research hints at the feelings of guilt that can accompany luxury purchases, which we discuss in more detail below.

16.4 HEDONIC PURCHASE MOTIVATIONS

16.4.1 Sensory and aesthetic pleasure from luxury brands

Clearly, one reason why consumers buy luxury products is simply for the hedonic or sensory pleasure they provide. In contrast to utilitarian products that perform a practical task or fill a basic need, hedonic products provide sensory pleasure, fantasy or fun.[12] Luxury scarves handmade from finest silk or luxury handbags hand-sewn from supple leather provide sensory and aesthetic pleasure in the form of sight, touch and smell. Similar hedonic benefits can motivate the purchase of luxury services as well, such as first-class airline travel, dining experiences at five-star restaurants and high-end spa vacations.

Research suggests that luxury brands, as distinct from utilitarian or value brands, confer certain marketplace advantages to the marketers of such brands. Indeed, luxury brands are more extendable to other product categories than are value-based brands, due to their greater promise of pleasure.[13] The broader acceptance of luxury brand extensions is driven by the brands' hedonic potential, that is, the fact that they are fun, thrilling and delightful.

Interestingly, some research suggests that consumers may overestimate the amount of pleasure or happiness that products will bring them. Although consumers predict that driving a more valuable and luxurious car will lead to more enjoyment, for example, one empirical analysis of car drivers' actual day-to-day experiences found no relationship between the level of enjoyment of driving and car value.[14] The general inaccuracy of individuals' efforts at predicting what will make them happy in the future, known as affective forecasting, is well established.[15] Because humans adapt so quickly to changes in their own circumstances, product acquisitions typically do not bring about permanent increases in satisfaction or happiness levels. Further research, however, is needed in this area, as few studies have focused specifically on the luxury market.

16.4.2 With pleasure comes guilt

It is well established that pleasure-based, indulgent consumption can generate mixed emotions in some consumers, such as feelings of guilt along with the feelings of pleasure.[16] For many consumers, buying and displaying luxury goods may be considered inegalitarian, immoral or unethical, despite the fact that some philosophers offer an economic justification for the selling and buying of luxury goods – suggesting that consumer greed and product acquisition efforts enhance the efficiency of the marketplace – echoing Adam Smith's notion of the "invisible hand".[17] Research shows that the link between sensory pleasure from luxury purchases and feelings of guilt is especially true of more prudent buyers as compared to more impulsive buyers.[18] One reason is that many religious and social traditions have historically frowned upon the pursuit of personal sensory pleasure.[19]

16.4.3 Aversion to indulgence

To avoid such feelings of guilt, some consumers exhibit behavior that demonstrates a chronic tendency to underindulge. A personality trait known as hyperopia refers to an individual's chronic aversion to indulgence.[20] A six-item scale has been developed to measure this trait. The scale includes items such as "I rarely enjoy the luxuries life has to offer" and "It's hard for me to make myself indulge". Hyperoptic consumers tend to view all luxury products as indulgent, and exhibit considerably lower preference levels for them. Interestingly, a key distinguishing aspect of hyperoptic consumers' psychological reaction to their behavior is lower levels of happiness and feelings of regret due to perceptions of having missed out on many of life's pleasures.[21] Therefore, encouraging such consumers to focus on the longer-term benefits of indulgence, such as the ability to mitigate such feelings of regret, may help motivate them to purchase luxury goods.[22]

16.4.4 Guilt laundering strategies

An alternative strategy for the luxury marketer could be to attempt to compensate for any guilt induced by luxury purchases. To offset the guilt associated with luxury products, marketers could bundle a guilt-inducing product with one that essentially "launders" part of the guilt. For example, a pleasure-driven purchase that is accompanied by a donation to charity may sufficiently offset the feelings of guilt to result in product purchase. Research in this vein suggests that cause-related marketing efforts will be more effective when tied to purchases that ordinarily induce guilt, such as luxury products, than to those that do not, such as utilitarian products.[23] Thus, we would expect that if a marketer offered to make a donation to UNICEF with product purchase, such an effort would be more effective if tied to a purchase of decadent chocolates, as compared to a healthy fruit salad. Similarly, for consumers who experience guilt when contemplating luxury brand purchases, an $X donation to charity made by the luxury marketer may be more effective at encouraging purchase than an equivalent sized price discount on the luxury good.

16.4.5 Frugality

Other research characterizes consumers on a continuous scale from being a tightwad to being a spendthrift. Tightwads are consumers who anticipate considerable psychological pain from indulging by spending money and thus tend to underspend. Spendthrifts, in contrast, are those who experience very little pain of paying and often have difficulty controlling their spending.[24] A scale that involves assessing one's spending style via short scenario-analysis has been developed to measure this personality trait.[25] One item states, "Some people have trouble limiting their spending: they often spend money – for example on clothes, meals, vacations, phone calls – when they would do better not to. Other people have trouble spending money. Perhaps because spending money makes them anxious, they often do not spend money on things they should spend it on. How well does the first description fit you? That is, do you have trouble limiting your spending? (from

1 = never to 5 = always). How well does the second description fit you? That is, do you have trouble spending money? (same scale)."[26] Certain strategies might be effective at reducing the pain of paying for tightwads, such as the use of credit cards rather than cash.[27]

16.4.6 Ego-depletion

Because resisting a luxury purchase requires the use of self-control resources, and because research shows that such mental resources are finite, consumers will be more likely to succumb to the desire to purchase luxury goods when they have exhausted such resources, that is, when they are "ego depleted".[28] Ego-depletion is caused by having just engaged in self-control behavior (for example, having resisted eating a tempting but unhealthy food item), or having engaged in activities requiring significant cognitive effort (for example, having made numerous prior choices).[29] Thus, just as studies have shown that consumers are more likely to purchase impulse items when they are ego-depleted,[30] it can be expected that consumers will also be more likely to purchase luxury products when ego-depleted.

16.5 SOCIAL PURCHASE MOTIVATIONS

It has long been recognized that possessions can signal aspects of one's identity, including those related to wealth, power and social status.[31] In today's marketplace, brands help individuals construct their self-concepts[32] – especially brands that are highly symbolic.[33] Brands allow consumers to: (a) achieve their self-identity goals, and (b) signal to others their actual or desired identities.[34] Thus, a consumer could buy a Toyota Prius in order to reduce their carbon footprint, supporting their belief or desire to be an environmentally conscious individual. Or, a consumer could buy a Toyota Prius in order to communicate to others that one is environmentally conscious. Thus, brands can be used to achieve a desired self or to communicate it to others, and this is especially true of luxury brands.

16.5.1 Signaling power, status, and wealth via luxury brands

It has long been known that there is a natural tendency to engage in social comparison to evaluate one's own standing in society.[35] Research shows that whether or not product acquisition makes consumers happy is highly dependent on what others around them have acquired: "People look to external reference information, such as what others acquire, to judge the merit of their own acquisitions."[36] Thus, we look to others to see how we ourselves are doing, in terms of relative wealth, power, status and so on. If such comparisons result in the conclusion that one is relatively powerless, one may be motivated to elevate one's standing via product purchases that can be displayed to others. The notion of conspicuous consumption has existed for centuries,[37] and refers to consumer expenditures on products for the purpose of displaying one's wealth and thus signaling one's status in society.

In a recent study investigating reasons why women buy luxury fashion brands, participants were asked to bring in 10–12 pictures of what "high fashion" meant to them.[38] Projective techniques were applied to the pictures, revealing that women perceive luxury fashion as timeless rather than trendy, as a form of "wearable art," and, importantly, as having transformative power – with high fashion brands, such as Louboutin high heels, a Gucci handbag, or a Bulgari ring, having the capacity to make the wearer feel more attractive and more powerful.

Recent research shows that feelings of powerlessness increase consumers' desire for products that confer social status, as a compensatory mechanism.[39] Powerlessness is an aversive state that individuals are motivated to eradicate. These researchers made feelings of power or powerlessness salient by asking study participants to recall an incident where they either had power over another person or another person had power over them. They found that making salient feelings of powerlessness increased the amount consumers were willing to pay for products strongly associated with status (such as cuff links, an executive pen, a briefcase, a fur coat or a silk tie), but not for products weakly associated with status (such as a ballpoint pen, a sofa, a dryer or a washer).

Reading about other successful individuals who are perceived to be similar to oneself also tends to increase preference for luxury goods.[40] Research suggests that product choices are more likely to be used to bolster one's self-image after it has been *threatened,* that is, when one's confidence in who one is has been shaken.[41] During economic recessions, it is therefore possible that threats to consumers' self-views regarding their wealth or status in society may motivate even *greater* luxury purchasing behavior. This need may explain why luxury marketers appear to be largely immune to the deleterious effects of economic downturns. It may also explain the results of a recent analysis of luxury handbag logos before and after the start of the 2008 recession. The study found that logos for luxury brands such as Louis Vuitton and Gucci were *more,* not less, prominently displayed on such items during the recession.[42] Luxury brands of handbags were observed to have altered their product lines to offer higher-priced bags with more prominently displayed logos rather than to have "toned down" their offerings during the downturn.

16.5.2 Eco fashion

Intuition might suggest that consumer purchases of environmentally friendly products, such as auto hybrids like the Toyota Prius, are driven by motivations opposite in nature to those driving luxury purchases. However, research suggests that "green" purchases are often driven by a similar set of motives, namely those related to signaling one's social status to others. Since purchasing pro-environmental products typically involves paying more and obtaining poorer performing products, engaging in such behavior acts as a signal to others regarding one's capacity to do so, in terms of excess resources. Thus, buying green can communicate both one's superior wealth and one's prosocial character.[43] Furthermore, research shows that activating a consumer's status motives increases the likelihood of choosing an environmentally friendly versus luxury brand – especially when purchased in public.[44] Understanding the motivations behind green consumption behavior[45] may have important implications for marketers of luxury brands, who might consider incorporating eco-friendly attributes into their offerings.

16.5.3 Segmenting the luxury market

Clearly, there exists a continuum along which luxury buyers lie in terms of the degree to which they are motivated to purchase luxury brands to signal to others in society. Indeed, one taxonomy of luxury buyers makes a distinction in their status between "patricians", who have a lower need for status, and "parvenus", who have strong motivations to dissociate themselves from the less affluent in society.[46] Patricians prefer more expensive but "quieter" handbags, that is, those with less-prominent logos. Parvenus, in contrast, prefer less-expensive but "louder" handbags with more-prominent brand logos.

Another research team similarly notes a bifurcation of the luxury market. They find that less-conspicuous consumption involving subtler brand signaling, such as through smaller or nonexistent brand logos, is preferred by consumers with more "cultural capital" – described as "insiders who have the necessary connoisseurship to decode their meaning".[47] This may explain why the most-expensive luxury goods often have no external markings to indicate brand origin. The public display of such items holds value for the wearer because other insiders will recognize the items' source.

16.5.4 Personality traits

Certain types of consumers may derive more or fewer psychological benefits from luxury products. A personality trait scale has been developed to measure the degree to which a consumer is susceptible to interpersonal influence, defined as the need to identify with or enhance one's self-image in the eyes of others by buying and using products and brands.[48] Examples of items in this scale are, "To make sure I buy the right product or brand, I often observe what others are buying and using" and "I rarely purchase the latest fashion styles until I am sure my friends approve of them." Those who score high on this trait tend to exhibit low self-esteem and low self-confidence. To the extent that luxury brands can confer social acceptance, individuals who score high on this trait will likely prefer such brands, especially if the logos are prominently displayed.

Consumers with interdependent (versus independent) self-concepts have weaker self-differentiation goals[49] and thus may also be more motivated to purchase luxury brands for social signaling reasons. Further, it may be that in societies with stronger interdependent cultures (e.g., in the East) luxury purchases are driven more by the desire to fit in and conform, whereas in societies with stronger independent cultures (e.g., in the West) luxury purchases are driven more by the desire to stand out. If this were the case, we might find a greater [lesser] willingness to purchase newer luxury brands that have not yet attained universal awareness levels where independent [interdependent] values dominate the cultural landscape. For example, well-established luxury brands with the highest levels of awareness, such as Chanel, Gucci and Prada, may be more highly valued in Eastern cultures, whereas newer and less-established luxury brands, such as Eterniti, a new niche luxury brand of automobiles from England, or Bardessono, a high-end niche hotel in Napa valley, might be more highly valued in Western cultures. The relative premium that consumers are willing to pay for established versus newer luxury brands would provide evidence in this regard.

16.5.5 Trade-ins

Research has found that when consumers trade-in a product and purchase a new product, at a new-car dealership, for example, they seem to be more concerned about getting a good trade-in deal than by the price they pay for the new product.[50] Consequently, they may be willing to pay more for the new product. This research offers an intriguing notion for luxury marketers, who may want to offer a trade-in policy to encourage consumers to trade up to higher priced products in their product lines (the older trade-ins could then be marketed separately). The availability of previously owned luxury products might also offset the appeal of counterfeit versions, due to a wider price range that appeals to more segments of the consumer population.

16.5.6 Counterfeits

Interesting research is emerging on the topic of luxury brand counterfeit products and why consumers knowingly purchase them. Counterfeit luxury products are lower-priced, lower-quality illegal replicas that may account for as much as $600 billion in value.[51] What drives the demand for counterfeit goods? Research supports the notion that consumers buy brands that are congruent with their actual or desired self-concept.[52] Consumers build their personal identities in part by consuming brands used by aspirational reference groups.[53] Research also shows that when consumers purchase products for socially motivated reasons, such as to signal their social status (for example, when they agree that "Luxury brands help me fit into important social situations"), rather than to express their values to others (for example, when they agree that "Luxury brands help me express myself"),[54] they are more likely to knowingly purchase counterfeit luxury products, and will do so without feeling very guilty about it. Exposure to counterfeit luxury products among socially motivated purchasers also reduces their preference for the "real thing" since a lower-priced alternative (the counterfeit) serves the purpose equally well. Counterfeit products are not equally effective for value-expressive purchasers however. Interestingly, this research found that prominently displayed luxury brand logos help socially motivated consumers achieve their goals. For this reason, luxury brand manufacturers may want to consider making their logos and other obvious stylistic elements *less* prominent to mitigate the effectiveness of counterfeit offerings. Luxury brands may also want to emphasize the hedonic or value-expressive benefits of their products in their advertising rather than the social-adjustive benefits.[55]

16.6 FUTURE RESEARCH

According to Mintel, from 2006 to 2010, the luxury markets in Asia-Pacific and the Middle East/Africa grew about three times as fast as those of Europe and the Americas. Whereas Europe has historically accounted for the majority of world's sales of luxury goods (38% in 2006), the emerging market regions now account for an equivalent share of the luxury goods market (35% each).[56] Yet most of the research on luxury product purchase motivations continues to be conducted in Western (especially North American) cultural settings. Clearly, there is a need to understand better the motivations of segments of markets where luxury sales are growing fastest – especially the Asia-Pacific region.

Another area that has been largely under-researched is that of on-line luxury marketing.[57] Luxury marketers will need to evolve to more electronic forms of both communication and sales and further research on electronic and mobile forms of communication is needed in the domain of luxury products.

NOTES

1. For Example: Hagtvedt, H. and Patrick, V. M. (2009). The broad embrace of luxury: Hedonic potential as a driver of brand extendability, *Journal of Consumer Psychology*, 19, 608–618. Han, Y. J., Nunes, J. C. and Dreze, X. (2010), Signaling status with luxury goods: The role of brand prominence, *Journal of Marketing*, 74(July), 15–30. Mandel, N., Petrova, P. K. and Cialdini, R. B. (2006). Images of success and the preference for luxury brands, *Journal of Consumer Psychology*, 16(1), 57–69. Nunes, J., Dreze, X. and Han, Y. J. (2011). Conspicuous consumption in a recession: Toning it down or turning it up? *Journal of Consumer Psychology*, 21, 199–205. Schwarz, N. and Xu, J. (2011), Why don't we learn from poor choices? The consistency of expectation, choice, and memory clouds the lessons of experience, *Journal of Consumer Psychology*, 21, 142–145. Venkatesh, A., Joy, A., Sherry, J. F. and Deschenes, J. (2010). The aesthetics of luxury fashion, body and identity formation, *Journal of Consumer Psychology*, 20, 459–470.
2. Kivetz, R. and Simonson, I. (2002). Self-control for the righteous: Toward a theory of precommitment to indulgence, *Journal of Consumer Research*, 29(September), 199–217.
3. Kivetz, R. and Keinen, A. (2006). Repenting hyperopia: An analysis of self-control regrets, *Journal of Consumer Research*, 33(September), 273–282.

4. Baumeister, R., Bratslavsky, E., Muraven, M. and Tice, D. M. (1998), Ego depletion: Is the active self a limited resource? *Journal of Personality & Social Psychology*, 74(5), 1252–1265.
5. See Chevalier, M. and Mazzalovo, G. (2008), *Luxury Brand Management: A World of Privilege,* Singapore: John Wiley & Sons; Kapferer, J. N. and Bastien, V. (2009), *The Luxury Strategy: Break the Rules of Marketing to Build Luxury Brands,* London: Kogan Page Limited; Okonkwo, Uche (2010), *Luxury Online: Styles, Systems, Strategies*. London: Palgrave Macmillan; Silverstein, M. J. and Fiske, N. (2008), *Trading Up: Why Consumers Want New Luxury Goods – and How Companies Create Them.* Boston, MA: Boston Consulting Group.
6. Chevalier, M. and Mazzalovo, G. (2008). *Luxury Brand Management: A World of Privilege.* Singapore: John Wiley & Sons, p. xi.
7. Kapferer, J. N. and Bastien, V. (2009), *The Luxury Strategy: Break the Rules of Marketing to Build Luxury Brands.* London: Kogan Page Limited, p. 18.
8. Freedman, P. (2008). *Out of the East: Spices and the Medieval Imagination.* New Haven, CT: Yale University Press, p. 7.
9. Silverstein, M. J. and Fiske, N. (2008). *Trading Up: Why Consumers Want New Luxury Goods – and How Companies Create Them.* Boston, MA: Boston Consulting Group.
10. Schaefer, M. and Rotte, M. (2007). Thinking on luxury or pragmatic brand products: Brain responses to different categories of culturally based brands. *Brain Research*, 1165, 98–104.
11. Also see: Lin, C. H., Tuan, H. P. and Chiu, Y. C. (2010). Medial frontal activity in brand-loyal consumers: A behavior and near-infrared ray study. *Journal of Neuroscience, Psychology, and Economics*, 3(2), 59–73.
12. Hirschman, E. and Holbrook, M. (1982). Hedonic consumption: Emerging concepts, methods, and propositions. *Journal of Marketing*, 46(Summer), 92–101.
13. Hagtvedt, H. and Patrick, V. M. (2009), The broad embrace of luxury: Hedonic potential as a driver of brand extendability. *Journal of Consumer Psychology*, 19, 608–618.
14. Schwarz, N. and Xu, J. (2011), Why don't we learn from poor choices? The consistency of expectation, choice, and memory

clouds the lessons of experience. *Journal of Consumer Psychology,* 21, 142–145.

15. Gilbert, D. (2005). *Stumbling on Happiness.* New York: Vintage Books.
16. Ramanathan, S. and Williams, P. (2007), Immediate and delayed emotional consequences of indulgence: The moderating influence of personality type on mixed emotions. *Journal of Consumer Research,* 34(August), 212–223.
17. Hilton, M. (2004). The legacy of luxury. *Journal of Consumer Culture,* 4(1), 101–123.
18. Ramanathan, S. and Williams, P. (2007). Immediate and delayed emotional consequences of indulgence: The moderating influence of personality type on mixed émotions. *Journal of Consumer Research,* 34(August), 212–223.
19. Strahilevitz, M. and Myers, J. G. (1998). Donations to charity as purchase incentives: How well they work may depend on what you are trying to sell. *Journal of Consumer Research,* 24(March), 434–446.
20. Kivetz, R. and Simonson, I. (2002). Self-control for the righteous: Toward a theory of precommitment to indulgence. *Journal of Consumer Research,* 29(September), 199–217.
21. Kivetz, R. and Keinen, A. (2006). Repenting hyperopia: An analysis of self-control regrets. *Journal of Consumer Research,* 33(September), 273–282.
22. Haws, K. L. and Poynor, C. (2008). Seize the day! Encouraging indulgence for the hyperopic consumer. *Journal of Consumer Research,* 35 (December), 680–691.
23. Strahilevitz, M. and Myers, J. G. (1998). Donations to charity as purchase incentives: How well they work may depend on what you are trying to sell. *Journal of Consumer Research,* 24(March), 434–446.
24. Rick, S. I., Cryder, C. E., and Loewenstein, G. (2008), Tightwads and spendthrifts. *Journal of Consumer Research,* 34(April), 767–782.
25. Rick, S. I., Cryder, C. E. and Loewenstein, G. (2008), Tightwads and spendthrifts. *Journal of Consumer Research,* 34(April), 767–782.
26. Rick, S. I., Cryder, C. E. and Loewenstein, G. (2008), Tightwads and spendthrifts. *Journal of Consumer Research,* 34(April), 767–782, p. 780.

27. Thomas, M., Desai, K. K, and Seenivasan, S. (forthcoming). How credit card payments increase unhealthy food purchases: Visceral regulation of vices. *Journal of Consumer Research.*
28. Baumeister, R., Bratslavsky, E., Muraven, M. and Tice, D. M. (1998), Ego déplétion: Is the active self a limited resource? *Journal of Personality & Social Psychology*, 74(5), 1252–1265.
29. Pocheptsova, A., Amir, O., Dhar, R. and Baumeister, R. F. (2009), Deciding without resources: Resource déplétion and choice in context. *Journal of Marketing Research*, XLVI(June), 344–355.
30. Vohs, K. (2007). Spent resources: Self-regulatory resource availability affects impulse buying. *Journal of Consumer Research*, 33(March), 537–547.
31. Berger, J. and Ward, M. (2010). Subtle signals of inconspicuous consumption. *Journal of Consumer Research*, 37(4), 555–569.
32. Belk, R. W. (1988). Possessions and the extende self. *Journal of Consumer Research*, 15(September), 139–168.
33. Escalas, J. E. and Bettman, J. R. (2005). Self-construal, reference groups, and brand meaning. *Journal of Consumer Research*, 32 (December), 378–389.
34. Kirmani, A. (2009). The self and the brand. *Journal of Consumer Psychology*, 19, 271–275.
35. Festinger, L. (1957). A theory of social comparison processes. *Human Relations*, 7, 117–140.
36. Hsee, C. K., Yang, Y., Li, N. and Shen, L. (2009). Wealth, warmth, and well-being: Whether happiness is relative or absolute depends on whether it is about money, acquisition, or consumption. *Journal of Marketing Research*, XLVI (June), 396–409.
37. Veblen, T. (1899/2009). *The Theory of the Leisure Class.* Oxford: Oxford University Press.
38. Venkatesh, A., Joy, A., Sherry, J. F. and Deschenes, J. (2010), The aesthetics of luxury fashion, body and identity formation. *Journal of Consumer Psychology*, 20, 459–470.
39. Rucker, D. D. and Galinsky, A. D. (2008), Desire to acquire: Powerlessness and compensatory consumption. *Journal of Consumer Research*, 35(August), 257–267.
40. Mandel, N., Petrova, P. K. and Cialdini, R. B. (2006). Images of success and the preference for luxury brands. *Journal of Consumer Psychology*, 16(1), 57–69.

41. Gao, L., Wheeler, S. C. and Shiv, B. (2009), The "shaken self": Product choices as a means of restoring self-view confidence. *Journal of Consumer Research*, 36(June), 29–38. White, K. and Argo, J. J. (2009), Social identity threat and consumer préférences. *Journal of Consumer Psychology*, 19, 313–325.
42. Nunes, J., Dreze, X. and Han, Y .J. (2011). Conspicuous consumption in a recession: Toning it down or turning it up? *Journal of Consumer Psychology*, 21, 199–205.
43. Griskevicius, V., Tybur, J.M. and Van den Bergh, B. (2010). Going green to be seen: Status, reputation and conspicuous conservation. Interpersonal Relations and Group Processes. *Journal of Personality and Social Psychology*, 98(3), 392–404.
44. Griskevicius, V., Tybur, J. M. and Van den Bergh, B. (2010). Going green to be seen: Status, reputation, and conspicuous conservation. Interpersonal Relations and Group Processes. *Journal of Personality and Social Psychology*, 98(3), 392–404.
45. Beard, N. D. (2008). The branding of ethical fashion and the consumer: A luxury niche or mass-market reality? *Fashion Theory*, 12(4), 447–468.
46. Han, Y. J., Nunes, J. C. and Dreze, X. (2010). Signaling status with luxury goods: The rôle of brand prominence. *Journal of Marketing*, 74(July), 15–30.
47. Berger, J. and Ward, M. (2010). Subtle signals of inconspicuous consumption. *Journal of Consumer Research*, 37(4), 555–569.
48. Bearden, W. O., Netemeyer, R. G. and Teel, J. E. (1998). Measurement of consumer susceptibility to interpersonal influence. *Journal of Consumer Research*, 15(March), 473–481.
49. Escalas, J. E. and Bettman, J. R. (2005). Self-construal, reference groups, and brand meaning. *Journal of Consumer Research*, 32(December), 378–389.
50. Zhu, R., Chen, X. and Dasgupta, S. (2009). Can trade-ins hurt you? Exploring the effect of a trade-in on consumers' willingness to pay for a new product. *Journal of Marketing Research*, XLV(April), 159–170.
51. Wilcox, K., Kim, H. M. and Sen, S. (2009). Why do consumers buy counterfeit luxury brands? *Journal of Marketing Research*, XLVI(April), 247–259.
52. Belk, R. W. (1988). Possessions and the extende self. *Journal of Consumer Research*, 15(September), 139–168.

53. Escalas, J. E. and Bettman, J. R. (2005). Self-construal, reference groups, and brand meaning. *Journal of Consumer Research*, 32(December), 378–389.
54. Wilcox, K., Kim, H. M. and Sen, S. (2009). Why do consumers buy counterfeit luxury brands? *Journal of Marketing Research*, XLVI(April), 247–259, p. 251.
55. Wilcox, K., Kim, H. M. and Sen, S. (2009). Why do consumers buy counterfeit luxury brands? *Journal of Marketing Research*, XLVI(April), 247–259.
56. Mintel report as of August 2011.
57. Okonkwo, Uche (2010). *Luxury Online: Styles, Systems, Strategies*. London: Palgrave Macmillan.

17

ELIE SAAB: STRATEGIC PRESENCE IN THE DIGITAL LUXURY SPACE

Rasa Stankeviciute

17.1 INTRODUCTION

ELIE SAAB made a decision to go online based on a belief that this was the future way of communicating with its supporters. Once the brand decided to get involved in web marketing, it did not hesitate to communicate its Haute Couture line alongside the Ready-to-Wear line online. The brand has successfully differentiated the Haute Couture and the Ready-to-Wear lines without diluting the couture-brand status. In addition, although ELIE SAAB has never used any online advertising, its web marketing, which runs counter to many other luxury brands' strategies, has brought fascinating results in just one year.

Due to the brand's relatively short online life, its online presence must and will be studied further in the years to come. This chapter will analyze ELIE SAAB strategies and achievements thus far.

17.2 HISTORY

Elie Saab opened his first workshop in Beirut at the age of 18, where he started creating evening and wedding gowns for royalty and special clients. Today, 30 years later, the brand is still very designer-oriented and Elie Saab's designs are made up by seamstresses who have been working in the atelier since the beginning. It is their talent, attention to the tiniest detail, perfectionism and passion for their work that the designer and the brand value the most.

In 2006 ELIE SAAB was nominated to become a correspondent member of *Chambre Syndicale de la Haute Couture*. Being a member of *Chambre Syndicale de la Haute Couture* adheres the brand to strict rules and conditions, laid down by the *Chambre Syndicale* and protected by the French government, one of which is to show Haute Couture collections twice a year.[1] For the Fall Winter 2012–2013 season the official schedule of the Haute Couture shows included only five correspondent members: ELIE SAAB, Valentino, Giorgio Armani Privé, Versace and Maison Martin Margiela.

Starting out as a couture brand, today ELIE SAAB offers, in addition to its Haute Couture gowns, a luxurious Ready-to-Wear line and an Accessories collection. One of the brand's latest additions to the family is ELIE SAAB fragrance: the first ELIE SAAB eau de parfum "Le Parfum" was launched in 2011, followed by the launch of eau de toilette in 2012.

An ELIE SAAB woman is strong and self-confident – "a heroine of her own life, a modern-day princess". Someone who values the brand's creations, be they a Ready-to-Wear piece, or a Haute Couture gown, because of their quality and ability to define the radiant femininity without ever "losing the magic". Many actresses, musicians and royal-family members are the loyal clients of the brand and fans of the exclusive Elie Saab's creations.

17.3 GOING ONLINE

Luxury brands have long-debated how to integrate the Internet – this powerful and intrusive channel of mass communication – into the intimacy of an exclusive luxury brand's strategy.[2] According to Suzy Menkes, the big fashion brands were used to having the control of everything in their hands, from what can be said about the brand to where the advertisement has to be placed; therefore, now when, with the help of social media every consumer has the ability to say something negative about the brand and attain thousands of comments that agree with what was said, the managers have become frightened.[3] Not surprisingly, with the increasing number of Internet users and with social media booming, luxury brand managers today are concerned about how to properly communicate their brands online without diluting the luxury brand image and status.

ELIE SAAB, in my opinion, could be a role model of how carefully implemented online marketing strategies and proper online communication can not only do no harm to the couture brand's image, but can also increase people's overall interest in the brand's universe. I have come to this recommendation after carefully studying the first year of ELIE SAAB's online presence. Two observations can be made. Firstly, the brand seems to have successfully differentiated the separate lines online to avoid confusing consumers and without diluting the couture brand status. Secondly, in less than a year and without any online advertising, ELIE SAAB has managed to successfully attract and maintain a constantly growing online audience on the official website, as well as on the social media platforms (see Figures 17.1 and 17.2). Importantly, both of these goals have been reached while maintaining ELIE SAAB qualities and values.

The number of Internet users worldwide has grown by 12–19 percent yearly from 2002, reaching over two billion users globally in 2011.[4] This makes the World Wide Web today an unavoidable tool to reach consumers. However, as the key element for luxury brands is to avoid taking actions that may harm the equity of a brand

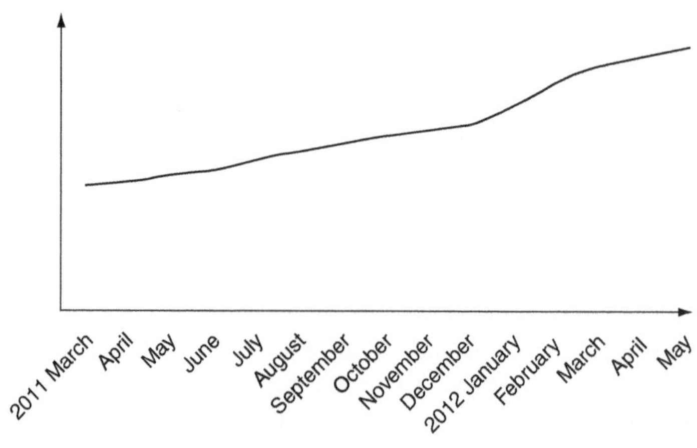

FIGURE 17.1 **The growth of ELIE SAAB Facebook fans-base**

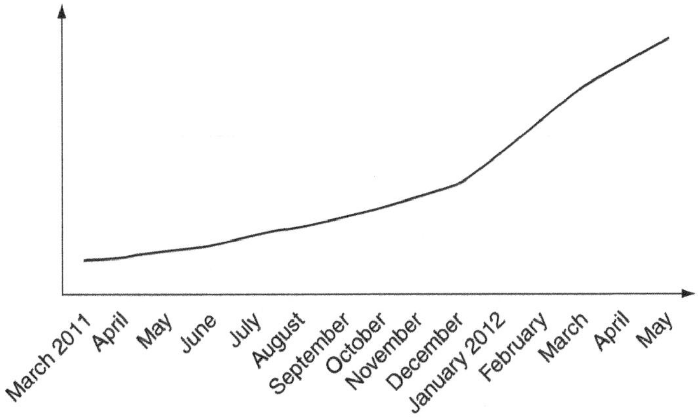

FIGURE 17.2 **The growth of ELIE SAAB Twitter followers-base**

with a well-established name for luxury,[5] serious considerations and careful preparation should be taken into account prior to any online act.

Jonas and Betina Hoffmann[6] in the book *Luxury Strategy in Action* suggest that the driving forces of technology and globalization are likely to redefine luxury innovation and creation in the future. Since the beginning of its online presence ELIE SAAB has had a strong faith in the importance of innovation in the luxury industry. The brand's decision to go online was based on the belief that this was the future way of communication and interaction with the brand's supporters. Moreover, ELIE SAAB had a clear vision of an innovative way of communicating the brand's values to their online audience. After a careful analysis I suggest that ELIE SAAB's creation and implementation of its online marketing strategies equate to the development of luxury innovation. Four steps of a PIER framework of luxury innovation, presented by the Jonas and Betina Hoffmann, are path, insight, execution excellence and rareness of experience.[7] All the steps of a PIER framework of luxury innovation can be seen in ELIE SAAB's web marketing.

The digital world surrounding ELIE SAAB and the developments of the brand's online platforms are a solid base for the future online establishments, be they an online selling platform, or any other challenge. The brand has not only noticed the lack of innovative decisions in portraying the luxury brands online and decided to fill this gap, but it has also decided to become a trendsetter in the field. I would like to take high-quality branded videos showing ELIE SAAB as cutting-edge, as one of many possible examples. ELIE SAAB currently co-operates with professionals in the field to create the short movies, but after realizing the need to be able to create the content more often and to ensure even higher quality of the content, the brand has planned to build an internal department dedicated solely to this purpose. You will read about the exclusive experience provided by ELIE SAAB to its online followers further in this chapter.

ELIE SAAB has always been willing to respond to attention and support received. Therefore, when growing numbers of visitors to the old website and the then discrete social media platforms of the brand showed people's desire to know more about the brand's world, this desire was recognized by ELIE SAAB. "We saw how the fan base was built up without us being active on social-media platforms and we felt that we had to give our attention to the fans in return. We felt we needed to exceed people's expectations online as we do in real world", says Elie Saab Jr, the eldest of three sons of Elie Saab, who joined the company in 2010 and has mainly concentrated on digital marketing since. Let us take the brand's decision to get involved in the social network Facebook to illustrate this. The growing numbers of unofficial fan-pages of ELIE SAAB on the social network led to the creation of its official Facebook page, initially as a way of reserving the name. From 2009, the brand saw its Facebook fan-base grow, even though it contributed a relatively small amount of information to the page in comparison to the present contribution. In response to this evident interest, ELIE SAAB re-launched its official website (www.eliesaab.com) in 2011 and actively started to communicate the brand on its social-media platforms. The number of people who liked the brand's official Facebook page more than doubled immediately after the re-launch, compared to the same time in 2010.

The year 2011 also saw the launch of the first ELIE SAAB fragrance "Le Parfum". The perfume, readily accessible to a broad consumer base, as well as the plans to launch an online store must obviously have contributed toward the brand's decision to become present online.

17.4 PORTRAYING THE BRAND'S UNIVERSE ONLINE

17.4.1 Differentiating the different lines online

The brand's website is the crucial element of the online marketing strategy. It is the central marketing tool to create an emotional relationship with potential customers;[8] therefore, the website's appearance and functionality contribute considerably to the success of the brand's online marketing.

On the ELIE SAAB website I notice the brand's decision to portray its digital universe just as it is in real life; the website is simple, clean, but at the same time elegant, sophisticated and magical in ELIE SAAB's well-known special way.

Visitors to the ELIE SAAB homepage must have noticed the possibility to zoom in on an outfit to see the tiniest detail of the dress. In fact, portraying the craftsmanship that the brand is known for and showing every single detail of the creation have been the main objectives of the newly designed website since it was launched in 2011.

Take, for example, the Haute Couture section. This section of the site confirms that luxury is an art by providing exclusive artistic material that leaves no one unmoved. With each look the brand tries to give its website visitors an exclusive preview of the dress. Everything from the intriguing close-up images of the dress details to the drawn sketches taken straight from the atelier and from the photographs of models wearing the ELIE SAAB dresses backstage to the high-definition videos has been carefully planned and created for the ELIE SAAB website. This experience provided to the visitors of the site corresponds to a story-telling principle, which enchains people's attention. The videos filmed, the photographs taken or the images fashioned that everyone sees on the site have been specially made to appear there.

ELIE SAAB makes sure that all the lines (Haute Couture, Ready-to-Wear, Accessories, Le Parfum) remain distinguishable. The presentation of the differentiated lines on the website corresponds to the esthetics of the same lines in real life. While the Haute Couture section makes one feel part of a fairy tale, the Ready-to-Wear section lets the visitor feel as if she was in the ELIE SAAB boutique, except, in the virtual world. The Ready-to-Wear and Accessories sections are interconnected. When browsing the Ready-to-Wear section, one is proposed a matching accessory and vice versa. Easy navigation of the site lets you jump between those two sections in a moment. Meanwhile, the Haute Couture universe is kept clearly separate.

17.4.2 The four Es: Experience, exclusivity, engagement, emotion

Luxury can be described as something exquisite, unique and rare; it is a combination of pleasure and aspiration; it represents a dream and gives you prestige.[9] Therefore, the well-known and long-used four Ps of the traditional marketing mix take second place when we deal with luxury brands. To be successful, luxury marketing requires "substantially different considerations, specifically the four Es: experience, exclusivity, engagement and emotion".[10] Although they may be viewed as four separate essentials of luxury marketing, the four Es of digital marketing for luxury brands are interconnected. I would describe them in this way: an indelible experience of exclusivity creates consumers' engagement and provides the emotion. The emotion is the key element of luxury marketing, as the luxury clientele, capable of buying anything, looks for the emotion when considering the brand.

With its online presence, ELIE SAAB's target segment is no longer limited to the existing or potential clients of the Haute Couture or the Ready-to-Wear lines. Now, the brand targets every woman with its first fragrance "Le Parfum", which gives everyone the possibility to feel that "exceptional moment", promised by ELIE SAAB, through the bottle of perfume. Still, as ELIE SAAB is first and foremost a Haute Couture brand, it remains faithful to the fundamentals of luxury in every step it takes, from the presentation of the perfume to the communication of the Haute Couture line to the online users. This eliminates the risk of brand status dilution.

In traditional marketing, the experience would correspond to the product. Although undoubtedly ELIE SAAB can be best experienced by feeling the luxurious product up-close and by having the ability to touch it, be it a couture dress, or a bottle of perfume, constraints of the online world obviously prevent such pleasure.

The experience of ELIE SAAB must therefore be conveyed through the brand's website.

Although all social media platforms of ELIE SAAB handle the information that is exclusive to that particular audience, the most important information is stored on the brand's website, as, at the end of the day, the website is where Internet users go first, and where traffic is directed by social media platforms. Notably, the right layout and a clear website menu increase user acceptance of the brand website and hopefully overall user satisfaction.[11] ELIE SAAB website is as user-friendly to navigate for inexperienced Internet users, as effective for the experienced ones. According to Elie Saab Jr, the reason why they decided to keep an ideal balance between advanced technology and easy navigation is because the brand wanted to please technically and visually the visitor of every age and every level of computer or Internet skill.

"Luxury innovation involves the capacity of someone at a certain moment to integrate unique skills ... to create something new, unique, an extraordinary product or experience".[12] What makes ELIE SAAB appear cutting-edge, a coveted position that leads directly to exclusivity,[13] is the TV-screen impression the visitors get when they are on the website. As well as the ability to switch from one look to another as if you pressed the fast forward and backward buttons on the DVD player remote. Let us clarify such comparison. Once the visitors are on one of the six sections of the site, they may browse the section either by using the arrows and sub-sections (SHOW, LOOK, DETAIL) on the computer screen or by using the arrows on the computer keyboard. As a result, with the easy use of four arrows on the keyboard, you jump from show to look to detail and from one outfit to another in seconds.

The brand's innovative decision to convey the experience and to communicate "a promise of an exceptional moment" to the online users by providing exclusive stories in a form of the high-quality short movies has been highly appreciated, as shown by the high-level users' reactions to particular stories. "In today's luxury marketplace, convincing consumers to buy isn't enough. Convincing them to join a brand on a journey is the key, and that's what stories do."[14] ELIE SAAB has offered its online audience many breath-taking stories, showing that luxury is an art, with the help of the videos (see Figures 17.3–17.6). For example,

FIGURE 17.3 **ELIE SAAB stories in the form of videos: *Balade À Paris* (I)**

FIGURE 17.4 **ELIE SAAB stories in the form of videos: *Balade À Paris* (II)**

visitors are welcomed on the brand's homepage with a short movie, which is either the runway video of the latest fashion show or an inspirational story, created to celebrate some kind of occasion. For example, a short movie "*Balade à Paris*", shot in the most beautiful places of Paris, announced ELIE SAAB pre-fall 2012 collection. Another brand's adventure worth mentioning was a short movie shared with the online audience following Paris Fashion Week Fall Winter 2012–2013. In addition to live-streaming its Fall Winter 2012–2013 Ready-to-Wear fashion show online, the brand gave photo cameras to three different insiders of the show: model Karlie

FIGURE 17.5 **ELIE SAAB stories in the form of videos: ELIE SAAB show through the eyes of Rosario Dawson, Karlie Kloss, Rene Celestin**

FIGURE 17.6 **ELIE SAAB stories in the form of videos: Against the fall of the night**

Kloss backstage, actress Rosario Dawson in the front row and the creative director of the show Rene Celestin, in order to capture the fashion-show experience from very different points of view.

The engagement of the online user can be considered achieved when the person restores the memories of the exclusive online experience when offline. It can be put this way: from a client point of view, value is derived each time a luxury product is used, or a service memory emerges;[15] from the website visitor point of view, the value is derived each time the memory of a website experience emerges. As a result, the visitor tends to return to the website. As we learn from this case, the returning visitors of the ELIE SAAB website tend to spend almost three times more minutes on the brand's online homepage than they did the first time they were there (see Figure 17.7). The average time spent on the ELIE SAAB website by the returning visitor is longer by 150–200 percent in comparison to the average time spent on the website by a new visitor. This shows a high visitor-engagement rate and proves the online users' acceptance of the luxury brand's online content. If we dig deeper, such results also imply that the brand succeeds in intriguing the new visitors to come back to the website, and when they do their expectations are being satisfied.

When dealing with online marketing of the luxury brands you have to satisfy the online users' expectations from the brand rather than make too many risky creative decisions. The luxury brand has to offer its online followers the material they would be willing

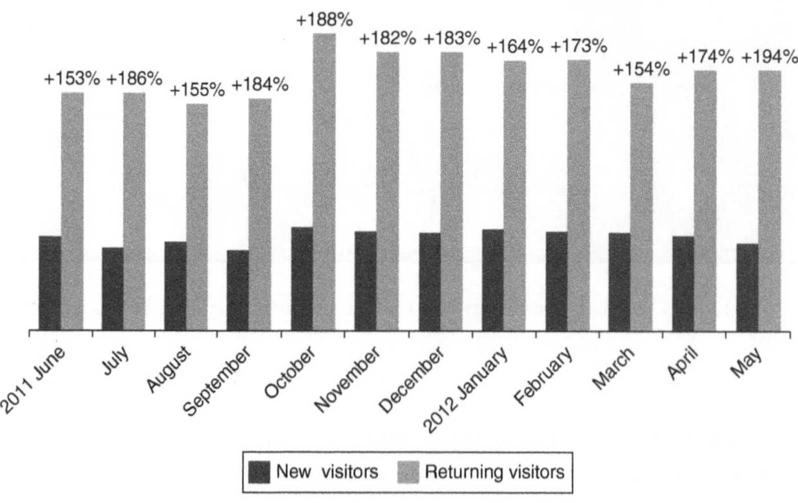

FIGURE 17.7 **The difference in average time spent on ELIE SAAB website by new and returning visitors**

to share and recommend to the others. This means, the provided online content has to create an emotion. ELIE SAAB has managed to find a good balance between the consistency and the creativity. As you will learn later in this chapter the followers of the brand's social media platforms show high engagement rates as well.

17.5 POWER TO ONLINE AUDIENCE

According to the study conducted by L2, fashion brands are embracing digital innovation with enthusiasm; however; most brands still approach digital as a series of pet projects rather than presenting a coherent multi-platform strategy.[16] In contrast with many brands, ELIE SAAB has been working on the implementation of the multi-platform strategy in order to ensure the consistency that is critical for the luxury brand. People behind the brand constantly interact with the consumers to know their needs and thoroughly studies the existing and potential audiences' reactions to particular online content presented by the brand in order to respond to their interests properly. And apparently the brand's audiences on different social media platforms differ surprisingly in their interests, needs, attitudes to luxury and fashion, and life in general. This outcome means that ELIE SAAB has to offer various materials to different online users in order to maintain their curiosity in and engagement to the brand. After all, knowing the audience is key to a web marketing strategy.[17] Thus, ELIE SAAB carefully tailors the message specifically to the audiences of different social media platforms for them to understand it.

Social media marketing is exceeding customer expectations in the online world through human connection and relationship building.[18] The purpose of the social media platforms is communication and interaction between the brand and its consumers and supporters. And as all brands are unique, so people want an authentic conversation with brands that speak as people expect them to.[19] Therefore, how you say things on the social media platforms is equally important as what you say. The social media voice of the brand is an inherent part of any brand's identity. A carefully developed brand voice is a key to meaningful and engaging communication between the brand and its followers. ELIE SAAB makes sure that its social media voice corresponds to the luxury brand image and status and always remains consistent. "The consistency of the brand voice we've preserved, was and continues to be a key component in the development of the ELIE SAAB online world", says Nathalie Mroue, the new media coordinator at ELIE SAAB.

Besides the website, ELIE SAAB's online activity began with the social network Facebook. The platform's velocity of adoption is unprecedented, and as it gets bigger, it grows faster, both in number of users and time spent.[20] With a population of over 800 million people this social network is an inexhaustible source of potential supporters and usually a starting point for those brands eager to get involved in the social media. However, winning on Facebook is more than just a "like" count.[21] Exemplary, in less than a year of active presence on Facebook in addition to the constantly growing fan-base ELIE SAAB has also earned high online user's engagement rates based on the volume of both comments received and post-likes received, calculated by Stylophane.[22] In order to illustrate these results I compared ELIE SAAB fans' engagement rates with two renowned luxury brands: BURBERRY, the luxury brand that has the biggest fan-base on the social network Facebook (as of June 2012), and CHRISTIAN DIOR, the luxury brand, offering both Haute Couture and Ready-to-Wear lines, that has the biggest fan-base on the social network Facebook (as of June 2012). See Figures 17.8 and 17.9 for the results.

Fascinatingly, although ELIE SAAB has a smaller fan-base than that of the other two brands, it has the biggest user-engagement rate based on the volume of comments received (C-Rate) and the leading user-engagement rate based on the volume of post-likes received (P-Rate). Moreover, the couture brand's C-Rate is far bigger than (in most cases double) that of the other two brands compared. As the engagement rate is a value that measures how effective posts have been for the brand based on the volume of comments and post-likes received,[23] so these results show that ELIE SAAB has managed to discover what the online users need and to provide them with the right material. As the brand has never used the platform to give out samples of its eau de parfum or eau de toilette (in contrast to BURBERRY, for example) and has no e-store, so does no promotions, the high C-Rate and P-Rate demonstrate that the brand has managed to attract and maintain the fans that are solely interested

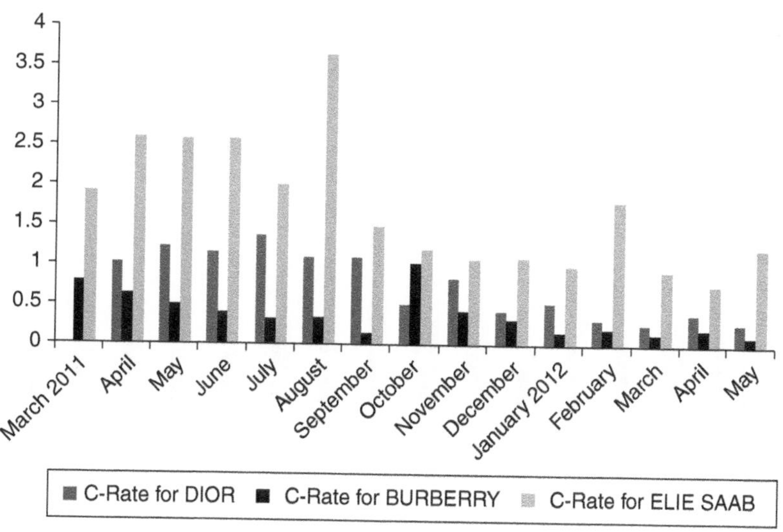

FIGURE 17.8 **The comparison of the user engagement rates (C-Rate) for comments for CHRISTIAN DIOR, BURBERRY and ELIE SAAB**
Source: Stylophane data.

in the brand's world and are looking for emotional rather than tangible benefits, such as discounts or samples. Moreover, knowing that ELIE SAAB has never used any online advertising, in contrast with other brands, the high engagement rates also prove that advertising can help attract big number of followers, but it certainly cannot buy their engagement and loyalty.

In addition to Facebook and Twitter, ELIE SAAB is also active on four other international social media platforms: Tumblr, Instagram, Youtube and Pinterest. Additionally, the brand is present on Weibo and Youku, the Chinese market's equivalents of Twitter and Youtube that have gained even more importance since ELIE SAAB opened its first boutique in Hong Kong in 2012. A new team member – a native Chinese – has been appointed to be responsible for the two Chinese social media platforms and to also work on the strategy of targeting the particular audience. The new recruit's ability to speak Mandarin and to better understand the audience's needs and communication manners will help the luxury brand respond properly. By using tactics such as these, ELIE SAAB has been trying to reach and please existing and potential consumers in

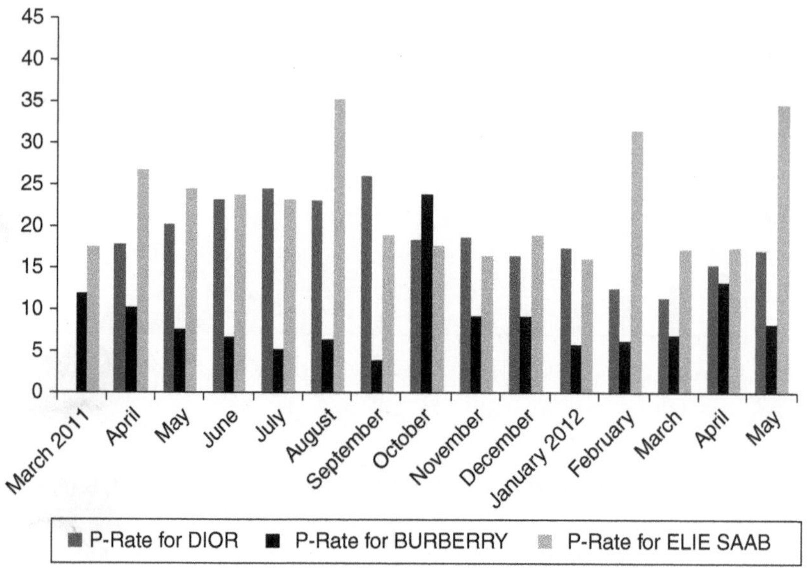

FIGURE 17.9 **The comparison of the user engagement rates (P-Rates) for post-likes for CHRISTIAN DIOR, BURBERRY and ELIE SAAB**
Source: Stylophane data.

many different regions of the world. And these tactics could serve as an example for many luxury fashion houses seeking to better understand and delight their clientele.

17.6 IN ONE YEAR – THE CONCLUSION

As we found, the brand's main online strategy had been to listen to its online users and meet their expectations. Consequently, in less than a year the brand has managed to successfully attract and maintain a constantly growing online audience. Moreover, the audience attracted by ELIE SAAB had shown much higher engagement rates than the relatively bigger audiences of other luxury brands. Therefore, knowing that there has not been any online advertising used so far, it can be concluded that though the advertising and promotion may attract followers, they cannot buy the followers' engagement and loyalty.

ELIE SAAB's accomplishments in web marketing are a continuous process. Nevertheless, the brand's first year in social media has been impressive.

ACKNOWLEDGMENTS

I thank Elie Saab Jr. and Nathalie Mroue.

NOTES

1. Robson, J. (2011), Paris Haute Couture: Azzedine Alaia's couture debut shrouded in secrecy, http://fashion.telegraph.co.uk/.
2. Gastaldi, F. (2012). "Internet, Social Media and Luxury Strategy", in Hoffmann, J. and Coste-Maniere, I. (eds), *Luxury Strategy in Action*, Palgrave Macmillan.
3. Amed, I. (22 January 2010) Fashion 2.0 | Suzy Menkes on the Growing Influence of Fashion Blogs. http://www.businessoffashion.com/
4. ITU Statistics (http://www.itu.int/ict/statistics).
5. Stankeviciute, R. and Hoffmann, J. (2011). "The Slippery Slope of Brand Expansion", *Marketing Management Magazine*, Winter.
6. Hoffmann, J. and Hoffmann, B. (2012). "The PIER Framework of Luxury Innovation", in Hoffmann, J. and Coste-Maniere, I. (eds), *Luxury Strategy in Action*, London: Palgrave Macmillan.
7. Hoffmann, J. and Hoffmann, B. (2012). "The PIER Framework of Luxury Innovation", in Hoffmann, J. and Coste-Maniere, I. (eds), *Luxury Strategy in Action*, Palgrave Macmillan.
8. Gastaldi, F. (2012). "Internet, Social Media and Luxury Strategy", in Hoffmann, J. and Coste-Maniere, I. (eds), *Luxury Strategy in Action*, Palgrave Macmillan, 2012.
9. Hoffmann, J. and Hoffmann, B. (2012). "The PIER Framework of Luxury Innovation", in Hoffmann, J. and Coste-Maniere, I. (eds), *Luxury Strategy in Action*, Palgrave Macmillan.
10. Greenhill, D. (29 November 2011). 4 Pillars of Digital Marketing for Luxury Brands, http://www.mashable.com/.
11. Gastaldi, F. (2012). "Internet, Social Media and Luxury Strategy", in Hoffmann, J. and Coste-Maniere, I. (eds), *Luxury Strategy in Action*, Palgrave Macmillan.

12. Hoffmann, J. and Hoffmann, B. (2012). "The PIER Framework of Luxury Innovation", in Hoffmann, J. and Coste-Maniere, I. (eds), *Luxury Strategy in Action*, Palgrave Macmillan.
13. Greenhill, D. (29 November 2011). 4 Pillars of Digital Marketing for Luxury Brands, http://www.mashable.com/.
14. Greenhill, D. (29 November 2011). 4 Pillars of Digital Marketing for Luxury Brands, http://www.mashable.com/.
15. Hoffmann, J. and Hoffmann, B. (2012). "The PIER Framework of Luxury Innovation", in Hoffmann, J. and Coste-Maniere, I. (eds), *Luxury Strategy in Action*, Palgrave Macmillan.
16. Kansara, V. A. (11 October 2011). Fashion 2.0 | L2 Study Reveals Shortfalls in Digital Competence, http://www.businessoffashion.com/.
17. Gastaldi, F. (2012). "Internet, Social Media and Luxury Strategy", in Hoffmann, J. and Coste-Maniere, I. (eds), *Luxury Strategy in Action*, Palgrave Macmillan.
18. Falls, J. and Deckers, E. (2012). *No Bullshit Social Media: The All-Business, No-Hype Guide To Social Media Marketing*, Pearson Education Inc.
19. Turner, K. (9 March 2009). Finding the Right "Brand Voice" on Twitter, http://www.mashable.com/.
20. Galloway, S., The L2 Prestige 100®: Facebook IQ, 2011, http://www.L2thinktank.com.
21. Galloway, S., The L2 Prestige 100®: Facebook IQ, 2011, http://www.L2thinktank.com.
22. http://stylophane.com/fbi/#.
23. http://stylophane.com/fbi/.

INDEX